How to Grow a
Connected
Family

How to Grow a
Connected
Family

With Contagious Love and Faith!

" . . . best parenting book I've ever read, and I've read a lot. It's simply life-changing!"
—Paul Johnson, Senior Vice President of the Baptist General Conference

James & Lynne Jackson

REDEMPTION ❧ PRESS

Unless otherwise noted, all Scriptures are taken from the *Holy Bible, New International Version*, NIV. Copyright © 1973, 1978, 1984 by Biblica, Inc.™ Used by permission of Zondervan. All rights reserved worldwide. www.zondervan.com

Scripture references marked KJV are taken from the *King James Version* of the Bible.

Scripture references marked NASB are taken from the *New American Standard Bible,* © 1960, 1963, 1968, 1971, 1972, 1973, 1975, 1977 by The Lockman Foundation. Used by permission.

ISBN - 978-1-63232-012-4

Library of Congress Catalog Card Number: 2005902785

Testimonials

"This is the best parenting book I've ever read, and I've read a lot. It is simply life-changing!"

—Paul Johnson
Senior Vice President of the Baptist General Conference

"A must read! I wish I'd had this book when I was a young parent."

—Roger Palms
author of fourteen books, and twenty-two years
as editor of Billy Graham's DECISION magazine

"I am recommending Jim & Lynne's teaching be embraced by our denomination as core teaching for parents."

—Greg Braly
Director of Evangelical Free Church of America's Family
and Children's Ministries

"This material is brilliant! It equips parents with a concrete, easy to learn framework for flexible, creative parenting. What a spiritually smart system! Jim and Lynne's practicality and authenticity simply ooze of God's grace.

—Charlene Ann Baumbich
Author of twelve books including *Don't Miss Your Kids*
and *365 Ways to Connect with Your Kids*

"I truly believe that I have never read anything by anyone that so thoughtfully melds solid scriptural doctrine with sound psychological principles. This is a resource of pure parenting and teaching gold."

—Warren Watson
MSW, LICSW, Clinical Psychology Director

"This book provides a biblical framework for consistently leading children towards God's loving purposes for their lives. It is also a great resource for nurturing transformation within the hearts of parents."

—Dr. Jean L. Leih
Director of Reformation Ministries

To our Hilarious Adventure,
our Journey in Intimacy,
and our Sunshine in Skin
(a.k.a. – our children Daniel, Bethany, & Noah)
May the fruit of God's love and purposes
grow full in you for generations to come.

Contents

SECTION III: PROACTION (Proactive Action)

SECTION IV: CORRECTION

Acknowledgments

WE'RE DEEPLY GRATEFUL to God for those who have stood behind our calling to write this book. From the parents who first encouraged us to write, to the key people who helped us push the project over the finish line, you have become to us a treasured community of contributors.

To the first, second, and third round of readers who helped us sharpen this content - you helped us become better writers. And Roger Palms, our editor – you greatly affirmed us and further helped us hone our skills.

To our pastors: At Brooklyn Park Vineyard, Dave and Donna Heinrich – you put wind under the wings of our hearts for children and families. You helped us trust God for the courage to begin again. At Westwood Community Church, Joel Johnson and team – you believe in the things God has grown in us and give us opportunities to share these things in our community.

To Jim's Family Hope Services supervisors and colleagues, and the youth we served together – through you God taught a "craft of grace" that will ever carry on in and through me. The threads of that gift are intricately woven through the pages of this book.

To Lynne's MOPS (Mothers Of Preschoolers) group: Your encouragement, support and trust were invaluable to us.

To our Board of Directors: Jay Allsup, Dan McCormick, Dave Scouler, Margene Vessel, and Jana Nelson. When God called us to launch Connected Families, you "held our arms up" with wisdom and encouragement. You believed in our passion and held us accountable to the vision.

To our faithful donors: There are scores of you. Your contributions have fueled this project.

To our community of friends (those not already mentioned): The Chapins, Freemans, Gundersons, Johansons, Littles, Nelsons, Pannings, Stafford, and Sweeneys. You feel like family. You love us as we are, and encourage us to be all God calls us to be.

And to our families: You taught us to live and to love. Through you God planted seeds that have become many of the concrete principles in this book and in our lives.

Preface
What can I expect from this book?

IN OUR OVER twenty years of working with parents, we've seen hundreds of families grow in a profound, passionate love for God and each other. The way it looks from family to family may differ greatly, but the basic principles that these families follow are quite consistent. We've captured what we've noticed by naming four simple but profound principles that are in place in every faithful, loving family we've seen. The principles are illustrated in a simple diagram and expanded throughout the book's four sections. While it is written primarily for parents of toddlers, pre-school, and elementary school-aged children, parents of pre-teens and teens have also found the principles quite valuable.

God has used these ideas in our lives and the lives of many others to produce peaceful, purposeful parents, and strong, connected families. These families love being together and with others, and others love being with them. Their joy is deep and their love and faith are truly contagious.

Though my wife Lynne and I contributed equally to the book's contents, it is written in a singular voice to make it more personal for you, the reader. In these pages you will get to know our family through numerous stories from our experience. Our children are free-spirited, transparent kids who are OK with Mom and Dad sharing the ups and downs of our family's adventures, in order to benefit others. We sometimes share examples from their lives as teens, mostly to show the fruit of persistently living according to the principles we promote in this book. We also share stories from many others who have learned and applied the powerful principles that are this book's subject. In these anecdotes the names are changed to ensure confidentiality.

Embedded in each chapter you will find questions that ask for your thoughtful response. Working through these questions will greatly maximize the benefit you receive from the book.

At the end of each chapter is an activity or discussion question to involve your children. Many people have stated that these questions are a culminating highlight of each chapter.

Throughout the book there are woven numerous Bible verses, since we believe that a great variety of Scripture sheds light on the challenge of parenting. Unless otherwise specified, the verses used are from the New International Version of the Bible.

May you be equipped through these principles to purposefully raise children who know, love, and serve God. And may yours be a strong, connected family, filled with contagious love and faith. Enjoy!

—Jim and Lynne

Introduction

"ARE YOU GOING to help me or not?" I snapped at Daniel, our son. He'd been asking for the past hour to go play at a friend's house. I'd dodged his request while badgering from a distance to enlist his help in a household project.

"Dad, get off my back!" he snapped back. "You keep ignoring me!" I was a bit stunned by his sharp tone. He waited briefly for a response. When none came he folded his arms and announced, "I'm leaving."

I was at a loss for words. Although he's definitely strong-willed, this was not typical for him. "Kids shouldn't talk to their parents that way!" I thought. I felt defensive and angry. I was tempted to quickly, firmly, and authoritatively "put him in his place." After all, he was being rude, selfish, and even a bit intimidating. But I was unsure. In my silence he started walking away.

My lack of peace and confidence about how to respond to this was my first clue that perhaps I needed to take a step back and think before acting. I held off my first impulse to firmly demand instant obedience. I paused instead, took a deep breath, tried to clear my head and invite some Holy Spirit wisdom. Something inside told me his was not the only misbehavior here.

Daniel's response held some truth I wanted to pay attention to. I had to admit that in some ways I had been as inconsiderate and selfish as he. In his own unrefined way, he was calling me on it. This realization calmed my frustration with him. I still didn't know what to do or say, but at least now I could respond calmly and more rational. Wanting the "right" words to say, I confessed to him, "I'm not sure what to say right now." I wanted to purposefully address his behavior, but in a way that might encourage him. I also felt compelled to admit my own bad attitudes. But I didn't yet know exactly how to deal with all that, and I wanted to get back to my project. So I decided to let it go for the time being. "Why don't you go now, and we'll figure this out later," I said. Then, with another deep breath, I smiled sincerely and proclaimed, "I love you." He winked back and said, "Thanks. I love you more."

This is real life. It's not always smooth and predictable. It can even get downright messy. But it is a life into which I can invite the transforming power of Jesus. It can then become a life of authenticity in which the whole family desires to keep growing in vibrant connection to God, to God's purposes, and to one another. This kind of life is not a destination. It's a journey. By journeying this way, I can build a solid, connected family that is able to withstand the inevitable difficulties and cultural influences that we will face.

Living this way may seem like a lofty goal. But we've found over and over again that when families live according to the principles in this book, their connection bears rich fruit in their relationships at home and in the world. Parents grow in a sense of peace, purpose and confidence for parenting. Children grow in respect for others and a sense of purpose for their lives. As God's love is welcomed into the everyday mix of life, the love in these families grows more and more contagious. The life of Christ overflows naturally to the world around them. This journey of knowing and sharing God's wonderful love in and through our family is what this book is all about.

Foundation

Chapter One

_____

A Life-Changing Perspective
The Connected Family Framework

"WHAT SHOULD I do?" This is the question most asked by parents struggling to figure out how to handle their children. It's an important question. "What should I do to get my daughter to quit making messes?" "What should I do about my son's laziness?" "What should I do when my child sasses back?" "How can I get them to do their homework?" If I figure out how to quickly and efficiently get my kids to do what I ask, life generally becomes peaceful – for them and for me. Most humans want a peaceful life. So most parents look for quick and effective methods to get their kids to behave. This is not necessarily a bad goal. Meeting it can lead to some short-term peace and quiet.

◆◆◆❖◆❖◆◆◆

**The parenting journey provides one of life's greatest
opportunities for spiritual growth.**

◆◆◆❖◆❖◆◆◆

If while working on the project I mentioned in the introduction, I had wondered only about how to quickly correct Daniel's behavior, I would have given all my energy to changing his defiant attitude and getting him to help me. Those could be good things to focus on. But there was more to this situation than just his misbehavior. There was mine too. To focus only on him would be to miss half the problem. So I decided to focus first on me. When I did, I realized that I had contributed at least as much to this problem as he had. I had to ask some deeper questions of myself. How and why had I been selfish? What was I thinking and feeling? How did those thoughts and feeling influence my actions? Where do I believe God is in the

1

everyday challenges of parenting? It is only through asking these deeper questions that *I* can change. These kinds of questions are about my own thoughts, motives, and behaviors. They address the way I relate to my children, and why. Through trying to answer them, I can begin to change the way I think and act as a parent. It is only when *I* change that I experience true, deep peace. This is perhaps the biggest gift I can give to my child, because when I am peaceful, I can make parenting decisions that achieve not only short-term results, but long-term transformation for both my children and me.

My wife Lynne and I have been parents for nineteen years, and worked as professionals with children, youth, and families for even longer. Through these experiences we are convinced that the parenting journey provides one of life's greatest opportunities for spiritual growth. To reduce parenting to a formula of dos and don'ts is to rob parents of this rich opportunity for personal discovery.

To suggest that there is some simple repeatable method for addressing my son's misbehavior begins with the assumption that I've got my act together. And, while I'm a work in some good progress (I trust and pray), I've not yet arrived at the perfection for which I so deeply long. I bring to every parenting encounter the baggage of my own struggles. So I must remain committed to my own journey of growth as a person and as a parent. As I am transformed, I can become more peaceful and purposeful as a parent.

At the root of my response to Daniel that day were four simple, transformational principles. They are principles we have seen in action in parents who work at raising children to want to follow Jesus. They are: **Connection, Proaction** (proactive action), **Correction,** and **Foundation.** This book reviews those principles and shares stories to illustrate them. Learning to thoughtfully apply these principles helps parents be more peaceful and purposeful through the ups, downs, and pressures of parenting.

Viewing parenting challenges through the lens of these principles changes how I view even the most mundane of interactions with my children. Instead of seeing these interactions as problems to fix and prevent, I am learning that these challenges can teach me more deeply about myself, my children, and God's love and purposes for our lives. It is this great premise that beckons us into an amazing journey.

The four principles led to the creation of a simple framework, a way of understanding how we give effort and energy to our own spiritual lives and to our children. It has been a tremendous source of encouragement and accountability. It has facilitated a deeper look at life as a parent and has stimulated growth in us as followers of Christ. As we have shared this framework with others, we have found that many report the same growth. This is *not* a parenting method to follow. Rather, it is a set of interrelated principles designed to fit any family's combination of personalities and developmental stages. Many parents have stated this framework is actually a whole new way to look at all their relationships, including with a spouse or co-workers. One dad exclaimed, "This isn't just about my kids, it's about life! It's really helped me at work."

The framework is built on this premise: Parents ultimately cannot change their children. They can only change the way they relate to them. Embracing this premise helps me be more peaceful, regardless of my children's behavior. I can enjoy my kids – even when they "act up." I can relax enough to see positive opportunities in difficult situations. I can address misbehavior peacefully and confidently. I recognize God's grace, mercy, and purposes even through difficulty. Knowing these three principles is by no means a guarantee that children will be great kids. But in most cases, parents who learn and apply the framework gradually begin to see changes in their children too.

The principles in this framework are consistent with biblical teaching. The first, **Connection,** is the starting place for relating to children. When I connect with my children I make sure they know my *unconditional love* for them. I give them my undivided attention. I have fun with them and enjoy them intensely. I tell them and show them my love in ways they will clearly understand. I convince them how significant and important they are. I learn to relate in this way in the context of all circumstances – even in conflict. Ideally, most of my parenting energy should be given to connecting with my children.

The next principle is about *proactively teaching* kids to learn character and responsibility. I affirm the unique gifts and traits of each child and create opportunities for each to use his or her gifts in a meaningful way. I put chore charts on the refrigerator alongside artwork, athletic awards, and fun photos. I work alongside my children and encourage their efforts. I help them learn to resolve conflict, not just avoid it. I energetically affirm responsibility, creativity, and kindness, and look for positive traits even in negative behaviors. I convince my children that they have important contributions to make to the world as children of God. This principle of **Proaction** is about guiding them toward their unique path and purpose in life.

Once **Connection** and **Proaction** are firmly in place, I can much more effectively use **Correction** when needed to *address misbehavior*. Children who know they are loved, valued, and are created for a purpose, are more likely to learn from corrective discipline. Effective correction involves enforcing consequences, withholding privileges, and using various strategies for addressing misbehavior with the child's best interest in mind.

MY RESPONSE...

How is my total parenting effort divided between each of my children?

	Child 1	Child 2	Child 3	Child 4
Effort per child	_____ +	_____ +	_____ +	_____ = 100%

Then, of the effort allotted to each child, how much is given to each of the framework's principles:

Effort in each principle:

Connection	_____	_____	_____	_____
Proaction	+ _____	+ _____	+ _____	+ _____
Correction	+ _____	+ _____	+ _____	+ _____
	= 100%	= 100%	= 100%	= 100%

(This is not a grading system. It is a tool for increased awareness. If the results seem imbalanced, parents can be encouraged by the opportunity for helpful improvement.)

What do the results tell me? What surprises me?

The fourth principle for parenting is more about me than about my kids. It is the basis from which I make my parenting decisions, and from which grows the energy and effort I give to parenting. It is called **Foundation.** In my **Foundation** I am strengthened for the tumultuous parenting experience. I learn about God's unconditional love. I fall more deeply in love with Him. I actively seek affirming, encouraging relationships. I discover who I am and what I'm called to do. I learn to understand the unhealthy messages and beliefs that I bring into parenting. I learn to rely on God's grace and mercy in the midst of any circumstance. I learn to face the challenges of parenting filled and defined by the truth of God's Word. As my **Foundation** is strengthened, I can effectively integrate my spiritual life and growth into my parenting.

The Connected Family Framework shows how these principles build on each other.

At the base is my **Foundation.** From it, I build to **Connection.** This area gets my biggest and best energy and effort. From a place of **Connection,** I take **Proactive Action.** This is where I develop and affirm my children's gifts and character. It is where I purposefully teach children the skills and values that they need to function within God's purposes. Finally, at the top is **Correction.** While **Proaction** is where I teach children how to stay "on track," **Correction** is where I help them to get back on track. This level is structurally dependent on all the levels below it. It

is the smallest section because ideally, the amount of effort I give to it is smaller than the levels below.

As parents learn these principles, many report a deeper sense of purpose for parenting. They also report that the principles seem to grow with them in their parenting experience. Perhaps most significant is the common discovery that when more parental effort is put into **Connection** and **Proaction**, there is generally much less need for **Correction**. Carrie and Mark's stories are a great example of this.

Carrie was quite concerned about Mark, one of her neighbors. He was a new step-dad and his highly structured, perfectionist way of life was on a collision course with the three lively sons in his new marriage. It was definitely a source of stress in the new family – particularly with his bride! Carrie grabbed a copy of the Connected Family Framework and with great conviction stuck it in Mark's face. "Here! You need this. When I looked at this I realized my relationships with my kids were upside down – my interaction with them was 90% correction. These ideas changed our whole family!" Mark was eager to do whatever would help his new family grow stronger. He began working to change his primary focus from correcting his stepchildren to connecting with them and giving proactive guidance. Over time, peace, joy and even obedience blossomed in their family as the boys responded to his affection and encouragement.

Lynne and I have been blessed as learners to apply these principles on a daily basis in our own family. We readily admit that parenting our three challenging, high-energy children does not always go very smoothly. Even though it sometimes gets downright messy in our home, both literally and figuratively, we are committed to relating to each other in a way that reflects God's no-strings-attached love.

The impact of these principles on our family to date has been profound. Currently twenty-one, eighteen, and sixteen years old, our children have a deep sense of our love and God's love for them. They enjoy one another deeply, in spite of the skirmishes that often occur. They are affectionate with each other – even in public or when friends are around. They love others with generosity and exuberance. They each have identified gifts and interests that God is already using in them to bless others. They are tremendous positive influences in their peer groups and are quite resistant to negative peer pressure. As they head off to college, they seek majors that will maximize their gifts, so they can go into the world to bless others.

We are grateful to God for helping us understand parenting through this framework. It has helped us become better spouses, parents, and Christ followers.

First Things First: Building my FOUNDATION

What shapes my ability to relate to my children?

When Daniel returned after leaving me to finish my project, he willingly sat down with me to discuss our earlier dispute, and gladly offered his help on another chore. I've found that as I have strengthened my **Foundation**, it has become normal to reconnect and resolve our conflicts.

> ◆◆◆❖◆❖◆◆◆
> **"These words I speak to you…are foundational words,
> words to build a life on."[1]**
> ◆◆◆❖◆❖◆◆◆

Jesus said that "smart carpenters"[2] build a sturdy house on solid rock. Then when the storms of life hit, nothing will move the house. This doesn't mean storms won't pelt the house from time to time, and even inflict some damage. It means the house will stand strong, able to endure even the most ferocious of storms. When I extend this metaphor into parenting, I realize that before I get too worried about the "house" of parenting skills, I need to build a strong **Foundation.** I build this foundation using four important "bricks." These bricks are an ever-growing *faith* in God, a sense of *purpose* in life, a *community* of supportive relationships, and a developing sense of *insight* into who I am and why I act the way I do. From this foundation flows my ability to relate to my children.

In contrast, a foolish carpenter builds on sand (that is, any beliefs, principles, or practices that are opposed to Christ's love and truth). This person finds his house collapsing around him in the winds of stress and hardship. A household with a weak or inadequate foundation (distance from God, a lack of identity and purpose, strained relationships with others, and lack of personal insight) will not stand strong against the normal storms of family life. Parents' weak foundations will reinforce unhealthy emotions and hurtful responses to their children. Even though it may *seem* that all is well, patterns develop that can perpetuate troubles of many kinds.

The Bible does not give specific instruction for how to deal with most daily parenting circumstances. Growth as a parent comes as I continually assess the "stuff" of life with my children against a growing understanding of the truth. As I do this, the challenges of family life drive me to deeper faith in the love and presence of God, deeper understanding of myself, and deeper peace about that which I cannot understand or control.

MY RESPONSE...

When do I feel confident as a parent? What makes me confident?

KID CONNECTION!

Ask your children, "What are our family's strengths? What helps us to be strong?"

Filled to Overflowing
The Cornerstone of FAITH

know yourself as unconditionally loved – that is, fully received – by God, ⌐⌐⌐, ⌐⌐⌐ ⌐urself,"[1] writes Henri Nouwen. In other words, to truly give love, I must first receive God's love. So to really love my children, I must know God's immense love for me. I can only know this love by faith. Once I receive that love, and God's forgiveness through Christ, I enter the lifelong fight of faith that helps me to remember and receive God's love.

One man describes the impact of trying to love with an empty heart. "All my Christian life I was challenged to love other people. But why? Why would anyone want my version of love? That's just asking for trouble. These were my love gifts: arrogance packaged as teaching; control disguised as protection; manipulation wrapped as concern; exploitation marketed as opportunities. How 'bout them love gifts! Until I learned how to *be* loved, my 'loving' just spewed all my junk and debris onto others."[2]

To effectively receive God's love and then give it away to my family is a step-by-step, day-by-day, year-by-year journey. It is only through this struggle that any of us can grow in an understanding of the presence and work of a loving God in our lives. Paul's prayer for the Ephesian church emphasizes with passion the significance of knowing Jesus' love:

I pray that you, being rooted and established in love may have power, together with all the saints, to grasp how wide and long and high and deep is the love of Christ, and to know this love that surpasses knowledge—that you may be filled to the measure of all the fullness of God.

—Ephesians 3:17-19

In the Bible, Moses, David, and Paul speak of the joy of receiving God's unconditional love,[3] being fully known,[4] and deeply enjoyed.[5] We learn from them that we too can love, know, and enjoy God because he first loves, knows, and enjoys us! In the journey of faith I discover that I am intimately known, down to the subtlest motive behind every thought; and yet in Christ I am fully accepted, embraced, enjoyed - fully loved! God's intimate knowledge of my life is not for condemning inspection but for his good pleasure, to savor and enjoy the miracle he created. Something in the deepest part of each of us longs to know and live in this love. This longing for love is what draws a person to Jesus Christ.

> ◆◆◆❖◆❖◆◆◆
> **"I can love, know, and enjoy God,**
> **because God loves, knows, and enjoys me."**
> ◆◆◆❖◆❖◆◆◆

Since this understanding of God's love is the means to being "filled to the measure of the fullness of God" and passing that fullness on to others, nothing can be more important in life. Discovering how to receive this love, by faith, is the basis for effective parenting.

Building FAITH: Pursuing God Uniquely

Do my spiritual practices reflect my individuality?

*"You will seek me and find me when you seek me with **all your heart**."*

—Jeremiah 29:13

Choosing and developing practices that *truly refresh* me with a deeper awareness of God's love is critically important for renewed strength as a parent. But understanding how I'm uniquely wired to do that may be a long process.

I remember the sign on the men's dorm wall during my freshman year at a Christian college. A spiritual disciplines checklist was posted for us to keep track of our "progress" (monitored by a well-meaning resident assistant). I am wired for variety, not daily routines, and I felt ashamed every time I missed checking off the boxes in the "Jim J." section: daily devotional time, prayer, fellowship, witnessing, tithing (At least I got tithing – 10% of 0 income). I felt ashamed that I wasn't measuring up, even to the point of checking boxes just so no one would know that I wasn't making very good Christian progress.

It was years later that a wise older friend and mentor taught me about true spiritual discipline. We laid aside the Bible study workbooks that had helped bring fulfillment to other men with whom he had met but had only frustrated me. He challenged me not to the discipline of a method but to the discipline of pursuing intimacy with God according to the way God wired me. I was no longer ashamed that I didn't have a typical daily devotional time. I felt graceful permission to grow in spurts. My love relationship with God continues to grow as I have greatly varied how I pursue that relationship.

While commitment to the *principle* of understanding God's love and truth is important, commitment to a particular *method* for spiritual growth may even be a hindrance. Many of the religious leaders of Jesus' day had rigorous spiritual practices, which became their idol and actually hardened their hearts to true matters of faith. A one-size-fits-all, "this is the right way to do it" approach to faith has left many followers of Christ discouraged and ultimately frustrated about pursuing a vital faith journey.

The authors of *Soul Types*[6] write, "Each psychological type[7] has a unique slant on spirituality." Nurturing my love relationship with God may happen through any variety or combination of regular devotional or Scripture reading, meditation, journaling, retreats, small groups, or mentorship, etc. Some people thrive on singing or writing worship music or other creative expressions of their faith, enjoying God in nature, serving those less fortunate. The possibilities are as endless as the individuality of people.

Aspects of the experience, such as a sense of accomplishment, learning, creativity, stimulating conversations, etc., may substitute for actual growth in God's love. Whatever the practice is, I can ask myself, "Does this really help me to better receive and respond to God's love?"

When I deepen my love for God in my own unique way, I can help others in my family to seek God according to their individuality. I can encourage them in all the possibilities and trust God to guide them. This models to them that spiritual practices must be meaningful and relevant for the purpose of loving God, and *not* for the purpose of impressing anyone, including myself!

MY RESPONSE...

Considering all the possibilities that I can think of, what practices might best help me to experience God's love? How might I develop these further? (Those who are new to this concept can start small and ask God for guidance.)

♦♦♦❖◆❖♦♦♦
**When I deepen my love for God in my own unique way, I can
help others in my family to seek God according
to their individuality.**
♦♦♦❖◆❖♦♦♦

Building FAITH: Selecting Activities Wisely

Do my time commitments deepen me, or drain and distract me?

"Everything is permissible for me, but not everything is beneficial."

—I Corinthians 6:12

Just as spiritual disciplines and practices can either strengthen or hinder my relationship with God, so can the activities and commitments I choose. Activities in and of themselves are not bad things, but it's important to consider their value before I make commitments. My family's activities can easily multiply to the point of running me ragged unless I am determined not to let those activities do that.

Our oldest child, Daniel, made a grand pronouncement one morning upon learning that we all had to go to church early and stay through three services because of our ministry commitments. "You are spread way too thin! You people are like good jelly that's wasted by being spread too thin on a big piece of toast. Nobody can taste how good you are. Why don't you work on spreading yourselves THICK!" Wow! Out of the mouths of babes…(Well, not exactly a babe at fourteen, but wise beyond his years.) We made a decision to "spread ourselves thick" and prayerfully simplified our lives over the next few months.

The toll that excessive busyness takes on people is enormous. Dr. Richard Swenson states four results or manifestations of what he calls the "Overload Syndrome":[8]

- Anxiety – feeling that the load is unmanageable, fearing failure.
- Hostility – blaming those around us for our stress.
- Depression – failing our own expectations and the expectations of others.
- Resentment – resenting the jobs and activities that overwhelm us.

There is growing concern about the pace kept by families today. Dr. Swenson reports that thirty-six percent of Americans say they feel rushed *all* the time. Parents in America work longer hours than anywhere in the world, including Japan.[9]

Research reveals the toll that this increasing busyness is taking on family connection time. The Center for Economic Policy research says we are becoming the "No Vacation Nation." (Unlike 127 other countries, the U.S. has no minimum paid-leave law.)[10] Over the course of two decades, the number of families[11] taking vacations declined from fifty-three percent to only thirty-eight percent,[12] and the number of families who say they have dinner together regularly decreased from fifty percent to thirty-four percent![13]

Building a quality relationship with God and with my children requires time and a peaceful heart. Clearly, the ability to draw the line on time commitments is a strong building block in my foundation as a parent. Certainly I am quick to protect my family from physical danger, financial ruin, or immoral influences, but it is easy to be oblivious to the danger of excessive busyness. To evaluate time commitments I can ask:

- Will the activity refresh and *deepen* my experience of God's word, love, and truth, or will it *drain* me?
- Is it consistent with my gifts and calling or will it *distract* me from God's true purposes for me?
- Are the commitments I make to my children's activities a *deterrent* either to their well-being and spiritual development or to mine?
- Is our level of busyness causing our family to feel *disconnected* from each other?

My Response...

What are the significant activities to which I've committed my children or myself?

Do these activities -
    Refresh my (or my children's) relationship with God
    Strengthen family connections
    Match my (or my children's) gifts and calling
Or do they -
    Drain my (or my children's) energy and relationship with God
    Weaken family connections
    Distract from God's purposes

What could I do to make helpful changes? (This may take some thoughtful consideration over time.)

Building FAITH: Listening Attentively to God

Do I anticipate that God may speak his love to me at any moment?

"God has poured out his love into our hearts by the Holy Spirit, whom he has given us."
—Romans 5:5

God loves me not because I am good. God loves me because God is good. So while I ought to wisely choose spiritual practices and activities to fuel my love for God, I must remember that I can love only because God first loved me. Just as a loving parent doesn't wait for a child to initiate affection, *God pursues me!* There will be unexpected moments when he will simply express his love to me through his Spirit. These may be while I am joyfully absorbing the miracle of creation or intimacy with a loved one. Or it may be in the very moments when I have abandoned all spiritual practices, I'm drained by a hectic schedule, and I am discouraged about my family, myself, or my difficult circumstances. When he whispers to me will I be listening? Will I notice and savor God's expressions of love?

> *The Sovereign LORD has given me an instructed tongue, to know the word that sustains the weary. He wakens me morning by morning, wakens my ear to listen like one being taught.*
> —Isaiah 50:4

In the book, *Abba's Child*, Brennan Manning asks a thought-provoking question: "Do you honestly believe God *likes* you, not just loves you because theologically God *has* to love you? …Could I answer with gut-level honesty, 'Oh, yes, my Abba (Daddy/Papa) is very fond of me.'[14]

> *"Because you are sons, God sent the Spirit of his Son into our hearts, the Spirit who calls out, 'Abba, Father.'"*
> —Galatians 4:6

The first time God the Almighty was addressed as "Abba," (a revolutionary shift in Jewish thinking) was by Jesus in his ultimate distress – in the garden of Gesthemane. In his darkest moments he was so aware of the loving presence of his Father that he used this needy, even helpless expression of his intimate trust and love for his Father. In those moments Jesus received comfort. It seems Jesus heard the Father's whispers of love and encouragement, giving him the strength he needed to face the cross.

Through the birth of our first-born son, I had a profound experience that powerfully shaped my understanding of God's love. When Daniel was born he was kept in an isolation incubator for the weekend because of an undiagnosed rash. I spent hours alone in the room just staring at him and stroking the glass. Here I was, a new dad, and I couldn't hold my son!

I was deeply troubled by his isolation. I wondered how or even if God was involved in this at all. Frankly, I had been asking that question about a lot of things. It had been a spiritually dry time for me and there were no easy answers or comfort. Late one evening, I found myself alone in the room, talking out loud to Daniel through the glass. I said the things I have since heard many new parents say to and about their babies: "What a miracle!" "I love you!" "What a gift you are!" "Just looking at you brings me joy!" and other unconditional expressions of love. In that moment, I sensed God saying to me,

"The love you are expressing to your son is the love I have for you!"

I began to weep uncontrollably as I received God's words of intense love for me – at a time in life when I felt the least deserving of it. It was a defining moment in my relationship with God. Through this experience I made a commitment to do my best throughout life to listen for, and to receive God's love for me – even in times of darkness. Then I committed myself to express those same messages of love to my wife and children throughout life.

♦♦❖◆❖♦♦

**To treasure and enjoy my children through the difficulties of childhood,
I must open my own heart to the love of God for me!**

♦♦❖◆❖♦♦

MY RESPONSE...

When have I felt deeply loved by Christ in a discouraging time? How did I respond?

Parenting can be an incredible setting for spiritual transformation. For this to be true, I must anchor my journey in the cornerstone of faith. It is the most significant building block in the foundation for parenting and for life. This "fight of faith" is not about "getting the Christian life right;" it's about growing in my awareness of God's heart for me, in me, and through me in the daily challenges with my children. Scripture reveals that Jesus Christ himself is the chief cornerstone of life (Ephesians 2:20), **"a precious cornerstone for a sure foundation; the one who trusts will never be dismayed"** (Isaiah 28:16).

And so this chapter ends as it began....

"I pray that you, being rooted and established in love may have power, together with all the saints, to grasp how wide and long and high and deep is the love of Christ, and to know this love that surpasses knowledge—that you may be filled to the measure of all the fullness of God."
                                                                          —Ephesians 3:17-19

KID CONNECTION:

Ask your children to describe what Jesus would be like if he were a parent. What stands out to you in their responses?

Chapter Three

Purpose-Full Parenting
The Cornerstone of PURPOSE

ONE OF THE key concepts of the Connected Family Framework that changed Carrie's life was the idea that each person in her family had been given unique gifts, herself included. Those gifts weren't given for their own enjoyment or ego building, but were to be used to bring the love of God to those in need. After learning this concept, Carrie's compassion and desire to serve prompted her to begin to reach out to a struggling single mom she knew. The whole family became involved – her husband Ron and occasionally even her boys joined her in meeting practical needs of this very overwhelmed mom. Sometimes this was very stressful for their family, but it provided a real life example to Carrie's boys of walking in faith and love. It was certainly much more powerful than any structured teaching about servanthood! They watched firsthand the impact of their family's friendship and service for this mom – she grew to be independent, encouraged and peaceful!

That shift in perspective – realizing their family was "blessed to be a blessing" – also impacted how Carrie and Ron parented. They gradually learned to view challenges as opportunities to shape the character of their boys in preparation for God's purposes for them. Clearly, a sense of purpose in life was a key "brick" in Carrie and Ron's **Foundation** for parenting. The joy and closeness that results from serving others builds strength into families.

◆ ◆ ❖ ◆ ❖ ◆ ◆

**"I don't know what your destiny will be, but one thing I know:
the only ones among you who will be really happy
are those who have sought and found how to serve."
Albert Schweitzer**

◆ ◆ ❖ ◆ ❖ ◆ ◆

Building PURPOSE: My Call to Parenting

Do I view parenting as a calling from God or as a role?

If I have a child, I have a God-given calling to parenting. To view parenting as a *calling* instead of a *role* can change my perspective on daily interaction with my children. My view of parenting challenges can change from, "What should I do about this problem?" to "What's the opportunity in this challenge to accomplish God's purposes?" Rather than just trying to immediately control behavior, I can prayerfully navigate through troubling times with a broader perspective.

MY RESPONSE...

In what ways do I sense God accomplishing his purposes for my child through my parenting? How might there be more opportunities for this that I haven't considered?

Viewing parenting as a calling also helps to establish a Christ-centered balance between the energy I give my children and the energy I give to other pursuits. It's easy to miss this balance.

I knew a pastor who had been in pastoral ministry for nearly fifty years. I asked him one day, "Looking back, what would you have done differently?"

He took a deep breath and with conviction told me that he wished he'd been there for his children. "I was so fervent about ministering to others that I forgot about those I could impact the most. My ministry was my life calling. Now I hardly know my children and they don't seem too interested in knowing me," he sadly reported.

The success, affirmation, and power that one often feels in the workplace can become addictive. Most jobs produce measurable outcomes and a sense of significance. There is also usually an effective authority structure. One dad put it, "I feel like I accomplish a lot at work. If someone doesn't do what I say, they're out of there! And then I come home, it's pure chaos, and I can't fire the little rascals!" It's easy to understand how climbing the corporate ladder or building a successful business can become an escape from challenges at home that make parents feel discouraged, powerless, and incapable. If I truly view parenting as a calling, however, I will passionately invest the time and energy my children need.

♦♦♦❖◆❖♦♦♦
If I have a child, I have a God-given calling to parenting!
♦♦♦❖◆❖♦♦♦

Building PURPOSE: My Purpose beyond Parenting

Do I realize parenting is only part of God's calling for me?

Before I can help my children discover their calling in life, I must be working to discover my own. Ephesians 2:10 says, **"We are God's workmanship, created in Christ Jesus to do good works, which God prepared in advance for us to do."** This means that each of us was uniquely created for a purpose – to use our gifts and talents in some way to enhance God's work on earth and in heaven. Discovering and functioning within that purpose is an important brick in my foundation for parenting.

Each of us should be on a journey to discover and function according to the miracle that God created in us - unique talents, spiritual gifts, passions, and personality. Purposefully identifying my calling begins by reflecting on the times I have felt fulfilled in the use of my gifts, not just as a parent, but in other areas of my life as well. Once I begin to notice those times of fulfillment, I can consider ways in which I can use those gifts to bless others. I can then involve my family in this pursuit. For those who feel stuck in this effort, there are numerous resources designed to help.[1]

While the pastor in the above story did not mention his wife's role in the family, it's easy to imagine this dynamic playing out: when one parent becomes wrapped up in his or her own professional world, the other is likely to compensate by making the family and its well-being the sole focus of life. One word of caution: parenting is a calling, but it is not my only purpose in life!

In contrast to men, who tend to measure success by accomplishments, women often get value from the quality of their relationships and the meeting of others' needs.[2] This sets mothers up to put their whole being into the needs of their families – their closest relationships. Emotions of a mom often rise and fall on the successes or failures, joys or sorrows, of her children. If the children are happy, Mom is happy; if they are not, she is not. In this scenario, it becomes Mom's job to keep the peace and prevent fighting because, after all, Mom is responsible for everyone's feelings about each other. One mom described it, "I feel like I'm a sponge, soaking up everyone's tension."

This dynamic unfortunately is detrimental for both the mother and the child. Mary Ellen Ashcroft states it this way: "Mothering, like fathering, is a relationship.... If motherhood becomes something else – a career or a popularity contest – it tends to warp the relationship and hurt the people involved."[3] Building my world only around my children can teach them that they are the center of the universe and can breed narcissism or a sense of entitlement. It also paves the way for the "empty nest syndrome" of purposelessness and depression when the focus of mom's entire life moves out of the house.

Certainly a parent can have a strong call to home and family. But God designs every believer to consider and act on how his or her gifts might best serve the Kingdom (see Ephesians 4:1- 13).

Particularly when my family is young or experiencing a particular challenge, it may be necessary to put tremendous energy into simply serving my family for a season. That's normal. But I can keep a vision that also serves the needs of the world around me. On numerous occasions Jesus communicated to his own mother that devotion to God took priority over family.[4] He lovingly challenged her to a life of discipleship.

Frederich Buechner defines our calling like this: "The place God calls me to is the place where my deep gladness and the world's deep hunger meet."[5] "The world's deep hunger" is outside the walls of my home. Thinking this way challenges me to consider how I can joyfully use the talents and gifts God gave me to accomplish his purposes through me beyond my own walls. This may feel like something that separates parents from children, but it is a great opportunity to model faith to my children and involve them, to whatever degree possible, in the calling I pursue.

◆ ◆ ❖ ◆ ❖ ◆ ◆

**The place God calls you to is the place where your
deep gladness and the world's deep hunger meet.**
◆ ◆ ❖ ◆ ❖ ◆ ◆

My Response…

What are several things I've done that gave me deep gladness? How did the elements of those activities fit with my unique talents, spiritual gifts, passions, or personality?

Kid Connection:

**Ask your children –
"What does Mom or Dad do that blesses or teaches you the most?"**

"What do you think Mom or Dad is good at that is helpful to other people?"

Chapter Four

It Takes a Team!
The Cornerstone of COMMUNITY

I VIVIDLY REMEMBER the cold, rainy night our 15-year-old child left a note saying: "I'm too mad to be at home. I've left. Don't come looking for me because you won't find me. Don't worry, I'll be safe."

I did what any panicked, desperate parent would do. I disobeyed my son. I worried madly, ignored the note, called close friends and went looking for him. I imagined every worse case scenario. My child could freeze to death in the rain, or be abducted from some dark, dreary hiding place, where only vagrants dwell. It's amazing how quickly our fear grips us when we feel our loved ones could be in danger. I started wondering which of my child's friends might offer a safe harbor. It was then I began to take some solace.

Our family has so prioritized the forming of a community of support, that as I reviewed the list of possibilities, my intense fear gave way to a twinkle of comfort and hope. If indeed our child landed in the home of any friend, we would have no worries, because all the possibilities were known to us, and felt safe. The only viable options for our child were kind of people who would care for and reinforce the values we hold so dear. The forming of this kind of community was no accident.

When parenting gets overwhelming, and it's bound to get overwhelming sometimes, there can be great comfort in the coming together of community in support of one another. This can be especially encouraging when there are others who will affirm and reinforce transforming love and guidance for my children.

There are different kinds of gifts, but the same Spirit. There are different kinds of service, but the same Lord. There are different kinds of working, but the same God works all of them in all men. Now to each one the manifestation of the Spirit is given for the common good.
—1 Corinthians 12: 4-7

These are familiar verses - each believer is called to contribute his or her unique gifts as part of the body of Christ. These verses are usually applied to the ministry of the local church. Could it be, however, that the first arena in which they could be applied is in the raising of my children?

Building COMMUNITY: With my Spouse

How can I protect my primary relationship?

Single and remarried parents often discover new depth in their relationship with God through the challenges they have faced. God's grace is abundant to all who walk this road. Most of them would agree however, that this is not a preferred road. The research about the devastation of divorce on children is extensive and convincing.

Marriage is the biblical starting place for families. God intended the union between man and woman to be intimate in every way—loving God and loving each other for a lifetime. A strong marriage is a key "brick" in the foundation of a strong family. This is powerfully stated in Malachi 2:15, as God's primary purpose for marriage is proclaimed – "**Has not the LORD made them one? In flesh and spirit they are his. And why one? Because he was seeking godly offspring.**"

One Christian psychologist, a friend of ours, recalls attending a class for psychology students on juvenile delinquency. When the professor invited students to share their reasons for taking the class, most gave lofty and intellectual answers. One student, a middle-aged man in army fatigues, looked tired and unimpressed. "The reason I'm taking this class," he said, "is that if something isn't done soon, my twelve-year-old boy will be majoring in juvenile delinquency."

The astute professor then said, "So you've come to this class to learn how to *prevent* delinquency?" The man replied, "Yes." The professor then sternly said, "I will give you the answer. The rest of the information provided this semester is only secondary in importance."

Of course the whole class jumped to attention with eager ears, waiting for the profound answer of this seasoned professor. They anticipated a scholarly dissertation backed by research. Instead, the professor looked this man in the eyes and with utmost sincerity said, "Love your wife. That's the greatest thing a man can do for his son."

That is easy to say, but it takes work to accomplish. The uniting of two unique people, with their diverse backgrounds and various beliefs, in this, the most intimate of relationships, is a profoundly difficult task. True unity requires a combination of solid commitment, great effort, and enduring patience on the part of each person. The best part of loving someone is the limitless acceptance that brings deep, safe intimacy and joy. To grow in such love, a man and a woman must first deeply pursue a love relationship with God. Then they must give great energy to nurturing their love for one another.

Too often, however, married couples lose their sense of adventure and connection with each other. Because the effort to keep the fire alive can be demanding, they resign themselves to an existence of daily routines, chores, activities, and responsibilities. When marriage reaches this place, a couple may slip into any of a number of distractions to deal with their relational dissatisfaction: a new house, job, leisure pursuits, even - kids! These couples are likely to support the over-commitment of their children because it gives them additional roles and responsibilities to fulfill. Many parents lament this excessive busyness, but very few actually do something about it. These activities become the essence of life. Removing them would strip away the false sense of significance the activities produce.

Many Christians simply accept this state in the name of commitment, while their marriage loses its vitality. When attempts to mask their dissatisfaction fail, some marriage partners choose infidelity. Many choose divorce. Others just stand firm in their commitment, living a busy but shallow existence. At some point, even if the appearance of a strong marriage is projected to the outside community, the children will know something is not right. This causes stress for them. It is only a matter of time before the children will act on this stress at home, in the community or, worst of all, internally.

Marriage is often considered the ultimate cure-all to a soul that is hungry for deep, abiding intimacy and fulfillment. It is only a reflection of the love of Christ, however, which is indeed perfect. The deepest longings of my soul for intimacy cannot be satisfied this side of heaven. So when I feel dissatisfied, I must recognize and confess my temptation to seek temporarily satisfying activities or relationships. If I am struggling this way, I can be honest with God and trusted friends about my disappointment. This will help me learn to be at peace regarding those things I cannot have or cannot change in this life.

Lynne shares her perspective on our journey with this concept:

When Jim and I were first married, I was sure that my fun-loving, handsome, gregarious husband was a real catch, the man of my dreams! Except... I wasn't sure he was as serious about the important things in life as I wanted him to be. I journaled specific spiritual goals for us as a couple. In retrospect, they were really more of an indirect listing of performance standards, unmet expectations, and fears. When he found out about it, he was hurt and angry that I had an agenda for his spiritual growth. He somewhat accurately interpreted this as my lack of acceptance and respect for him as he was.

A few months later, we attended a seminar about letting God's grace transform the subtle performance standards Christians unknowingly attach to themselves and each other. These standards, if not revealed, tend to lead Christians down a path of "fixing" and controlling others. Only through the lens of God's grace can the Christian family function in the joy, freedom, and potential that God intends. This message not only changed our relationships with God and how we viewed all of life, but it built into our marriage a solid understanding of grace and acceptance for each other. That understanding was invaluable in weathering the difficulties of having three intense children.

Some time later, Jim came to me excitedly – "Honey, I figured it out. You're not the wife of my dreams, you're the wife of my reality!!" Wow. How do you take that statement? I wasn't sure if I should be insulted that I wasn't the wife of his dreams or relieved by the lack of the expectation attached to his fantasy wife. I decided (by faith) to be relieved. His insight took our family's understanding of the grace of God to a deeper level. Jim exhorts and humors me through my ongoing struggle with insecurity and self-criticism; his thinning hair and thickening waistline have become kind of cute. And we find it easier to adore the children of our reality. Ironically, as we learn to live in this graceful definition, our marriage grows ever closer to a dream come true.

Whether my marriage is thriving or on a rocky road, I try to remember that it is only by God's love and grace that marriage can be fulfilling. Parents feeling stuck in marriage can seek the help of a friend, pastor, or professional who will gracefully listen and help them explore their deepest longings and beliefs.

MY RESPONSE...

What is my first inclination when my marriage is stressful? Do I talk to my spouse? To a friend? Do I stay silent? Do I seek ways to distract myself from the stress? Do I pray? What has been the result of my various choices?

In what ways do I see the character of Christ in my spouse? How might I find a way to express this to him or her?

Building COMMUNITY: As a Single Parent

How can I strengthen my foundation for parenting?

The trauma of divorce or the death of a spouse fractures a life at its very core. The way many single parents deal with this reality is a great gift to the body of Christ! The need all parents have to build a strong **Foundation** can be more obvious for single parents than for those married. Because two-parent resources and energy are simply not a part of daily life, single parents can become models of growth in dependence on God's word and very presence in their lives each day, and dependence on the community of faith for even the most practical of support and encouragement.

As a single parent I have a great opportunity to model for my children how to deal with crisis. My children can learn more from my life in a difficult time than from years of Sunday school lessons. Will they see someone who brings their struggles authentically to God and who doesn't measure God's love by how life has unfolded? Many strong believers have been inspired by the exceptional courage, commitment, and selflessness of a parent who raised them alone.

Jane shared her story with us. As a young child, life changed both emotionally and financially after the death of her father. Her mother raised five children alone, including one with a handicap.

"My mother reminded me often that her Creator was her true soul-mate[1] and would meet her needs. She relied strongly on God's Word and the fellowship of other believers in the challenge of raising the five of us. She also took an interesting approach to her financial challenges, one that many people would not consider. Sometimes there was no money to put gas in the car, or to even own a car, but she gave generously to the poor, regularly took in and fed those in need, and taught her children the importance of giving and serving God no matter what their circumstance. Later in life, as a single mother myself, I gained much strength from her example, and still find great joy in helping those in need."

In addition to loneliness and other challenges, those single parents who are divorced also must deal with a culture that is often cynical about marriage. Bitterness toward ex-spouses is rampant and "congratulations on your divorce" greeting cards are readily available. A divorced parent benefits from close friendships that provide strong encouragement to pursue the **"God of all comfort"** (2 Corinthians 1:3) instead of cynical resentment. The heartache of divorce can easily grow into a **"bitter root** (that) **grows up to cause trouble and defile many"** (Hebrews 12:15).

♦ ♦ ❖ ◆ ❖ ♦ ♦

A great challenge provides *a great opportunity* to model
to children how to deal with crisis.

♦ ♦ ❖ ◆ ❖ ♦ ♦

Jesus had a special joy in connecting with broken, discouraged people of all types because they understood their need for him. Just as Jesus readily embraced people in need, the body of Christ is designed by God to be a surrogate family for orphans, widows, and any other family unit that needs support, encouragement, and love.

MY RESPONSE...

What aspect of single parenting is particularly difficult for me? What opportunity is hidden in the difficulty?

Building COMMUNITY: In Spite of Parenting Differences

How can we decrease the stress of parenting together?

For most of us, whether married or single, our children's other parent is involved with the kids to one degree or another. Every parent is different and those differences are bound to cause stress.

Choosing to avoid the effort of dealing with these differences can cause a growing wedge in the marital relationship. Parents often attempt to compensate for what they perceive as the other person's parenting mistakes, (i.e., too lenient or too strict). As both parents do this, it polarizes their parenting styles, creates greater inconsistency for the children, and increases conflict between the parents.

For others, the stress of parenting differences can be a motivator to make the effort to address, understand, and support those differences. A parent can address the stress while demonstrating godly character, forgiveness, wisdom, and self-control in dealing with the other parent.

Focus on principles

It is helpful in addressing conflicts to begin by discovering and discussing areas of agreement on basic parenting principles and values. These might include children's need for **unconditional** love, the importance of certain values and responsibilities, and respectful discipline when the children are off track. If parents can agree on the needs but allow each other to have different *methods* and *styles* in meeting their children's needs, it can greatly decrease conflict.

Lynne and I are opposite personality types and our parenting challenges are quite different from each other. I tend to be fast-paced, expressive, and emotional. A common weakness is a quick, harsh temper. She is more analytical and guarded, and is prone to critical nagging. After two decades of marriage, our differences continue to present challenges (and they probably always will), but we have greatly decreased them by agreeing on fundamental principles. A couple in a class we taught explained that learning to agree on parenting principles, implemented in their own styles, relieved an enormous pressure on their relationship and may have even saved their marriage.

Strengthen the child

Regardless of typical differences, it is almost inevitable that at some point I will be tempted to jump in the middle of a harsh conflict between my child and his or her other parent. In this story, Lynne's perspective illustrates how this can work.

Jim was crabby and responded harshly and loudly to Bethany, our five-year-old daughter. She ran to me in tears and sobbed out her hurt feelings. I was angry and judgmental of his impatience with her. My impulse was to criticize him and tell him to apologize to Bethany. Instead I took a deep breath and put my focus on helping my daughter, "You seem scared and sad. Is that right?" "Yeah." "Could you tell your daddy how you feel?" "I can't!" "How about if I go with you and we can snuggle while you talk to him?" "O.K."

Jim appreciated my approach. He listened while Bethany told him how she felt when he yelled at her. His apology gave her increased confidence in her ability to resolve her own conflicts, even with someone five times her size.

Strengthening children to resolve their own conflicts with a parent is a very helpful principle in the context of working together as parents. Years ago, Lynne and I made a commitment to support each other's decisions in response to our children's requests. The children quickly learned that one parent's no meant no, and they would be held responsible for disobeying one parent's no, no matter what the other parent might say. If I disagree with Lynne's answer I will either support her decision or guide the children in respectfully negotiating with her. This might be as simple as, "If your mom said no, you'll have to work it out with her." Or it might involve problem solving a respectful way for the child to articulate his or her needs and viewpoint.

But of course it doesn't always go this well if the other parent in the situation is prone to defensiveness or harshness. When the one parent is not open to dialogue with a child about a situation, sometimes the other parent's best option is to help the child understand what's happening, what he or she can and can't control, and where God fits into all this. "How are you feeling after what Dad/Mom said (or did)? What could you do about feeling _____ (i.e. sad or mad)? What might help the situation with Dad/Mom?" And trying as it may be, when a child's other parent presents difficulties, there is an important opportunity to teach children about God's love and value of them. As children get older, they can learn to look at the example of each parent and their heavenly Father's example and decide how they will live life.

**Discover and discuss areas of agreement
on parenting principles and values,
not methods or styles.**

MY RESPONSE...

Is there a recurring conflict with my children's other parent? (If so, what is that conflict?)

(Choose one or more)
1. **On what basic parenting principles might we agree? How might I begin that discussion without prompting a defensive response?**
2. **How could we each implement in our own way the parenting principles on which we agree?**
3. **How can I strengthen my children to solve conflicts with their other parent?**

Building COMMUNITY with Others of Faith

What role can other people play in my parenting journey?

For too many parents, church is an *activity* they attend once or twice a week. From a biblical perspective, however, "church" is the *community of faith* and is at the core of the believer's identity. For the church to function properly as the body of Christ and display God's presence on earth, connection with one another must be an integral part of daily life – including family life. We all need a safe community to provide acceptance and encouragement in family struggles. This community is also designed to be a partnership between adults who are committed to loving one another's children with Christ's love.

Christians are given many "one another" commands in the New Testament. Love one another,[2] encourage one another,[3] and bear one another's burdens,[4] are some of the important commands. The power of such connected relationships in the church is an essential characteristic of grace-filled Christian community. To have a strong foundation of faith, I must constantly seek relationships with other believers that feed my soul and strengthen me to love Christ more deeply. Conversely, if I am shy or have had wounding experiences in relationships, it may be an act of faith just to be authentic and open with others.

According to a George Gallup survey, "Americans are among the loneliest people in the entire world."[5] Houses have grown bigger and have fewer people in them. Kids, following their parents' example, can escape to entertainment centers, computers, and anonymous lives – in their own rooms. Excessive work demands take parents away from their families, and high mobility jobs take families away from their rooted relationships. This is accepted as normal. Robert Putnam reports that involvement in local civic organizations, leagues, and clubs has fallen roughly fifty percent since 1975.[6] Larry Crabb interprets the effect of this on the church. Unless the church focuses on community now, he says, it will become "stale [and] irrelevant. A place where sufferers suffer alone, where pressure generates conformity rather than the Spirit creating life."[7]

Love one another

It doesn't have to be that way. I was created for gut-level, honest, grace-filled connection with other believers.

Lynne explains how she benefited greatly from connection and support from others:

In the difficult early years of my parenting journey, I confided in others out of desperation. During one particularly discouraging phase, two of my close friends (who didn't know each other) called me within a few hours of each other. They each stated nearly identical versions of this message: "I felt like the Lord told me to call you and tell you he was pleased with you." I remember hanging up the phone on that second, confirming phone call. I was stunned and amazed at God's very personal love and care for me when I felt as though I least deserved it. I still reflect back on that phone call in times of discouragement and will forever be grateful to people who brought the healing light of Christ into my darkest moments.

MY RESPONSE...

Who are the people in my life who really encourage me (fill me with courage) for my journey? What sets them apart from other relationships? What will it take to arrange to spend more time with them?

Connected, supportive relationships with other families are important for parents. And these connections are essential for kids! Sometimes they seem difficult to achieve in this culture. It's not impossible, and it is well worth the persistence to achieve them.

Carry one another's burdens

When Moses told the nation of Israel to follow God's commandments and **"impress them on your children,"**[8] he was not speaking just to parents but to an entire community. He knew individual families were vulnerable. He knew that a family was only as strong as its community. He knew they would need each other in almost every way if their faith was to be passed on from generation to generation.

In our individualized, isolationist culture, parents may communicate carefully *about* their struggles but still continue to deal with them alone. After teaching our parenting class, I had what has become a fairly common conversation. A couple described the difficulties that they were experiencing with their children. The struggles they shared were very painful for them. I listened intently and asked questions to help me further understand. I then asked whom they had invited to help them carry their load with them. Each stated that they were involved in a women's or men's group and frequently shared prayer requests.

I questioned further, "At what point have you asked someone in your community to carry your burden by coming to your home for a few hours so you could get out and connect with each other or with Jesus?"

Their confused look preceded the husband's response, "We could never do that! That would be too much to ask." His wife nodded in agreement.

In the context of struggling with sin, the Bible tells us to carry each other's burdens.[9] Yet, most parents try to take care of their problems themselves to avoid embarrassment or imposition. As a result, parents often deny their family the outside support that they need. And the body of Christ loses the opportunity to function as God designed it.

We were been blessed to be part of a little community of families that rallied around Linda, a single mom from our church. She was struggling to raise three very lively young boys without financial support from her ex-husband. One family provides practical help and childcare, another family provides budgeting and financial help, we coach her in her parenting challenges. Linda blesses *us* with her example of faith and determination. We all gather periodically to share meals and fellowship. The gatherings are lively as the dozen children ages 3 – 18 integrate with every aspect.

On one such occasion all the parents arrived stressed for various reasons, particularly Linda. The low energy level of the adults was quite a contrast to the off-the-charts intensity of the children. We are nearly all irritable. The drone of whines was constant. Our 15-year-old son Noah sensed the need to give the adults some space and led the boys in fun, active play. Soon the adults could re-engage to calm and encourage the kids. Linda's liveliest son seemed to relish periodically snuggling in my lap. The whining subsided and the boys began to feel really important as they were invited to contribute to the dinner prep. As calm fell over us, the youngsters even took delight in helping to clean and then play peacefully together. When the night was done, the peace and joy we all felt was exhilarating. We knew we had been in the presence of Christ, functioning like he had designed his body of believers to function.

◆◆◆❖◆❖◆◆◆
**The body of Christ is designed to be
a source of encouragement in family struggles and a partnership
between adults who love each other's children.**
◆◆◆❖◆❖◆◆◆

So as a member of the Body of Christ, with the amazing capacity to love my family and me, it is important for me to consider whom I can invite to help me carry the burden of my lively and sometimes difficult children.

MY RESPONSE...

What is my initial gut response to the idea of calling a friend in my faith community and asking him or her to share my burden of parenting in some way? Why? How could I do this in a way that will help me to feel comfortable when I need help?

KID CONNECTION!

Choose one or both –

1. Ask your children to describe your parenting style. Older children can choose from a list of descriptive words: Firm, lenient, expressive, reserved, spontaneous, organized/ orderly, playful, hard working, etc. Ask them what they see as each parent's most important strengths. Younger children can choose animals that seem similar to Mommy and Daddy: strong lion, hard-working beaver, playful puppy, quiet kitty, snuggly teddy bear, etc.

2. With what other family, do your children wish you could all spend more time? Consider a plan to get together.

Chapter Five

Why Do I Stay Stuck?
The Cornerstone of INSIGHT

"the Lord…will bring to light what is hidden in darkness and will expose the motives of men's hearts."

—I Corinthians 4:5

CHERYL AND TINA enjoyed their playdates with their two preschool boys. The boys generally played together quite well, but today they were a little *too* quiet. When the moms went to check on them, they found them engaged in "learning" about each other through a little game of Doctor. Cheryl was concerned, but also somewhat amused. Tina, who is normally a very gentle and patient mother, immediately lost her composure and began screaming at her son. "Jack, what in the world are you doing? That is NOT o.k.! Pull your pants back up right now, and don't EVER do that again!! Go to the time out chair!" Same situation, two very different responses by the moms. So what fed their different responses?

Dr. John Gottman, psychologist and family researcher, wisely stated, "The path to becoming a better parent – like most every road to personal growth and mastery begins with self-examination."[1] Better parenting starts not with better techniques, but with a careful look at myself and why I respond the way I do as a parent. Paul's prayer for the Philippians gives us encouragement to seek to truly understand ourselves, **"And this is my prayer: that your love may abound more and more in knowledge and *depth of insight*, so that you may be able to discern what is best…"** (Philippians 1:9,10).

It is from this perspective that I can bring my parenting challenges to God, *not* asking, "What should I do?" but asking, "What am I thinking and feeling?" "What am I believing?" and "How do these things hold up to God's truth?" Answering the first question, "What should I do?" in isolation is simply an exercise in behavior management. Answering the other questions is a rich adventure into spiritual growth. Once these foundational questions are addressed, parents can make wiser decisions about responses to their children. We know that Cheryl has learned to ask such questions, and that they guided her gentle response. We can only wonder whether, if Tina had understood her own feelings by asking these questions, she might have chosen a different response. Instead, we know that hers was the kind of response that can create shame in her son about a child's natural curiosity about bodies. This shame, reinforced over time, can lead to all kinds of sexual struggles.

So we always encourage parents, along with addressing the "what should I do?" question, to be growing in awareness of how what's going on inside them and how God's truth might speak to their parenting challenges.

> ♦ ♦ ♦ ❖ ◆ ❖ ♦ ♦ ♦
> **"The path to becoming a better parent –
> like most every road to personal growth and mastery
> begins with self-examination."**
> ♦ ♦ ♦ ❖ ◆ ❖ ♦ ♦ ♦

Building INSIGHT: Understanding Core Beliefs

What are they and where do they come from?

Caryn grew up in a strict Christian home. Her mom was the primary family caregiver and her dad was the provider. She was frequently criticized for what she did that was wrong or "sinful," but rarely affirmed for anything. Through these experiences she developed numerous underlying beliefs:

- God loves me more when I do well.
- Parents are responsible for their kids' choices.
- Maintaining a good impression is more important than admitting problems.
- Faith in God is life's most important virtue, but don't admit if you struggle with it.
- Doing "right" is more important than learning from mistakes.
- Conflict and anger are "unchristian."

For years Caryn lived according to these beliefs, which were powerful, unidentified influences. While she admitted to a deep, perpetual sense that something was "off," she basically learned to ignore this sense and manage life according to these beliefs - until her oldest child became a teenager. The strong-willed child put each belief to the test – either intentionally or by virtue of rebellious behavior. Caryn could no longer keep the façade of a peaceful life. Tempers flared and abusive words and hurtful actions occurred almost daily. As the conflict escalated, she felt judged by church friends and incapable of implementing the rigid solutions they gave.

Only when she began to identify her core beliefs was she willing to let go of her desire for a quick and easy solution. She began to take those beliefs to God, to allow him to transform them. Gradually, in a process of humility and honesty, Caryn's relationship with her teen has been transformed.

There is in each person a set of core beliefs, which guide that person's choices and actions. These are beliefs about God, values, relationships, comfort, purpose, etc. Some people are quite aware of these deep-seated beliefs; other people are not. Whether we are aware or not, we all bring our core beliefs to marriage and parenting. Some of these beliefs are rooted in truth; some are not. Whether or not I am aware of them, whether or not they are rooted in truth, these beliefs are the major influence behind my thoughts, feelings, and decisions in family interactions. These beliefs are first shaped in the family in which I grew up.

Core beliefs do not come only from families of origin. Peers, teachers, pastors, or other outside factors such as media, advertising, and popular culture also shape these core beliefs. How I interact with this complex mosaic of influences largely determines my beliefs about what is acceptable, safe, desirable, important, etc., and what is not.

Growing to understand these beliefs and how they affect my actions can be a life long pursuit. This is both a courageous and scary pursuit because in it, we invite God to expose what we have hidden in the darkness of secrecy or ignorance, and shine the light of his truth on the ugly things we might believe about ourselves and others.

MY RESPONSE…

What are some possible core beliefs (reference Caryn's underlying beliefs above for examples) that I learned from my parents…

…about what's important in life?

…about roles and relationships between men and women/husbands and wives?

…about relationships between parents and children?
In what ways does my parenting style reflect these beliefs?

Building INSIGHT: Noticing the Effect of Core Beliefs

In what circumstances are they most easily identified?

A friend once shared a fairly common viewpoint with me: "When I'm with friends and people at work or church, I feel successful and positive. When I'm at home, I become somebody else, short-tempered and harsh. It's as if I lose the real me!" While the joy of working with others can be a reflection of real God-given gifts and desires, our inner struggles or "baggage" can be easily protected or hidden behind a "mask" well-managed behavior. Most people can control themselves well enough in public so that what others see, and what they themselves experience, is in line with core beliefs such as, "I should always be successful and positive"; "I am only valuable when people approve of me"; or "Christians should always be nice." Due to the superficial nature of most public interactions, these beliefs are not readily challenged and revealed. But at home, when our masks are stripped away, the "real me" is sure to be revealed. And it's not always a pretty sight. But it is a reality God can work with if we are willing to grow in insight about our "baggage" and learn to let God keep transforming us from the inside out. Here's how it can work:

When my life is going smoothly, it can be difficult to identify any false beliefs that adversely affect my life and my parenting. However, life at home is much less easy to control. Parenting tends to bring people to greater extremes of emotions and responses than they ever thought possible! In my closest relationships, raw opinions, beliefs, and emotions are most readily provoked and exposed. This provides a rich opportunity to identify and examine any false beliefs that perpetuate my family struggles.

I had an opportunity to gain insight into my own core beliefs during one of our early vacations. We had looked forward to this warm-weather family vacation all winter. It was our first with all three children. I had just settled into a fulfilling new job and God seemed to be smiling brightly on our young family. Our favorite babysitter was even coming along to ensure an enjoyable time for all. As we started down the road I was overwhelmed with a sense of God's goodness to us. I joyfully anticipated a rich family time ahead.

That was when I learned an important lesson: No matter how you slice it, packing three extremely active preschool children into any sized vehicle for a fourteen-hour drive can turn the brightest expectations into a hopeless nightmare. The kids grew crabby and restless. They fought constantly with each other and I frequently fought them to keep their seat belts on. Lynne did her best but needed me to engage as well. The babysitter was overwhelmed, certainly wondering what she'd gotten herself into. I tried to ignore the chaos while I was straining to see the stripes on the road through a dense fog. By the time the kids fell asleep, I had a pounding headache and a white knuckled grip on the steering wheel. I was out of control of everything but the steering wheel and I was determined to get to our destination where I could relax.

Any remaining "blessings" evaporated quickly as kids got sick, we all fought, and the weather grew so cold it snowed. Our daughter's screaming meltdown under the table in a restaurant pushed my sanity to the edge. A private tantrum of my own (complete with panic attack symptoms) made me realize something was terribly wrong – not with the children, but with *me*.

And where did God fit in to what had happened? I had no clue. At the time, I just wanted the feelings to go away. I prayed that God would settle my children, that things would go smoothly the rest of the trip. I hated how I felt and I wanted it to end. I begged, "God! Come and calm the storm!"

Looking back, I see now that this was a tremendous, but missed, opportunity to let my thoughts, feelings, and responses lead me to a place of deeper insight about me, God, and my relationship with God. It was a couple of years later that I learned to realize that events or situations do not cause my thoughts, feelings, and actions. Rather, those responses grow out of my core beliefs. Generally speaking, the stronger my response is to a given situation, the stronger the belief I have about some aspect of that situation.

My Response....

What do I relate to in Jim's story? When do I most often experience strong emotions in my parenting?

For most people, strong feelings and responses such as these provide helpful clues about their core beliefs. However, when some people encounter stress, they avoid it. They will work hard to present a positive impression and act as if everything is OK when it is not. This reaction gives less of a clue about underlying beliefs because it may look like an appropriate response. At some point, however, that avoidance may cause infrequent but intense emotional outbursts, or even intense emotional "inbursts" such as depression, self-destructive behaviors, or social withdrawal.

**Usually the stronger my response is to a given situation,
the stronger the belief I have about some aspect of that situation.**

Building INSIGHT: Identifying My False Core Beliefs

What do my intense responses tell me about my own core beliefs?

Jesus experienced intense emotions and responses that were anchored in biblical truth and justice![2] For most people, however, intense responses (particularly those involving anger, deep frustration, or anxiety) are usually driven by false beliefs. These beliefs can be powerful but subtle. Understanding them usually requires intentional or purposeful reflection. As parents grow to better understand the relationship between responses, thoughts, feelings, and beliefs, their foundation for parenting is strengthened and they are better equipped to give effective energy to their children. The following chart lists some common parenting responses, strong emotions, and the possible false beliefs that drive them.

Response:	Strong emotions:	Possible false beliefs:
Controlling – Making sure things always go my way.	-Frustration -Anxiety -Irritation	-My children's behavior defines me. -We'll be rejected if we behave badly. -Happiness depends on getting my way.
Mean words or actions – Saying or doing things to hurt or make my child look bad. Condescension.	-Hurt -Vindictiveness -Anger	-I must keep my children in their place. -I "get even" by hurting others. -They deserve a harsh response. -I am superior.
Outbursts – Loud, intimidating displays.	-Anger -Fear -Rage	-I must control my children at all times. -I must protect myself. -Life is terrible, and God doesn't care.
Avoidance – Acting as if things are OK when they're not. Peacekeeping at all costs.	-Anxiety -Discouragement -Shame	-Christians shouldn't have conflict. -Things must look good. -I'm not worth listening to.
Escape – Extreme avoidance, like addictions and obsessions. Absence.	-Despair -Hopelessness -Fear	-God has given up on me. -I'm a failure. Life is hopeless. -The pain of my problems is unbearable.

MY RESPONSE...

After taking a few minutes to look at the chart, to which emotions and beliefs do I most relate? What stands out to me?

◆◆◆❖◆❖◆◆◆
**As I grow to better understand the relationship
between responses, thoughts, feelings, and beliefs,
my foundation for parenting is strengthened.**
◆◆◆❖◆❖◆◆◆

Building INSIGHT: Valuing a Difficult Process

What benefit is there to identifying false beliefs?

Addictive or destructive patterns are rooted in people's inability or unwillingness to examine their false beliefs. It somehow seems easier to ignore the problems they create, or to hope and pray that God will somehow just take them away. Even when people try to ignore the pain of recurring problems, it remains a primary factor in their relationships and behavior.

As much as I might like them to go away, difficult emotions and responses are God's gift to me – a valuable window into my soul. They tell me when something is not as it should be. They can lead me to healing that changes more than just my parenting. If I view pain as negative, it can cause me to escape, deny, or try to cover it up.

Consider this beautiful story from the life of Dr. Paul Brand, as recorded by Philip Yancey.

"Most people view pain as an enemy. Yet, as my leprosy patients prove, it forces us to pay attention to threats against our bodies. Without it, heart attacks, strokes, ruptured appendixes, and stomach ulcers would occur without warning. I noticed that the symptoms my patients complained about were actually a display of bodily healing at work. Virtually every response of our bodies that we view with irritation or disgust – blister, callus, swelling, fever, sneeze, cough, vomiting, and especially pain – demonstrates a *reflex toward health*. In all these things normally considered enemies, we can find reason to be grateful." [3]

No matter how much I might whine, plead, or bargain, God won't just *deliver* me from the chaos and painful emotions of family life. It is my false belief that needs healing, not my emotional symptoms. God will not take away my symptoms at the expense of my spiritual growth. He wants my frustration, confusion, and even despair, to drive me to *him* – not to another formula

to make the pain go away. He is inviting me to boldly enter a process of transformation. Only by working to identify false beliefs and to hold them up against truth can those beliefs and the "stuck" patterns be transformed.

**Difficult emotions and responses are God's gift to me,
a valuable window into my soul. They can lead me to healing
that changes more than just my parenting.**

MY RESPONSE...

When has a difficult process been the source of helpful change in my life?

KID CONNECTION:

Next time you're sharing a book, movie, or TV show with your child, talk about what one of the characters might have been thinking, feeling, and believing that caused his or her response. What did you learn? (This is a helpful way to teach discernment and values to your children.)

Chapter Six

━━━━━━━━━━━━━━━━━━

Transformed Parenting
Insight + Faith = True Change

"Do not be conformed to this world, but be transformed by the renewing of your mind."
—Romans 12:2

IN JOHN 5:24, Jesus said, "The truth will set you free." When I am anchoring myself in God's truths, I find incredible freedom as a parent. But how is this accomplished practically?

Building INSIGHT: Discovering the Power of True Beliefs

How does scriptural truth affect parenting in everyday life?

The Scriptures are filled with principles that have repeatedly corrected people's beliefs. Most false beliefs are related to subtle ways in which I feel inadequate or defective. This makes me dependent on circumstances or other people's responses to me (including my children) to feel successful, loved, or happy. The Scriptures speak loud and clear. Because of God's love and his forgiveness through Christ, I am full, complete, and deeply loved. And so are my kids. The more I can remind myself of those truths, even in tense situations, the more my parenting changes from the ground up. This is why studying and applying the Bible is the most important step to correcting my false core beliefs.

The following is a list of biblical truths applied to parenting. I am learning to hold these truths up against false core beliefs and allow God to transform my mind and emotions.

Truthful Core Beliefs for Parenting:

Each family member is beloved and treasured by God, despite failings or imperfections.
Romans 8:1, 37-39   **Ephesians 2:4,5**

God is at work in our midst, desiring to transform each person for his good pleasure.
Philippians 1:6, 2:13   **1 Corinthians 3:6,7**

God has a plan and a purpose for each one of us.
1 Corinthians 12:4-7,11   **Ephesians 2:10**

God is present in our worst situations and will guide and counsel us.
Psalm 73:21-25   **Isaiah 43:1-5**

God can use our struggles for eternal good.
Romans 8:28   **2 Corinthians 4:17**   **Hebrews 12:11**

When things go bad, Jesus is enough.
Ephesians 1:3-6   **Hebrews 4:16**   **2 Corinthians 12:9,10**

My children are responsible for their own behavior. I am responsible for *my* behavior.
(The fruit of the Spirit is *self*-control, not control of others!)
Matthew 16:27   **Romans 14:4**   **Galatians 5:22,23**

My value is only from God's value of me, neither from my behavior nor my children's.
Titus 3:4-7   **Philippians 3:3-9**

God delights in me because I am his creation and his child.
Zephaniah 3:17   **Psalm 139**   **1 John 3:1**   **Galatians 4:6**

The most important thing when family life is difficult or confusing is to love and value my
children.
1 Corinthians 13:13 1   **Corinthians 16:14**   **Romans 13:8**

God is the source of my love for my children.
1 Thessalonians 3:12   **Ephesians 3:16-19**   **Colossians 3:12**

◆◆❖◆❖◆◆

**If I receive God's love and his forgiveness through Christ,
I am full, complete, and deeply loved.**
◆◆❖◆❖◆◆

My Response...

Which of my parenting responses do I recognize as rooted in truth? What truth is the source of that response?

Which of the truths would I like to build more firmly into my Foundation? (This may take some thoughtful reflection with an open heart and an open Bible.) How could I remind myself of those truths so that they sink deeper into my spirit?

Building INSIGHT: Transforming my Beliefs

What does this process involve?

Let's look at two different ways of addressing children's misbehavior. The first starts with the question "What should I do?" As we've said, this can be an important question. It is a question about parenting strategies. Here's how it works:

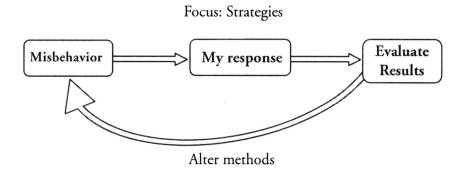

When my child misbehaves, I respond. From my response there is a result. I evaluate the results. Based on whether my response effectively addressed the misbehavior, I plot a strategy for the next time it happens. I can go to books or talk to others to determine what to do differently. Sometimes this approach effectively modifies or corrects my child's behavior.

However, if I keep trying new strategies but my child still misbehaves, it could be a signal that I need to take a look at my own thoughts, feelings, and actions. It's possible that these elements are contributing to my child's responses. Each of us can think of times when someone's words to us seemed appropriate but something about their response aggravated us. Children are experts at discerning and reacting to anxiety, anger, or other emotions that drive parent's responses, no matter what the technique.

Remembering that events (i.e., a child's misbehavior) do not really *cause* responses, I can look below the surface to the beliefs, thoughts, and feelings that may be driving my responses. The question, "What am I believing about this?" sets up a whole different focus for reflection and evaluation. I begin to realize that if my kids are to change, then I need to change first. I have to change not only what I am doing, but what I believe.

Focus: Beliefs

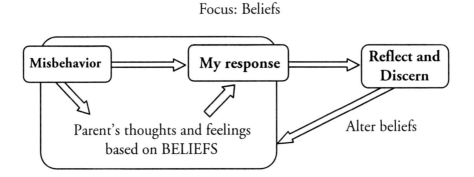

From this perspective, I can see that all of my responses to my kids' misbehavior actually flow through my beliefs. This is why a young mother or father can get so bent out of shape by a child's persistent messiness while the grandparents can just laugh. The parent's belief might be that kids shouldn't leave messes, that messiness is disrespectful, or that children are never going to learn to clean up after themselves. The grandparent's belief is that making messes is just a part of being a child and that learning to clean up after themselves is a *long* process for children. Same event. Different beliefs. Different responses. Hopefully, through a process of discerning false beliefs, I won't have to wait to be a grandparent to find the peace needed to smile through my children's difficult behavior.

The question, "What might I be *believing* that is driving this repeated problem with my child?" is a vulnerable question. But the Bible encourages authentic, not superficial, relationships among believers. My growth has been accelerated by blatant honesty with God and a few close friends who encourage me to grab hold of God's truth in my challenges.

"(The Lord) knows the secrets of the heart."

—Psalm 44:21

"Surely you desire truth in the inner parts, you teach me wisdom in the inmost place."

—Psalm 51:6

"Therefore confess your sins [including unbelief] to each other and pray for each other so that you may be healed."

—James 5:16

Replacing false beliefs with God's truth is certainly not simple, but it starts with one situation and one truth at a time – like building bricks in a foundation. It is a journey that will have its ups and downs but will yield long-lasting results.

While working with youth and families, I have seen many whose extreme false beliefs have been deeply engrained through traumatic experiences or relationships. These people often find it very beneficial to seek the help of professional ministers or Christian therapists who specialize in these dynamics. They can skillfully address the issues and walk people through spiritual and emotional healing. Parents will probably benefit from additional help if, after doing their best to apply these principles, they still frequently relate to at least one of these statements:

>...*I feel out of control or overwhelmed.* I lack the resources to deal with life's challenges.
>...*I don't understand.* I don't know why I respond and feel the way I do in situations.
>...*I feel stuck.* My problem seems to be getting worse, even though I have tried to change.

**Replacing false beliefs with God's truth is certainly not simple,
but it starts with one situation and one truth at a time –
like building bricks in a foundation.**

My Response…

In a recent difficult situation with one of my children in which I had a strong, emotional response, what possible false belief might have contributed to my response? What true belief could I focus on in a similar situation in the future?

Building INSIGHT: Learning from Practical Examples

How does this process work with different types of parents?

You may have empathized with my Murphy's Law vacation in the last chapter – fog and snow; sick, out-of-control kids; and a teetering-on-the-edge-of-sanity dad. This experience was disturbing, but eventually taught me some important lessons. That day was loaded with the kind of strong emotions and reactions in which I could either stay stuck or that could lead me toward spiritual transformation. Conventional anger management might teach me just to breathe and relax. But that would do nothing to help me assess and address my false beliefs.

My first false belief was that *family vacations should be fun and relaxing*. Since that first vacation I have adopted a new belief that there's really no such thing as a "fun and relaxing" vacation with young children. We now call them family trips! Even the name change helps to redefine the belief: these trips are very important, but not relaxing. Ironically, from that belief I find it easier to actually experience relaxation.

On that trip however, my anxiety exposed another, even deeper false belief. I believed *God needed to be invited to be fully present, and that when he came, things would get better.* The intensity of my private tantrum and demanding prayers revealed it - "God, come and calm the storm." Conversely, this must mean that *God's presence and blessing must cease when circumstances become difficult.* I have since learned, and continue to learn, that God never leaves us or forsakes us.[1] God's love and presence are not evidenced by smooth circumstances. In fact, difficult circumstances are actually a primary opportunity to know and experience God's love and presence by faith. When similar situations occur these days, I sometimes find myself whispering under my breath, "Jesus, you are with me." Because of his presence I am learning the secret of being **"content whatever the circumstances,"**[2] even in family stress and conflict. There are times now when I am able to smile with sincere peace and joy during the chaos surrounding family trips.

Lynne is very different from me, although engaged in the same process. I tend to have significant "Aha" moments, often achieved by talking about it. She's prone to persistent analysis and likes to journal. Each parent finds his or her own style of seeking to transform false beliefs. She tells her story:

During the very difficult years of early parenting, I would go through long times of despair, as well as periods of dislike for one or more of my children. I felt horribly guilty as well as angry with my family and myself. I was frustrated because I couldn't find methods and answers to fix my extremely lively, strong-willed, struggling kids.

I remember one of those dreadful nights: Jim was working. The youngest child was sick, and the other two were overwhelmed with homework. I grew more and more frustrated, resentful, and harsh at the simultaneous requests for assistance. Kids fought, whined, criticized dinner, and frequently disobeyed me. I was too frazzled to figure out what was really happening.

The next morning, I dragged myself to God's Word, as I often do when discouraged, and received the reorientation to the truth that helped me see more clearly. Looking back on the experience of the previous night, I prayed through the following helpful questions. In the years since then, I've realized that seeking God's truth with these kinds of questions has been far more significant than any parenting methods I ever acquired.

What were my emotions and responses?
- I was frustrated by the chaos.
- I was resentful of Jim's absence and the kids' simultaneous requests for help.
- I became increasingly impatient and harsh, and then felt guilty.

What underlying false beliefs produced those emotions/responses?
- Life should *not* be chaotic. Or, at least, I shouldn't get stuck with the chaos by myself.
- My children shouldn't be asking for more than I can give.
- It's my job to keep my children happy, or at least stop them from whining and demanding.

What did I inadvertently communicate to my children by my response?
- Life is stressful and that's bad.
- Your needs make me upset.
- Jesus doesn't help me when I'm upset.

What is true?
- "Chaos happens." I don't have to make it stop or try to keep everyone happy.
- It's OK, and even good, for children to wait for help.
- Jesus' presence can bring peace in chaos, and mercy when I struggle.

As Lynne's experience shows, chaos as a parent is virtually inevitable! But what's not inevitable is how I respond. Do I blow up or melt down? Do I try to manage life so similar situations can't occur? Do I revisit and pray about what happened? Do I seek Scripture and the wisdom and teaching of mentors? Do I talk with others and with God? Do I identify my false core beliefs and repeat the true biblical beliefs that I'm seeking to embrace. Do I stumble? Do I start over again?

KID CONNECTION:

Read and discuss Romans 8:1, 37-39 and/or Ephesians 2:4,5 with your children. Talk about how those verses are true for all of you, even when things get crazy in your house. Figure out ways to remind each other about your value in Christ. Write your ideas here.

The challenge of the Christian life is to always be "pressing on" to build a solid **Foundation** for life and parenting. I know that as long as I'm on this earth, there will be more bricks to lay. It is from a solid **Foundation** that I can effectively **connect** unconditionally with my children, take **proactive action** to build their character and skills, and **correct** in love!

◆◆◆❖◆❖◆◆◆
"Never will I leave you;
Never will I forsake you."
(Hebrews 13:5)
◆◆◆❖◆❖◆◆◆

Connection

Chapter Seven

Love No Matter What
The Essence of CONNECTION

"IF YOU REALLY love me, I think you'd show it by liking me better." This bold, honest statement from a teenaged daughter to her mother added a new dimension to our session together. The mom had previously defended all of her punishments, criticisms, and lectures, saying, "I do all these things because I love you so much." Somehow, though, as time progressed, the daughter began to doubt her mom's love and felt more like her mother's project. She reported disappointment, anger, and a desire for control as her mom's primary attitudes about her. Even though it was clear to me that the mom loved her daughter, the daughter no longer felt loved by her mom. For the rest of our sessions together, we worked less on managing the daughter's behavior and more on rebuilding the sense of love between mother and daughter. As the daughter began to feel loved again, she became more motivated to behave better.

Parents almost unanimously agree that the number-one thing they want their children to know is how much they are loved. This is a critical element of parenting, because as children feel loved, they generally do much better in life. When children are young, it is quite easy to show them love. But as they grow older the strength of their will and their ability to challenge parents increase, and the simplicity and purity of the love between parents and children becomes more complicated and difficult. As a result, heart-felt connection between parents and children often fades. Prominent author Josh McDowell names "disconnection" as the core reason that increasingly young Christians are succumbing to the values of their peer culture. "Many young people, even those from good Christian homes, feel disconnected and alienated from their parents, from adults in general, and from society as a whole."[1]

To really connect with our kids requires effective communication of that love. It has been said, "The goal of communication is not to communicate so that you can be understood, but to communicate in such a way that you *cannot be misunderstood.*"[2] As this relates to communicating love, it must be done in a way the child *cannot misunderstand*, and is able to fully *receive* it. Particularly when an endearing sibling is in the picture, children may easily believe they are not truly loved, despite parents' attempts at communicating love. A child receives a parent's love in the same way people receive God's love: by understanding that they are fully loved, known, and enjoyed. **Connection** is the bond formed when these aspects of love are shared between parent and child.

◆ ◆ ◆ ❖ ◆ ❖ ◆ ◆ ◆

**Connection is the bond formed when a parent and child
love, know, and enjoy each other.**

◆ ◆ ◆ ❖ ◆ ❖ ◆ ◆ ◆

The sophistication of today's youth and the many pressures our world puts on families, threaten real connection perhaps more than at any time in history. To wait until children become teens to address these realities is to wait too long. As children grow and life becomes more complicated, parents who learn to stay connected through their kids' ages and stages find their relationships and their children's growth much stronger.

Loving My Children

How can I know if my love is truly unconditional?

Unconditional love is *not* praise for positive behavior. When I express love in any context where children can possibly interpret my affection as conditional (based on their behavior), it loses its power as an expression of love! When this happens, children can begin to believe that love is earned. For example, I once worked with a teen who reported that the only time her father expressed affection for her in her early years was when she got dressed up. She grew up believing that she was lovable only when she looked pretty. She was very conscious about her appearance, and struggled with self-esteem and eating disorders as a teen. Another young man related how his dad would show up at his football games and beam with pride, but it was the only time this young man received affirmation or affection from his dad. When an injury forced him to quit football, his resulting despair led to depression and thoughts of suicide. In his mind, there was nothing about him to love anymore.

Unconditional love is devotion and affection for someone, *regardless* of his or her behavior, appearance, performance, or ability to meet my needs. This means I affirm my children simply for who they *are*, not for what they *do*. Remember the messages of love I communicated to my newborn son? "I love you; you are a miracle, a gift, you are infinitely valuable." Learning to communicate those messages throughout my children's lives is the essence of unconditional love.

Jesus' parable of the father's response to his prodigal son depicts powerful love in response to a child who had sunk to the depths of failure (Luke 15:11-31). The watchful father longs for the return of his lost son. When he finally sees him he leaps into unmistakably loving action. Running to the child, he greets him with a joyous embrace. He then throws a great welcome party to honor his returned lost son. This story challenges us to look at the times when our children blow it the worst and ask ourselves if we have a heart of unconditional love for them. This love is unwavering – ever providing, defending, nurturing, comforting, and forgiving. It says, "I'm here for you, no matter what" (2Timothy 2:13). "I want the best for you" (Jeremiah 29:11). "Nothing can separate you from my love" (Romans 8:38, 39).

Timing is everything

The timing of my communication of love to my children is critical. Hugs, smiles, and "I love you's" consistently given only in response to positive behavior can breed insecurity and a performance-based sense of self-worth in children. If I want my love to be understood regardless, I will be thoughtful about communicating my love during regular routines, such as bedtime or returning from work. I will intentionally communicate love messages when the children are not doing anything particularly noteworthy. In addition, I will even see times when they have "messed up" as unique opportunities to powerfully communicate a message of unconditional love. The less children feel they deserve love, the greater the impact of lavishing it on them anyway.

A huge variation in the grade point average of our children's report cards left one of them quite discouraged. This child's dejection made it obvious that this was a great opportunity for encouragement and to communicate to all three children that our love for them is unrelated to their success. We decided to have a "Report Card Party" to celebrate our children regardless of their grades. Problem-solving about raising the low grades could wait. We had a special dinner and then ran around the house like loonies, whooping and hollering and firing Nerf guns at each other. We all had a blast, but the child with the lowest grades seemed to have the most fun!

◆◆◆❖◆❖◆◆◆
**The *less* children feel they deserve love,
the *greater* the impact of lavishing it on them anyway.**
◆◆◆❖◆❖◆◆◆

MY RESPONSE...

When do I most often express love to my children? How does it relate to my mood and/or their behavior? What messages might they conclude from the timing of my affection?

As I consider the affection expressed toward the prodigal son, what is a typical difficult struggle for each of my children that could be a great opportunity to express unconditional love to that child?

Knowing My Children

How can I uniquely communicate love to each child?

To love my children requires that I truly *know* them and how they perceive love. This means I adapt to their developmental level, learning style, personality and values. Doing this well also requires that I know myself and can discern and act on my unique God-given capacities to connect with each of the children.

My child's unique needs

Both Paul and Jesus demonstrated an ability to use their own styles to connect at the level of others when sharing the good news of the gospel. In 1 Corinthians 9:22, Paul states, "I have become all things to all people..." (in order to build a bridge for the love of Christ). Jesus had an amazing ability to effectively communicate the love of God to people from every age and socioeconomic group.

As Lynne and I grew more intentional about communicating love effectively to our young children, we asked them one day what it was that made them feel the most loved. One preferred special dates. Another loved snuggling. And one said, "Mercy when I blow it." Their answers were not ones that we would have predicted and were as diverse from one another as could be imagined. Just asking this simple question helped us understand and honor our children's uniqueness.

I can also be a keen observer of my children, in order to learn how they might receive my love. The way they express themselves and interact with the world can give great clues. Lynne's work with a discouraged mom put this principle to work:

Diane's tears revealed the depth of her struggle. In spite of her best efforts to express love to her challenging 8-year-old daughter Greta, nothing seemed to get through. Diane lamented to me, "I honestly don't think she cares. I'm trying so hard to figure out how to connect with Greta. Nothing works. When I tell her I love her, she says, 'Oh stop it, Mom!'"

I asked about Greta's interests. Diane sadly replied, "She loves books and she loves to write, but those things seem to carry her farther from me." I probed deeper, "Might you find a way to communicate with Greta through writing or reading?" In an 'Aha moment' of hope, Diane decided to buy a journal for Greta.

The next time we met, Diane reported that she had given the journal to Greta explaining, "You have such deep feelings and you love to write, so I thought you might enjoy this journal. I'd like you to save the first page for me to write on!" Greta took the journal with no expression or gratitude. But several days later she handed the journal back to her mom filled with sticky notes on the pages. In a monotone voice Greta informed her, "These are the pages for you to write on, Mom," and walked away.

With guarded hope, the mom carefully wrote on the designated pages and described in detail several things she loved about Greta. She expectantly handed the journal back to her daughter...still no response from Greta!

A few days later Greta was reading the journal, not realizing her mom was watching her from across the room. Diane's heart soared as she saw Greta's face light up with joy and amazement while reading her mother's entries.

That one moment energized Diane's perseverance in connecting with her daughter! Through journaling, Diane's relationship with Greta is being transformed. Greta even wrote some apologies for her difficult behavior and proclaimed her love for her parents. Diane has started speaking the words of love she first wrote in the journal, and Greta enjoys hearing it! The discerning eyes of a parent to know her child and persevere in communicating love, freed this little girl's sensitive soul to give and receive love!

MY RESPONSE...

These questions may require some keen observations: Toward what type of people does my child gravitate? How does my child interact with friends, siblings, a favorite doll – is it primarily a verbal, physical, or tactile expression? How does he or she express affection to me? To what extent is silliness, humor, helpfulness, generosity, dramatic expression, etc., a value of my child? What special interests bring each child joy?

Based on the questions above, how might each child best receive love?

My unique path to Connection

The road I travel to connect with my children will also grow out of *my* unique gifts and interests, an important aspect of my **Foundation** for parenting. If God has given me a particular child, he has given me the unique capacity to connect with that child. With a child who loves physical touch, that could either be gentle affection or wrestling and rough play. A verbally oriented child may go on long, chatty dates with a gregarious parent and exchange silly emails with a quieter parent. When I discover the intersections of interests/personalities I have with each child, I can nurture these as "intersections of joy." The effort to discover the combination of my unique capacity and my child's unique needs may require some trial and error and searching, but it is a worthwhile search.

I know one particular father and daughter who seem as opposite as night and day. He is introverted. She is extroverted. She loves loud music and flashing lights, while he loves a quiet evening with a book. He loves the outdoors and solitude, but she loves the action of the city. She is abstract. He is concrete. These differences drove them apart as she approached adolescence. Her lifestyle choices strained their relationship further. The dad wanted desperately to connect with his daughter, but his efforts were unnatural and she met them with resistance. After much encouragement to try to find some intersection of passion or interest, he discovered that she loves racecars – and he does too! His efforts to connect with her by taking her to a few races meant the world to her and renewed some of the sense of connection they shared when she was younger.

◆ ◆ ◆ ❖ ◆ ❖ ◆ ◆ ◆
If God has given me a particular child,
he has given me the unique capacity to connect with that child.
◆ ◆ ◆ ❖ ◆ ❖ ◆ ◆ ◆

My Response…

What unique God-given gifts and capacities for connection has God given me?

With a willingness to stretch my creativity and expressiveness a bit, how could I use them to connect better with family members?

<u>Enjoying</u> My Children

How can I strengthen the joy I share with each child?

Jane Nelsen, Ed D, internationally acclaimed speaker and author of the Positive Discipline series of books, stated, "Not too long ago I had a great idea for a book that would be so profound and effective that I would offer a 'triple your money back' guarantee if parents didn't experience fabulous results with their children. The book would contain just three words: *Enjoy your children.*"[3]

Keeping enjoyment of my children alive over the years can be a challenge. Frustration and resentment can slowly seep into parent-child relationships until it is draining to be together. A Christian therapist we respect reports that his teenage clients frequently express, "Deep down, I believe my parents love me; I just can't stand to be with them. I structure my whole life not to be home when they are and never do any family activities." Even if the parents of these teenagers were successful in communicating basic elements of love to their child, connection and joy in being together was clearly lacking.

Conversely, we know of many families in which the value of connection is a high priority. In these families, the adults and children of all ages enjoy being together, sharing experiences, and even serving others together as families. The teens in these families learn independence, but not at the expense of family relationships. So what can be done early in life to keep children appropriately connected to their families as they grow toward the teenage years?

The joy of laughter

Few things in life feel better than hearty laughter. Few things are more connective than enjoying that feeling together with those you love. Unfortunately, in many families, as children age, they enjoy less and less laughter with their parents. This is certainly not inevitable, however, and parents can make a commitment to keep laughter alive as their children grow.

The importance of laughter is well documented. So is the impact of its absence. Homes where laughter is absent are more stressful and less physically healthy. One doctor has actually developed a survey to identify which types of humor his patients prefer so he can prescribe the humorous books, films, and audiotapes that best fit his patients! His research about laughter reveals:

- Laughter increases antibodies and decreases infection.
- Laughter decreases stress hormones.[4]

Again, a lack of laughter can be symptomatic of either some simple or complex issues. Sometimes parents simply need to be more thoughtful and prayerful about making laughter and humor a daily part of family life. There are many resources to aid parents in creating joyful family experiences.[5] These experiences can be as simple as typical games in your yard, or as involved as making up special creative activities and adventures. If a parent feels burdened by the idea of sharing joy and laughter with his children, it might be a helpful signal to look at more complex emotional issues of discouragement, resentment, or depression.

The joy of friendship

Some professionals strongly assert that I can't be my child's friend because I must first and foremost be his or her parent. While I want to be careful about how to communicate this, I propose that being a friend to my child is one essential aspect of Connection. Healthy parenting includes a complexity of aspects or roles, including friend and playmate, disciplinarian or confronter, encourager, advocate, consultant, etc. An effective parent can easily shift between roles according to a child's needs.

I am unable to parent effectively if I am unable to switch roles. The parent who always *needs* to be a friend and be accepted by his or her child creates an unhealthy dependence on the child and is unable to discipline effectively. In contrast, parents committed to an authoritarian role can't let their guard down, and they forfeit joy and connection with their children. They generally choose to keep a distance in order to maintain control.

A friend is a person on my level with whom I *choose* to spend time, to play, laugh, and share my life. In true friendship there is no agenda, but simply joy in being together. The freedom to function as my children's friend helps me connect with them on their level, whether it's playing on the floor with a preschooler or talking about Lego's or ponies with an elementary- age child. In this way, I can have a relaxed, nonjudgmental (even amused) response to the outrageous things that may slip out of the mouth of my hormonally charged adolescent.

As children grow older and more independent, they have an increasing, valid need for strong connection with friends. If parents can't ever function in the role of a friend, their relationship with their children will gradually diminish to that of an authority figure (and how many teenagers are eager to pursue *that* type of relationship?). If a "fun outing" with me frequently disintegrates into a lecture or confrontation, why would my kids choose to spend time with me? No wonder so many parents are losing their teenagers to their peer culture as the primary influence!

Lynne has worked hard to keep connection alive with Daniel as he grows through the teen years. Some of the learning comes by trial and error:

Daniel and I had planned for quite some time to go to dinner and a comedy play for his fourteenth birthday. We both had high expectations of an evening of great fun together! Just before we left, he had one of those delightful sibling squabbles with his sister. I was fuming irrationally at his behavior as we drove downtown. Unable to foresee the possibility of ruining our night together, I felt compelled to address the issue. He was hurt and angry at both my criticism and my timing. No matter what I said to apologize and regroup, I had put a cloud over the evening that tainted the experience for both of us. Even the great comedy didn't dispel it. If I could "rewind the tape," I would have chosen the role of Friend instead of Disciplinarian, once we got in the car.

◆ ◆ ❖ ◆ ❖ ◆ ◆
An effective parent can easily shift between roles according to a child's needs.
◆ ◆ ❖ ◆ ❖ ◆ ◆

MY RESPONSE...

In what ways am I a good friend to each of my children? In what ways is that hard for me? How could I deepen the element of friendship in my relationships with my children?

In my attempts to connect fully with my children, I must truly seek to **know** them and myself, and what each of us brings to the relationship. There will be times for unfailing **love** and support in struggle, and times for exuberant **joy**, laughter and friendship.

John Gottman has completed scientific (laboratory-based) research on marriage and families. He dispels the common myth that learning to resolve conflicts is the critical success factor for happy relationships.[6] His research shows that, "Happy families* are based on a deep *friendship* (italics added)...a mutual respect for and *enjoyment* of each other's company. These families *know* each other intimately – they are well versed in each other's likes, dislikes, personality quirks, hopes and dreams. They have an abiding regard for each other and express this *fondness* not just in big ways but in little ways day in and day out."[7] These statements summarize not only the nature but also the importance of **Connection** with my children - the bond formed when we **know, love,** and **enjoy** each other.

The Blessing of Connection

Jesus said, **"Whoever embraces one of these children as I do, embraces me, and far more than me – God who sent me."**[8] One translation says whoever welcomes one child, welcomes God himself.[9] What more powerful blessing than to welcome God! This is perhaps my highest calling as a parent - to embrace, welcome, and love my child as Jesus would.

These experiences then cultivate in my children a receptivity to God's intimate love. When I fill my child's soul with my love and delight, I cultivate "fertile soil" for an accurate perception of God's love. This is the infinite value of connection.

One day I was reflecting on God's delight in me as recorded in Zephaniah 3:17, which finishes, **"He will rejoice over you with shouts of joy!"**[10] I deeply enjoyed just soaking that up in the quiet of the morning. As the children woke, I felt compelled to model that kind of love for them. So, one by one, I went to them and began, well, rejoicing and dancing over them with shouts of joy. It was not the prettiest thing they'd ever seen. In their own way each one communicated to me what a weirdo I was. But upon my explanation of what I was doing and why, each smiled a receiving smile, knowing my love for them is deep and full, not withheld if their chores aren't done or their rooms are a mess (which was the case that day). Most important, they understood that my love for them is only a sliver of their heavenly Father's love for them.

♦ ♦ ❖ ◆ ❖ ♦ ♦

**When I fill my child's soul with my love and delight,
I cultivate "fertile soil" for an accurate perception of God's love.**

♦ ♦ ❖ ◆ ❖ ♦ ♦

KID CONNECTION!

Ask each of your children, "What makes you feel the most loved?" Record their answers and examples of how you can meet those needs on a deeper level. Then make a plan to do it.

Chapter Eight

Eye to Eye, Heart to Heart
Connection through ENGAGEMENT

DEB NEVER FELT accepted by her mother, much less enjoyed. Her energetic and fun-loving personality was a grating mismatch for her mother's depression and bitterness. While other people responded to her engaging personality with delight and pleasure, her mom responded by ignoring her and emotionally pushing her away. Deb tearfully recalled, "I remember intentionally screwing up, just so I could get her to pay attention to me. I wanted so much for her just to look at me and talk to me!"

How often is it said, "Oh, she's just doing that to get attention"? Or, "He's just trying to get a rise out of you." These statements imply that the child's motivations are invalid, manipulative, even sinful. A deeper look reveals that getting our attention is exactly what a child should be doing. The child who doesn't seek attention is a child in serious trouble. Whether behaving or misbehaving, children desperately want their parents to engage with them – to give them energized, focused attention. I like Webster's definition of engage —- "to draw into; involve... to attract and hold... to occupy or involve oneself; take part; be active."[1]

For this engagement to communicate God's heart for my children, it must be filled with my interest and affection. It is a "dance" of responsive interaction, the expression of delight in connection with them. Objectively, this kind of engagement occurs when I give all of my energy toward listening, giving attention, and being with my child. On a deeper level, it is about fully absorbing and savoring the miracle that is my child. It has no personal agenda and is free of expectation. There is no prescription for how to do this. What works for one parent may not work for another. Attention to some basic principles will provide good learning opportunities.

Engaging through <u>Attention</u>

How can I meet my child's need for attention in positive ways?

For my children to truly understand unconditional love, they must experience regular, intense engagement. When I take time to focus my undivided attention on my children and intentionally engage them, it lets them know they have high value.

Special activities

I remember learning about this idea of "focused attention."[2] I decided to bring our then five-year-old son to the annual Outdoor Sports Show at the local convention center. I attend this event each year and eagerly look forward to checking out all the new, high-tech fishing stuff. What a great time of father and son bonding this would be! I could give Daniel a whole day of focused attention, while at the same time taking in the show.

We excitedly entered the center and immediately Daniel was attracted to the dock display and pontoon boats. "Maybe later," I said as I whisked him off to the fishing boats. But he was not to be deterred and became increasingly determined. I tried to persuade him that my interests were more practical for our family. Unconvinced, he began to whine in loud frustration. I tried to convince him that the fishing boats were faster and more exciting than pontoons, but to no avail.

My frustration grew as this noisy power struggle escalated. Then it dawned on me. I had been dishonest with myself – and with Daniel. This was not focused attention at all! I had dragged him along to "my thing" in hopes that I might convince him to be interested. [3]

I remembered my original intent, and decided that for the rest of the day I would follow him wherever he wanted to go while fully engaging in him and his interests. We rode the fastest pontoons in the history of the world and caught whales. We got lost in the middle of the ocean on a floating dock and fought off the attacking sharks. We ate hot dogs, ice cream, and French fries 'til our stomachs hurt. What a glorious afternoon!

I left the convention center having missed my own agenda but having fully participated in his. We were both overwhelmed with the joy of being together and the connection we shared.

The point of this story is to illustrate the significance of highly-engaged focused attention. It may not be possible to regularly take children on daylong excursions. It is not appropriate to give extended focused attention too frequently or children may begin to conclude that the universe revolves around them and their needs and desires. However, occasional outings such as these can be vivid memories that children treasure as a marker of a parent's love and delight in them.

Small, daily doses of focused attention will reinforce messages of unconditional love. I can regularly carve out special times by arranging little "dates" or shared activities with my children. As my commitment and ability to give focused attention grows, I learn to find opportunities in many varying situations. Even diapering or getting a child dressed can be a great connection time involving eye contact, touch, verbal interaction, and playfulness.

Daily routines

First-thing-in-the-morning interactions tend to set a tone for the day. In our home we try to make sure each day's first interaction is filled with positive energy toward each child. This communicates, "I'm really glad to see you before you've had a chance to do anything to earn my affection." The importance of making this a routine is captured in Lynne's experience with Daniel:

When Daniel was a toddler, I developed the habit of greeting him when he first came down the stairs, with a grin and an enthusiastic, "Oh, boy, IT'S MY BOY!!!" followed by a hug. There was excitement in his eyes as he would stand on the steps waiting for my greeting. One morning I was reading when he came down, and my response to him, if I made one at all, must have been bland and non-engaging. The part of the memory that is still vivid is the sad look on his face and the little, disappointed voice, "You didn't say, 'Oh, boy, it's my boy.'"

Sometimes Lynne and I forget and greet our children by revisiting last night's conflict or reminding them of an unfinished job. Because of our commitment to set a positive tone, we have actually sent kids back to their rooms and asked them if we could start over on a more positive note. What a difference it would make if we really knew the significance of even our "small" interactions with our children.

Mealtime can be a practical time to regularly give positive attention. The impact of simply sharing mealtimes regularly has been well documented. A university study discovered that "more mealtime at home was the single strongest predictor of better achievement scores and fewer behavioral problems. Mealtime was far more powerful than time spent in school, studying, church, playing sports and art activities."[4]

Bedtime is a great opportunity for storytelling, snuggling, giggling, talking about each other's day, or praying together. A friend of ours gives focused attention at bedtime by giving the children time to ask any questions on their minds. He reported his amazement at the depth of their thoughts and questions. As children begin to relax in a quiet environment they are often able to talk about significant thoughts or feelings that they may not have been able to identify in the busyness of the day.

Fashioning routines in which giving focused attention can be natural sometimes requires creative new thinking. I may have to give up, or reposition, some task or pursuit. But the effort is almost always worth it in the long run.

Engaging through <u>Interest</u>

What message do I communicate about my child's interests?

Another way to engage with children is to enter their world: watch, ask, listen! Take an active interest in learning from them about things they enjoy. One mom felt her connection with her teenage son diminishing. She had never previously paid much attention to his baseball card collection so she bridged the growing disconnection by having him "teach her the ropes" of his baseball card interest. (Now that's dedication!) When I immerse myself in something my child treasures, I communicate an important message: "You are so valuable, the things that are important to you are important to me!"

This message is also communicated when parents display genuine interest in the details of their child's communication. A mother of five told us that her older children once "busted" her and her husband with an insightful observation, "We know you're not listening when you say, 'Wow, that's great!'" The children were able to discern that the parents were really not listening or observing very closely. Fortunately, they could state their disappointment aloud and the parents could respond. Many kids in this pattern just grow up believing that perhaps they are not so important.

Lynne experienced the following satisfying application of this principle:

Noah asked me to look at a sketchpad of artwork he had recently completed. Unfortunately, it was during dinner prep and I knew that I would be an easily detectable fraud if I pretended I was really looking at it while trying not to chop my finger in with the vegetables. I looked at him intently and said, "Noah, I can see you've worked hard on this. It's really important to me to look at it closely with you. Let's do it after dinner when we have lots of time."

After dinner I sat down to admire an incredible collection of drawings. I made sure we were positioned so I could look into his eyes, which lit up while he talked. He was unusually verbal and animated as we journeyed through his black and white world together. He told me stories about many of his favorite drawings, explained how he'd gotten his ideas, what he liked or disliked about each picture. I asked questions about the drawings I didn't understand and commented on the incredible detail I noticed in his artwork. It was such a delightful experience for both of us, I tipped Jim off to this golden opportunity and he arranged a similar "Tour de Sketchpad" at a later time.

MY RESPONSE…

As I consider my listening style with my children, do I ask a lot of questions? Do I give answers or judgments about what they say? What might make me a better listener?

While getting into my children's world as an observer, listener, and learner is a critical aspect of *Connection*, inviting them into my world to participate in my interests, plans, activities, and ministries is an opportunity for both *Connection* and *Proaction.*

Engaging with my <u>Face</u>!!

What does my child discern from my expression and tone?

The eyes have been appropriately called, the windows to the soul. When I look my children in the eyes there is an intensity that can be powerfully positive or negative. Consider a typical scenario: I barely glance up from my task or newspaper to greet my child. "Hi, Honey" (monotone). My expression is as exciting as leftover oatmeal. I follow with, "How was your day?" not expecting (or wanting) any more than the typical, "OK." No soul gazing here. No **Connection** either. My words may have been right but my face was in a different world.

Let's rewind and try again, engaging my face. This time I'm watching for my child (remember the parable of the lost son and his father?). I see her coming up the street. I enjoy watching her tread slowly across the lawn to the front door. When she steps through it, I look her in the eyes proclaiming energetically, "Hi, Honey!" She's used to this and continues her routine. I follow with a sincere question. "How was your day?" "OK," she says, half wondering if I'm really all that interested. I am, so I probe a little deeper, "What was the best part of your day?" Now, knowing I am truly interested, she spends a few minutes telling me a bit about her day. She then goes on to her after-school chores and I go back to my tasks.

Children are incredible discerners. If I say the "right things," but my expression and tone of voice don't follow, the tone of voice and lack of facial engagement will communicate a different message. In research interviews of children on their understanding of love, four-year-old Billy observed, "When someone loves you, the way they say your name is different. You know that your name is safe in their mouth."[5] I'm convinced that "the way they say your name" is less about the words used and much more about the way the eyes, voice, and face engage in saying them.

> ✦✦✦✤◆✤✦✦✦
> **When I look my children in the eyes there is an intensity**
> **that can be powerfully positive or negative.**
> ✦✦✦✤◆✤✦✦✦

It is important that the "energy of my eyes and face" be used in a positive way to communicate the intensity of my love for my children and not just the intensity of my disapproval. If I usually meet their need for face-to-face connection while communicating disapproval, I may wound my children's desire and ability to pursue connection with God and others. They will likely conclude that intimacy represents pain and therefore it should be avoided. Ross Campbell, a noted pediatric psychiatrist, describes further problems that can occur:

"Eye contact is one of the main sources of a child's emotional nurturing. When a parent uses this powerful means of control at his disposal in a primarily negative way, a child cannot but see his parent in a primarily negative way. And though this may seem to have good results when a child is young, this child is obedient and docile because of fear. As he grows older, the fear gives way to anger, resentment, and depression."[6]

Lynne has worked to keep connection alive in spite of conflicts with the children:

I had a challenging day with our oldest son Daniel, a day of butting heads with his strong will, and dealing with numerous sibling conflicts in which he was....uh, assertive! As the day wore on, I had grown increasingly frustrated with him – and he knew it. I realized I needed to re-connect with him. When he was happily playing in the bathtub covered with bubbles, I went in and just looked into his eyes with a contented smile on my face. He looked at me quizzically, "What are ya doing?" "I just like looking at you!" I replied. We smiled at each other silently for a sweet, long moment, and I quietly left. At the end of the night, I noticed that he had been unbelievably affectionate and gentle with his little sister all night. A little bit of loving eye contact had "filled his soul." Just as importantly, I was refreshed in my delight in my child.

It's simple but powerful: If I can set aside the activity of the moment and gaze directly into the eyes of my children and listen intently to them, I may well find myself delightfully distracted by how adorable and endearing they are.

MY RESPONSE...

Thinking back to the last few times my children entered the room I was in, what were the first messages communicated to them by my facial expressions, my body language, and my tone of voice?

KID CONNECTION!

Take time to interview each child about something that interests them: a favorite game, activity, or hobby. Find out everything you can about that interest.

And/or-

Give each family member some focused attention with no agenda except to enjoy him/her. (This does not have to be an outing or "date.") What did you learn or experience?

Chapter Nine

Read My Lips — "I Love You!"
Connection through WORDS

"PEOPLE JUDGE YOU by the words you use; to make a powerful impression, you need a powerful vocabulary." This slogan from a vocabulary program's ad campaign rings even truer when related to the words I use to connect with my child. The truth is, my children are always listening for my words of love. They desperately need those words if they are to be securely convinced of my love for them. Psychologists John Trent and Gary Smalley elaborate:

"Words have incredible power to build us up or tear us down emotionally. This is particularly true when it comes to giving or gaining family approval... We should not be surprised, then, that the family blessing hinges on being a spoken message. Abraham spoke a blessing to Isaac, Isaac spoke it to his son Jacob. Jacob spoke it to each of his twelve sons... In the Scriptures, a blessing is not a blessing unless it is spoken." [1]

Consider the only instance recorded in Scripture of God speaking audibly to a public gathering. Jesus had just been baptized when his Father's voice boomed a spoken blessing from heaven, **"You are My Son, whom I love. With you I am well pleased."**[2] Although Jesus had already **"grown in wisdom, stature, and favor with God and man"**,[3] he had not yet started his public ministry. The Father's strong proclamation of his love was not a response to Jesus' ministry but the foundation for it. What a powerful impression! What powerful **Connection**! What a great example!

The following principles for speaking love and affirmation help parents make a powerful impression on their children.

Affirmation that is <u>Strongly Proclaimed</u>

How can I be sure my child receives my words of love?

The day Daniel was born, God gave me a gift that I have taken into my parenting life. At some point it dawned on me that the words I spoke to Daniel then, in his incubator, were important words to express to him in various ways throughout his life:

- What a miracle!
- I love you!
- What a gift you are!
- You make my heart burst with love!
- You are so beautiful.
- I'm so proud you are my child!

My first responsibility related to words and messages like these is to protect my belief that they are true. My children will not believe the messages if I don't believe they are true. This is why I continue to do the **Foundation** work of allowing God to fill me with his love for my children. Then I am empowered to sincerely, confidently, and frequently speak these messages of love. The way I say them, my timing, and a heart attitude that my children cannot misunderstand, are all critically important. At different stages of growth and development, and with different children, the messages may be more of a challenge to communicate. But I will not give up. I know that I must seek God's wisdom so I can change as necessary to keep clearly convincing them of my love. As I learn to speak these messages, I also learn to adapt with my growing children.

Noah, our youngest son, is less verbal than the others. As a four-year-old, he would quickly respond to a simple "I love you" with a big grin or by jumping into my lap. Over the years he has become less responsive. It has been a challenge to learn to speak words of love in ways he cannot misunderstand. As he emerges into his teen years, he can appear to respond to "I love you" with indifference. It's almost as if he's heard it spoken so much that it just sort of rolls off him like water off a duck's back. Not wanting to wonder if he understands, we have to work a bit wiser and harder at communicating. So sometimes we are very specific, stopping whatever we're doing, engaging him, and saying things like, "I really love you. I'm so glad you're my youngest son. What a joy it is to be your parent!" His smile lets us know that he's not misunderstanding.

Many parents don't make these adjustments as their children grow. As a result, the connection between parents and their growing children often weakens. While there is a natural, healthy part about children separating from their parents as they grow up, if that separation is driven by the children's lack of feeling loved, they may well end up "looking for love in all the wrong places." While it can be more difficult to learn to express unconditional love to teens, it is by no means impossible. Many parents have done the hard work of growing from their **Foundation** to freely express love to their teens.

MY RESPONSE....

When have I recently spoken words of unconditional love to each of my children? What evidence is there that they fully understood?

The words of love that parents speak to their children in private are multiplied in power when spoken publicly. Imagine the joy that welled up in Jesus when his Father spoke so boldly about him before the gathered crowd. This same dynamic comes to life when parents speak highly of their children in public – even in front of their children. Again, to do this requires a sincerity that can come only from a strong **Foundation**. One mom so understood the damage of publicly criticizing her children that she made a covenant with her husband to speak only words of encouragement about their children "publicly, privately, and prayerfully." This covenant changed not only how she spoke, but also how she viewed her children – for the better!

Sometimes expressions of love are best received visually. Particularly for less verbal children, visual communication of messages of love can be very effective. This can include sign language, gestures, journaling, notes, emails, and text messages. One dad we coached had a breakthrough with his teen daughter when he learned to send text messages. It had never occurred to him to let her know he was thinking of her by sending silly little "love texts." This simple practice opened a whole new dimension to their relationship. He was particularly delighted one day when, after forgetting to bring his phone to work, his daughter scolded him for not sending the love texts.

Another dad wanted to make sure that his words of love had a lasting impression. He wrote each of his children a letter on their birthdays, stating his deep love for them and describing the growth and positive traits he had observed in their life in the past year. When parents take the time to handwrite a thoughtful, insightful note to their child, it can be a keepsake that brings a blessing every time it is read, even beyond the life of the parent. *Love Letters to a Child,* by Tracey Finck gives great ideas for expressing love through writing.

MY RESPONSE....

What are some "unconditional" messages I want my children to fully receive from me? Some may be for all my children and some may be unique to each child.

How could each child best receive these messages from me?
(This may warrant several times of thoughtful, prayerful consideration.)

Affirmation that is <u>Silly and Playful</u>

How can playfulness communicate my love more effectively?

Words of affirmation that are silly or playful communicate not just "I love you and I enjoy you," but also "I'm really having fun loving you!" Playful, affirming words can be a tremendous source of connection with my children. Here are some ideas from our experience:

Songs created specially for my child express love in a silly, fun way. The songs do not have to be fancy, only heartfelt. Consider the following:

When Daniel was a toddler, we made up a little love song to the tune of Chitty, Chitty, Bang-Bang: "Doobie, doobie, Daniel (repeat 3x's); We love you!" We would sing it in the car over and over in different harmonies, and with progressively wilder endings. Probably not going to get a Grammy Award for that one, but he loved it and, as unashamedly doting parents, we did too. As he got older we would occasionally dust it off and belt it out again.

Years later, he was an intense and impulsive adolescent struggling with the challenges of middle school. He was deeply discouraged by the frequent criticism by his teachers and rejection from the brutal peer culture that engulfed him. Lynne asked him one day, "It's really tough for you at school these days – how do you make it?" Without hesitation he told her, "Well, sometimes when I'm in the halls, I sing that song to myself that you guys used to sing..." When the world's message to him was, "You're worthless," "You're a jerk," those silly but powerful words strengthened him to know the truth – that he was valuable and deeply loved.

Nicknames used in affirming, playful ways can create a special bond between two people. We've had fun with a variety of silly nicknames for the kids - Doobie Daniel, Danny-Jimmy, Peaches, Buffers, Noah-Balboa, Noaski, etc. Obviously nothing particularly clever, but it was a source of great fun and connection. It was a pleasant surprise when our children started to follow our example. Bethany and Daniel can sometimes argue intensely, but when we hear them calling each other "Boof" and "Doof", we know they have resolved their conflict. No one else uses their special names for each other, and the fun they have using them strengthens their friendship.

Affectionate phrases, like nicknames, reinforce connection again and again. Phrases our children loved to hear over and over were: "When I look at you, I think to myself… my goodness, what a boy!" (endings varied); "You're my girly, girl, girl; who I lovey, love, love!" Note the lack of cleverness that is needed to engage kids. We have also known several parents who have silly competitions with their children to express love with exaggeration, wit, creativity, or by simply getting in the final word: "I love you as much as _____" or "I love you more than you love me!"

Fun stories about our children help them know we treasure our memories about them. Children love to hear the drama of how they were born, the silly words they said when learning to talk, their hilarious statements as they got older, the adventures and scrapes they got themselves into. They feel like the star of the show, the hero of the adventure, the world's greatest comedian. For years we kept a running list of quotables and short anecdotes on layers of paper taped to the inside of a cupboard for easy access. We've had much fun rereading them over the years.

These exact ideas may not fit every family. But the principle of playful affirmation definitely fits my home as I work to discover ways my family can laugh together and enjoy each other. A friend of mine recently shared the impact of this in his family growing up. "We sure had our share of dysfunction, but we managed to laugh and have fun together. That has made such a difference in how we now all relate as adults."

My Response....

Considering the kinds of humor my family enjoys, how could I adapt these ideas to playfully affirm my children?

◆◆◆❖◆❖◆◆◆

Words of affirmation that are silly or playful communicate
"I'm really having fun loving you!"

◆◆◆❖◆❖◆◆◆

Affirmation that is <u>Specific</u>

How can details increase the impact of my words?

How does my son hold his fork? What are my daughter's mannerisms when she talks on the phone or reads a book? How would I describe my children's favorite sleeping positions? Answering these questions requires keen observation. Keen observation requires a desire to notice and delight in even mundane things about my children. Once I make such observations, I can verbalize them. My delight in these things, and the effort to speak my observations, communicates a powerful message of unconditional love. The message, when I take delight in even the simplest of my children's activities, is that I really take delight in them.

When I practice watching my children this way, I can get more deeply in touch with my love for them. By describing what I see, I communicate that love. For example: "I enjoyed watching you work so intently on your picture. Your tongue would stick out and you'd frown a little when you were working your hardest. I noticed you picked your favorite animal to color and you carefully filled in the areas with bright colors. You even worked hard to outline the clouds in the background."

Howard Glasser describes this concept.[4] He coined the term, "Video Moments," in which the parents take a few moments repeatedly through the day to describe in detail what they see their child doing in ordinary (non-misbehavior) moments.

Detailed observations like this communicate important messages, "You are seen. You are worthy of recognition. I appreciate and enjoy who you are. I look carefully because I love deeply."

◆◆◆❖◆❖◆◆◆
Detailed observations of my children tell them
"I look carefully because I love deeply."
◆◆◆❖◆❖◆◆◆

MY RESPONSE…

What recent affirmation did I give my child (or what is a typical one I might give)? How could I be more specific in order to increase the impact?

Some parents might say, "Why is this (connection and expression of love) such a big deal? My parents never really told me they loved me and I turned out OK." While it's true that many people "turn out OK" without verbal love expressions from their parents, the culture that surrounds our children is critically different than just a generation ago. There are numerous voices in our world that seek our children's affection in subtle, sophisticated, and powerful ways. When parents do not learn how to clearly communicate words of true love to their children, the children become highly vulnerable to the voices of advertisers, media, peer groups, and alternative lifestyles.

It is imperative for parents to do the **Foundation** work necessary to understand and develop an ability to lavish their children with words of love. The price of missing this principle is too great. Gary Smalley and John Trent explain:

"Let's look at what commonly happens in homes where spoken words of blessing are withheld. What we will see is that *silence does communicate a message*; and like an eloquent speech, silence too can set a course for a person's life. But it's not the path most parents would like their children to take."[5]

There are countless ways to use words that connect children to my love for them. Most families have their own unique way of expressing God's work in their midst. As I consider these principles, Proverbs 12:18 is a reminder of the power of my words: **"Reckless words pierce like a sword, but the words of the wise bring healing."** When the world speaks lies to my children – "You're not cool enough, smart enough, athletic enough, popular enough, good-looking enough..." may my words of love sing truth in their hearts!

KID CONNECTION!

Make a point to look each of your children in the eyes and tell them in your own words that you love them. Try to be specific and use some detail that is unique to your relationship with each child.

Chapter Ten

The "Magic Touch"
Connection through TOUCH

I MET LENNY in a home for displaced children on his eleventh birthday. He was there because his neglectful, abusive parents had lost their parental rights. He'd already been kicked out of two foster homes and another residential facility. I was enlisted to help him reconnect with the world in a positive way. The first thing he said to me was, "Go home!" When I began to respond he threw out some nasty profanity and angrily proclaimed, "Shut up!" This deeply wounded young man was not interested in me, or in my words. Looking for some way to connect, I asked if I could watch him as he continued playing his video game. He did not respond. I figured if he'd had strong feelings about it he would have said so, so I sat near him on the couch in front of the TV. He was pretty good. I said so.

Still no response.

When he successfully completed a level, I congratulated him by nudging him with my elbow and announcing, "You're awesome!" The nudge got his attention. He gave me a confused look and continued the game. I wasn't sure if he liked or disliked the touch, so I continued my verbal affirmation but kept a small distance between us. As he excitedly bounced while operating the controls, I noticed him inching toward me. I stayed in place.

When he successfully completed the second round, he elbowed me and proudly announced, "That's the first time I made it that far!" I patted his back. He looked up at me with puppy dog eyes and asked, "You gonna stay for a while?" I nodded as he proceeded to the next level of the game. Touch opened the door to what has become a significant healing relationship for Lenny.

The human need for loving touch is as crucial to healthy development as the need to hear words of love. The Bible is filled with stories depicting both the practical and symbolic importance of touch.[1] Imagine the despair of the man covered with leprosy,[2] absolutely never touched by anyone, isolated behind an invisible wall of illness and shame. Unable even to look in Jesus' eyes, he fell with his face in the dirt at Jesus' feet, begging for healing. How might it have felt when Jesus reached out and touched him, oozing sores and all, before Jesus proclaimed his healing? Exhilaration, acceptance, intimacy, and freedom must have flooded the leper's whole being!

Jesus frequently touched those he met. He touched children to bless them. He touched many of those he healed, when certainly he could have healed with a simple word. In his last night with his disciples, he touched them in a most memorable way by washing their feet. It seems Jesus was very intentional about the use of touch to communicate love because he understood people's longing for a loving touch. Nurturing, connective touch strongly impacts our physical, emotional, and spiritual health!

How might life change if parents acted daily in the power of loving touch? Could it be that families would be happier, healthier, and more relaxed simply by touching each other more? Research says yes! Clearly those who grow up in environments where healthy, nurturing touch is a frequent expression of connection and love grow up feeling loved and secure.

Benefits of Touch

What is really accomplished when I touch my child?

Some people feel that touch is a rather nonessential aspect of parenting, left to the dictates of a family's style. Recent research, however, has substantiated the incredible benefits of touch for people of all ages, and particularly for children. Consider this scientist's conclusion: "Our research suggests that touch is as important to infants and children as eating and sleeping." [3] Babies who are touched frequently develop brains twenty percent larger than those who are not. Infants who received massage therapy (compared to those who were only rocked) weighed more, slept better, and were more content and social.[4] Daily massage even improved cognitive testing results in preschoolers.[5]

While the various physical and cognitive benefits are important, the greatest benefits to touch seem to be emotional and social in nature. Touch decreases anxiety and depression,[6] and builds positive feelings between people.

"In one experiment in a library, a slight hand brush in the course of returning library cards to patrons was enough to influence patrons' positive attitudes towards the library and its staff. In another study, waitresses who touched their customers on the hand or shoulder as they returned change received a larger percentage of the bill as their tip."[7]

In both of these studies the people did not necessarily even recall being touched, but the impression of friendliness and caring was established by a brief, casual touch. Imagine the emotional benefits our children receive from regular, nurturing touch!

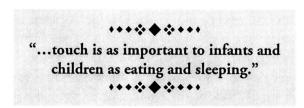

"...touch is as important to infants and children as eating and sleeping."

When our son Noah was a toddler, he was a high-speed mover and a shaker, but absolutely not a snuggler. One time he even reached around and removed Lynne's hand as she tried to gently pat his back. When he was about a year and a half old, we began to provide a type of therapeutic massage for brief but frequent periods. The changes were dramatic in his ability to sit and focus. But most importantly, by age two he began to really enjoy snuggling and hasn't stopped to this day. What a difference it made in our relationship!

Purposeful affectionate touch can communicate these powerful messages:

- Affection - I value and enjoy you.
- Nurture - I want to meet your needs.
- Intimacy - There are no barriers between us. I like being close to you.
- Trust - You are safe with me. (This is an essential message that teaches intimacy can be safe.)
- Peace - If a relationship is strained, affectionate touch might communicate: I long to be closer to you. I want to bridge the gap between us.

In addition to the direct benefits to my children as I touch them, research shows that increased touch also improves the way in which I will relate to them. For example, fathers who gave their infants daily massages prior to bedtime for one month showed improved interaction with their infants in general.[8] It only makes sense that the connection that occurs with touch benefits both parent and child, and builds a stronger bond that influences the relationship at other times.

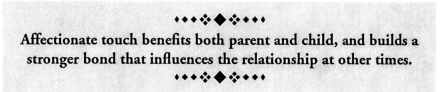

Affectionate touch benefits both parent and child, and builds a stronger bond that influences the relationship at other times.

Intersections of Touch

How do unique beliefs, needs, and style influence touching?

It is important for parents to spend some time considering their own experience and core beliefs about touch. Some people come from highly affectionate families, while others come from caring but reserved, unexpressive families. For some families touch may even have negative, controlling or even abusive connotations. Spouses often have very different past experiences regarding touch and affection. What an adventure to be on the journey of figuring this out in my life and in my family.

My Response...

Thinking back on the role of physical affection in my family of origin, who touched me? When? Was it pleasant or unpleasant? How does it affect how I touch my family now?

The diverse backgrounds and unique personalities of the parents are not the only issue to address. Each of my children is wired uniquely as well. One child eagerly crawls into my lap and covers me with kisses. Another may deftly escape my affection. The third is unpredictable. Just when I think I've got them figured out, they change. So not only do I have to figure out me and my issues, I need to stay attentive to my children's varying moods and styles.

Just as with other forms of connection, parents' unique needs and style of touch can intersect with their child's. The attentive parent will discern how their children's unique personalities wire them to best receive touch. An expressive extrovert is probably quite comfortable with lively bear hugs and kisses, and may be comfortable both initiating and spontaneously receiving affectionate touch. A reserved introvert would be overwhelmed and embarrassed by the same delivery mode and probably needs to have affectionate touch be on his or her terms and timing. Expressing physical affection is a "dance" in which parents alternate between leading and following their children's lead.

For some children the way they enjoy touch can be quite unique, but still very effective. A father in a small-group discussion shocked us by sharing, "My daughter loves it when I kick her!" He laughed and explained he had taken up Tai Kwando in an effort to connect with her. He inadvertently discovered that the easiest way she could accept hugs, was to start with some martial arts roughhousing. They're both quite athletic and competitive, so this was a great discovery!

It's important to be on the alert for what our children initiate and capitalize on it. A mother in one of our classes relays her experience.

"I was praying about how I could connect more with my intense, challenging teenage son. Many of my attempts seemed to be awkward and he was not always receptive. Instead, he kept trying to engage me in an interaction almost like tag. He'd poke me, yell, "Last Touch!" and run off, expecting me to chase him. Initially I was a little irritated. Then I realized that this was what I had been looking for—a fun way to connect with him through affectionate touch.

With that realization the game became so much fun my daughter wanted to join in. I talked with her about the special, unique ways she and I easily connected and my son's need to have his own special way. She was able to laugh and enjoy our antics as we thundered and squealed around the house after each other. He gradually became more comfortable with hugs and other playful forms of affection, and I noticed our relationship seemed much more relaxed. Who would have thought a goofy little game of tag could be so significant."

The following list describes various ways parents and children can share physical affection. The list starts with minimal, low-risk possibilities and works toward more intimate physical expressions.

- "High fives," special handshakes.
- Little nudges/jostling, contact during sports.
- Patting or briefly touching a child's shoulders or back.
- Arm wrestling, wrestling, piggyback rides, other physical fun.
- Back/shoulder rubs. (Some kids enjoy these if they strongly desire touch but are unwilling to exchange hugs.)
- Sitting close together or on your lap.
- Holding hands.
- Hugs of varying intensities of intimacy, from a quick squeeze around the shoulders to a noisy, affectionate bear hug.
- Touch to a child's face. (This is intimate and powerful but must be appropriately timed.)

My Response...

What are my children's favorite ways of touching/being touched? How might I touch them this way more often?

The Timing of Touch

When is touch hurtful or helpful?

A person's emotional state changes his or her perception of touch. For example, a light touch greeting on the shoulder from a spouse feels good, but a touch to the shoulder from a large stranger late at night in a dark alley may spark shock waves of terror. The touch is the same, but the difference in the emotional state results in vastly different perceptions.

I love to give vigorous little backrubs to my kids. Bethany is particularly fond of robust massages as she starts winding down at the end of the day. But if she's not fully awake or cheerful, I can get myself in a bit of trouble. I recently initiated such a massage when she was feeling overwhelmed with her schoolwork and cleaning responsibilities. She was lying down on her bed and I started to rub her shoulders by briskly bouncing her on the pillow. Oops. Bethany erupted with anger and tears before I even knew what was happening. Bad timing on my part.

If my children are angry or conflicting with me, touch can be very detrimental. One of our children in particular perceives touch during an argument as uncomfortable, offensive, and an attempt to control him, thus increasing his anger. I've learned to respect that by giving him space at such times. Research supports that when touch "is interpreted as a status or power play, or when it is too prolonged or intimate, it may evoke anxiety, anger, or other reactions".[9]

When emotions are intense, touch can be very soothing, but it is essential for the child to feel in control of any physical contact. Simply saying, "Let me know if you decide you want a hug," expresses affection and support without violating the boundaries of an upset child.

Although touch during conflict can sometimes be hurtful, in every family's routines there are built-in opportunities for helpful physical contact. Identifying these times and making a habit of touching during them, provides a positive connection at key times of the day. Connecting with a hug or a kiss at transitions (right before and after work/school) influences how I leave them for the day or send them off to school. It can also set the tone for my interaction with them when I return home. Snuggling or backrubs in the morning or at bedtime are powerful ways to start and end the day with affection and capitalize on everyone's relaxed mood. Lynne illustrates with a story from one of her patients:

I once consulted for a family with a teenager who had sensory and behavioral challenges. I made recommendations to provide calming input in several important sensory systems. A few months later his mother reported, "We haven't tried everything you recommended, but one of the suggestions you made was really valuable. We still give our son backrubs every night when he goes to bed. It's made a huge difference." This form of touch opened up relaxed conversation and had a significant impact on him and their relationship, which was no longer exclusively defined by the conflicts they were having. They were ending every day with physical and emotional connection in a way in which he could truly receive their love.

Barriers and Boundaries

What should I do when my child doesn't want to be touched?

Some parents are disheartened in their attempts to express affectionate touch.

- "My child doesn't want my touch."
- "My son gets irritated and withdraws when I try to hug him."
- "I feel awkward and phony when I try to express physical affection to her."

Trying new ways of touch can be very difficult. Perhaps touch has been used to manipulate, so the child doesn't trust the parent. Resentment toward a parent may cause resistance. Children may perceive the parent's discomfort with touch and avoid the awkwardness. Growth in this area with children of all ages is possible, assuming the parents are working in their **Foundation** to come to the relationship prepared to meet their child's needs.

Trust must be reestablished. It can be a slow process.

I once worked with a teen that had a history of physical, possibly sexual, abuse. When we first met, Gail would not allow any eye contact and wouldn't let me come physically closer than eight or ten feet. I affirmed her boundary simply by respecting it. I gave her permission to tell me when she was uncomfortable. When she did, I did not argue even if I thought she was unreasonable.

It was several weeks before Gail allowed me close enough for a handshake. When I welcomed her one night by extending my hand, she put her head down and extended hers just within reach. I shook lightly and briefly. Each week I tried to find a way to pat her back, give a high five, or even give a friendly nudge. Our female volunteers were encouraged to do the same. She was more open to them. If she seemed wary, I gave her space. It was more than a year before Gail gave me permission to put my arm around her. Over time we became closer as I won her trust. She became a leader in the program and went on to become a nurse, a profession in which healing touch is central. When I moved away to open a new ministry site, she wrote this note:

> The gifts you've shared have made me feel
> So much real joy it seems unreal.

> I once thought that I'd seen my end.
> But I was wrong my dear old friend.
>   Thanks forever, Gail

Connecting through touch with a resistant child is more than worth the effort and patience required. It can start with non-contact playfulness and positive interaction and then move to playful touch and physical affection, as listed in detail in the "Intersections of Touch" section. Thoughtful parents will look for opportunities to gradually increase this aspect of their relationship without having an agenda to connect in a certain way. Had Gail felt at any time that I needed her to respond to me, particularly in the early days of our relationship, she likely would have never come back.

Some parents find resistance to even their best thoughtful and prayerful efforts to initiate affectionate touch. This may indicate some valid reason other than just personality-style differences. These parents may need to take a deeper look. They may have subtle attitudes that build resentment in their children. They may be unknowingly acting in ways toward their children that hurt them or posture them defensively. When parents feel stuck, it is critical to discuss it with their spouse or a good friend. Also it may be appropriate to seek professional help if you can't begin to make progress.

Resistance may also be due to a child's physical wiring. Some children actually experience touch as physically unpleasant, due to hypersensitivity in how the sensory input is processed. If this is the case, it is extremely helpful for parents to be well informed about the challenge called "tactile defensiveness"[10] that their child faces.

MY RESPONSE...

Are any of my children resistant to my touch? What do I think might be some reasons for this? What could I do to encourage them?

Whether or not children have challenges related to touch, it is important to protect them from unwanted touch. Almost everyone has bad memories of an overbearing relative who obligated all young nieces, nephews, or grandchildren to an uncomfortable, bone crushing hug, complete with a smelly and/or wet kiss. The messages communicated to the child are hurtful and, to a lesser degree, the same as those received repeatedly and intensely by victims of sexual abuse – "You are here for my needs and pleasure, and your feelings and needs don't matter."

It is the responsibility of parents to protect children from this, even if it means offending a relative. It is helpful to teach children respectful ways to say no to the pressure from an overly affectionate person and to support them in their choices. This strengthens children's ability to keep the touch they experience safe and positive, and lays the foundation for good boundaries in their adolescent years.

KID CONNECTION!

Offer backrubs to each of your kids after connecting with them verbally or playfully, or at bedtime. Find out what kind of rub they want – gentle, tickly, firm; back or arms/legs, etc. (If any say no, seek other ways to give them focused attention and acceptable affectionate touch.) What did you learn from their responses?

The ideas in the last three chapters are not a formula for success. They are merely ideas and examples to spark creativity and determination for communicating love to children. Each family is a unique combination of parents' and children's values, personalities, gifts, and histories. Within each family mosaic are thousands of possibilities for learning to express messages of love through engagement, words, and touch. The only way to really get it wrong is to stay stuck in disconnectedness. Getting it right is about being on the journey to grow. This is the adventure of connection, of asking God for insight into my unique abilities and my children's needs, and then asking for guidance on our journey. It is in the context of this adventure that effort can be effectively given to **Proaction** and **Correction**.

**The adventure of connection is asking God for insight
into my unique abilities and my children's needs,
and then asking for guidance on our journey.**

Chapter Eleven

When Connection is Difficult
The Struggle to Connect

"CONNECTION WITH GOD happens when I love, know, and enjoy God, because he loves, knows, and enjoys me."[1] Similarly, connection with my children occurs when they respond to my unconditional love and enjoyment of them, when they feel known, understood, and accepted. It is a dynamic bond that holds a relationship together. People were designed to experience delight and pleasure in their family relationships, to truly love and enjoy their children.

"May your father and mother be glad: may she who gave you birth rejoice."
—Proverbs 23: 25

In Scripture, children are described as a heritage, a reward, a blessing from God, and lots of kids in the family means lots of blessing! (Psalm 127: 3-5). This is the ideal, but what's real is that children are not always perceived as a blessing. For numerous reasons, parents often struggle to connect with one or more of their children. Sometimes they even struggle with the desire to connect.

I spoke recently with a mother who confessed that her feelings of love for her six-year-old son are gone. He is challenged by high intelligence and extreme physical and emotional sensitivity. He has little self-control. She and her husband are growing increasingly resentful of his outbursts and arguments about even the slightest nuances of daily life. They are quite knowledgeable about various techniques for handling their son. But they have lost the desire to connect with their child. They are angry with the child and angry at God – because of how difficult the boy makes their lives at every turn. Clearly these parents have a difficult child. But unless they can regain their joy in connection with him, he will likely grow up believing that he is a disappointment, a failure, and a burden.

We've heard many statements from parents that voice this common challenge:

"Our daughter's behavior ruined our vacation. Why does one kid have to wreck it for everyone? I'd like to leave her at home next time."

"I wish someone else would just raise my son for a while and give me a break. Things are so difficult right now that I don't like being around him."

"When he comes into the room I'm not glad to see him. I feel this anxious little twinge and think, 'Here we go again. Now what's he gonna do?'"

"No one ever expressed unconditional love to me when I was a kid. It feels awkward doing that for my kids."

"I love my daughter, I just don't enjoy her. We're so different. It's impossible to have fun together because we don't really like being with each other."

These parents' statements describe how hard it can be sometimes to even *want* to connect with their children, let alone to effectively do so. Most parents, Lynne and myself included, relate to this frustration at some point in the parenting experience.

Barriers to Connection

What keeps me from joyfully, affectionately loving my child?

As parents determine to connect more often and more deeply with their children, they may discover personal barriers to emotional intimacy or physical affection that make attempts at deep connection with their children seem stiff and awkward. It takes courage to honestly look at these inner barriers. These barriers could be rooted simply in personality differences, but also they may be due to discouragement, resentment, or even important core beliefs about intimacy. Whatever the case, it is essential to develop awareness of whatever factors make connection difficult and pursue help if needed.

No model for the parents

She was in the front row. For the first three weeks of our class she had listened wide-eyed and engaged enthusiastically as we talked about the principles of **Foundation** and **Connection**.

This day was different. During the class she avoided eye contact and spent much of the time looking at the floor. She never spoke a word. After the class I approached her. "You seemed a bit distant today. Is everything OK?"

The tears formed instantly and were falling by the time she spoke. "For the first time in my life I've realized that the reason I have such a hard time connecting with my son is that no one ever really connected with me."

We have found this to be the primary reason parents struggle to connect with their children. Parents are not usually quick to make this confession because it can be so painful. Instead, there is a tendency to scapegoat the child or the difficult behaviors. But time after time, beneath these superficial problems is an intense sense of grief and loss due to the unmet longing for deep, loving connection with parents, or at least with someone. Some parents, like the one mentioned above, can readily identify with this. Others spend a lifetime trying either to compensate for this loss, protect themselves from the pain, or both. Addiction, anger, depression, overachievement, and superficial relationships are some of the symptoms.

Parents who have not experienced connection should not lose hope. They can return to their **Foundation**. They can fight to learn God's perfect connective love for them. They can find true spiritual friends who will love them with Christ's love. They can make a priority of discovering and functioning in God's purposes for them. It's never too late!

My Response…

How frequently was I told that I was loved? When I was told, did it seem conditional or unconditional? How has this affected my ability to communicate unconditional love?

Awkwardness

Parents sometimes express, "We just aren't a huggy family." This may be an indication that their family has other unique and effective ways to express love, or it could be a symptom of discomfort with affection.

If I take a moment to imagine looking into the eyes of each of my children, touching them affectionately, and telling them I love them, certain feelings emerge. These are significant. For some people this activity might evoke pleasant feelings of love and closeness. Or it might make them feel awkward and uncomfortable. They might even feel anxious, forced, or numb. There may be other feelings as well. The feelings may relate to how love was expressed (or not expressed) during a person's own childhood.

Awkwardness may also stem from anticipated rejection by my child, particularly if that child is older. Many parents report that at some point they are hurt when their child rejects their attempt to express love. But strong feelings are an opportunity to look at my core beliefs.

If I feel hurt, it might be that I believe my value depends on my child's acceptance. It might be that I'm feeling unloved in another relationship and am using my child to meet needs in me that he or she can't meet. Understanding my beliefs and how they affect me is never simple work. But it must be done in order to overcome these barriers to connection.

MY RESPONSE...

As I imagine giving appropriate, affectionate touch and eye contact to each person in my family and telling them I love them, how do I feel?

What does that tell me about the presence or absence of barriers to intimacy with each person?

What could be some possible core beliefs I hold about affection and vulnerability that might be an influence?

Self-criticism

Many people beat themselves up over their shortcomings as parents. They measure their success by their children's behavior, and then project their disappointment onto their children. These parents stay stuck in discouragement and a sense of failure because they have unrealistic expectations for themselves. This cultivates an environment in which family members typically feel a great deal of guilt and shame because they never measure up to excessive standards. Lynne wrestled in depth with this sense of failure:

> Face down on the carpet, I pounded my fist and cried. "I'm so irritable and hard on the kids - it seems as if I'm always angry!" I was equally sick of my children's behavior (hyperactivity, strong wills, and frequent tantrums) and angry at God for the whole mess. "Sometimes I can't stand them! What is *wrong* with me? Why did You make us this way?!!"

> During my early years of parenting I was deeply discouraged by my failure to live up to the standard of the "ideal Christian mother" (always patient, positive, loving, and full of faith). Much of what I read or heard suggested that I could attain this ideal if I was committed and worked hard enough at it. But the harder I tried, the more I realized this standard was unattainable for me, which only fueled my discouragement. Since my children were the 3-D display of my failure, my desire to truly connect with them was greatly hindered.

God gradually helped me see that my desire to be the ideal Christian mother was more about my need to feel good about myself than it was about the needs of my children. True change finally began when I was able to let go of unrealistic expectations and embrace myself as an imperfect parent in whom God was at work. This revelation in no way encouraged me to parent carelessly but helped me to forgive myself (and my children) and see our whole process as part of God's work and plan for our lives.

Many Christian parents never get beyond this dynamic. Self-criticism can short-circuit parents' desire to connect with their children. Parents filled with high expectations for themselves are usually too discouraged to express love joyfully and unconditionally.

My Response...

What is my standard for parenting? How do I compare to it? How does this comparison affect me?

Disappointment and resentment

Some parents experience deep disappointment with their child. He or she is not the excellent student, athlete, or social butterfly for whom they had hoped. Other parents simply dream of having a reasonably compliant child. While parents of children with obvious handicaps usually get sympathy and support, an intense or behaviorally challenging child is likely to elicit criticism from others, which adds to more guilt and stress for the parent.[2] Parents may deeply resent their challenging child because of the public embarrassment he or she brings.

Disappointment with, or resentment toward a particularly challenging child may cause parents to not even want to be around the child, let alone to express unconditional love and affection. Parents are continually frustrated that children won't change in response to their diligent parenting efforts. Even attempts at "connection" may be part of a parent's strategy to change them, and therefore they do not communicate unconditional love to their children. Children generally respond to their parents' disappointment by either working hard (because of fear of failure), fighting the expectations (because of resentment), or by giving up (because it's too hard to measure up).

When our second child was born, Daniel didn't seem to like this invasion of his secure place at the center of our lives. He became aggressive, defiant, and irritable. Up to this point, he had mostly been the child of our dreams. But we were losing our sense of connection with him. It was quite upsetting.

I decided to take him on a special father-son outing to the mall, hoping to reestablish some of his sense of security that came from being an only child for almost three years. Perhaps he would then be less edgy at home.

From the moment we arrived at the mall, Daniel seemed to have an insatiable desire to get exactly what he wanted and stay as long as he wanted. He finally found a favorite toy, and out of frustration I just let him play with it while I shopped nearby. When it was time to go he stubbornly resisted my attempts to get him out of there. "I'm NOT leaving!" he yelled. It seemed every eye in the place was riveted on us as the conflict continued to escalate. Infuriated, I finally grabbed him, flung him over my shoulder, and headed for the nearest exit. His frantic screams echoed through the mall. My anger boiled. When we reached the parking garage, I looked to be sure no one was watching and spanked him.

I decided not to take Daniel to the mall again for a long time. We arrived home angry, defeated, and in worse shape than before we left.

Looking back I can see that what may have looked like an attempt to connect with my son was actually an attempt (rooted in my feelings of disappointment) to manipulate Daniel's behavior. When it was clear that my tactic was not working, I grew angry and resentful. If I had been able to accept him and the challenging stage he was in, I could have helped him verbalize his difficult feelings and communicated, "I love you no matter what."

My Response...

In what ways do I struggle to accept and enjoy my children just as they are? How does this affect my ability to connect with them in ways that express unconditional love?

The Strength to Connect

What can I do to help besides "just try harder"?

I desire that my daily experience as a parent be closer to the truth of Scripture so that I can fully enjoy each of my children. Whatever my barriers to connection, the starting place is honesty with God and with a few trusted people who will encourage and pray for me. Pretending that all is well will only perpetuate troubles. Once I've been "brutally honest" about the situation, there are practical ways that I can build my Foundation for the joy of Connection with my children.

Contentment - Embrace reality in the light of God's truth

Everyone has dreams for themselves and their children. Most, if not all, of the difficulties parents encounter along the way run counter to these dreams. If the difficulties deepen, parents often work to keep the dreams alive. They exert pressure on themselves and on their children to live up to these expectations. Particularly with firstborn children, there is a desire to be a perfect parent and have a child who is the reflection of that perfection. At some point there grows a tension between the dream and what is real. It becomes clear that the dream is perhaps more fantasy than possibility. The key to true growth is to let go of the dreams and accept myself and my child, roses, thorns, and all! Only then can my love and dreams for my child be communicated freely, with the child's best interest in mind.

This means that I:

- Accept the reality that neither my child nor I can or will ever get it entirely right.
- Admit that parenting is not what I expected. This may mean letting go of a false standard for myself, or grieving as I release hope for the "child of my dreams."
- Learn to get my self-worth not from my children's behavior but from God's delight in me.
- Embrace core beliefs in line with Scripture: This child is a gift, created for eternally valuable purposes.
- Realize—perhaps more difficult to believe—that I am a gift to my child, uniquely matched to my child for God's good purposes.

Freedom, joy, and connection come alive when I embrace myself as an imperfect parent, raising imperfect children, on a journey together to discover the love of God.

A good friend of ours has young children, wired similarly to our children: intense, hypersensitive to sensory experiences, and exceptionally active. He stated this realization for himself succinctly and wisely: "Our children will struggle, but we are going to be OK. Jesus is enough."

As this statement became a core belief, it transformed his relationship with his children. His frustration due to unmet, unrealistic high expectations was replaced with encouragement and joyful connection.

◆◆◆❖◆❖◆◆◆

**The key to true growth is to let go of the dreams and
accept myself and my child, roses, thorns, and all!**

◆◆◆❖◆❖◆◆◆

What real frustrations do I face (or wish would go away)? How might I summarize these issues in light of God's truth?

Conviction - Prioritize connection

The priority of connection is expressed in the truth of Galatians 5:6: **"The only thing that counts is faith expressing itself through love."**

Families are strong when parents "drive a stake in the ground" about the priority of **Connection** – connection to God and with each other, and then with their children. **Connection** is the bottom line in healthy relationships with children. It is the glue that strengthens families. It requires a lot: commitment, time, insight, vulnerability, and perseverance. But from this place of strong connection, children are equipped to connect well to the world around them.

There are still many intense moments in the Jackson household. The "ballast in our boat" that keeps us balanced and rights us when we tip in a storm is the shared core belief/value that connection with God and with each other is primary. As we have prioritized, practiced, and discussed with our children the importance of connection, we have seen them begin to adopt the same conviction.

After a particularly intense conflict with Lynne, Daniel (at age 12) said to her, "Mom, we've been mad at each other a lot this morning, so I think we should go play tennis together." She was shocked, and marveled that he valued connection so deeply. Clearly he had established a vital core belief, one that will serve him well when he eventually parents his own children, who may well inherit his spunk.

Revisiting this important issue of building the **Foundation** is important to each aspect of parenting. It is the place I must continually go if I am to grow as a parent.

MY RESPONSE...

What has stood out to me as an important way to strengthen my Foundation so that I can better connect with my children?

◆◆◆❖◆❖◆◆
Freedom, joy, and connection come alive
when we embrace ourselves as imperfect parents,
raising imperfect children, on a journey together
to discover the love of God.
◆◆◆❖◆❖◆◆

KID CONNECTION!

Thoughtfully consider Luke 3:22, "You are my son, whom I love; with you I am well pleased." In Christ we have been given the Father's love and pleasure. Repeat the phrase Jesus heard several times (substituting "daughter" if appropriate), and imagine the Father saying it to you. How does it feel? Do you believe it?

Choose one child, possibly one with whom you've struggled. Say this sentence to that child (paraphrased as needed to be comfortable) at a time when you can express it with full conviction. What did you glean from this experience, either about your relationship with God or with your child?

Proaction
(Proactive Action)

Chapter Twelve

Training for Life
Introduction to PROACTION

BUILDING A STRONG **Foundation** is like filling a reservoir with the faith, supportive relationships, sense of purpose, and personal insights that I need for effective parenting. Out of that reservoir flows my **Connection** with my children. But if all I do is connect, my children will become overly dependent and prone to weakness, bobbing aimlessly in my love for them. Children need "swimming lessons" that teach them to function purposefully in the love they've been given.

"Proaction" is a word we coined to express this concept. It means to take proactive action to prepare my children for life. Instead of waiting for misbehavior, and then trying to teach lessons through **Correction, Proaction** is about being thoughtful, watchful for ways to teach and train my children. I mentor success in important life skills and build character in everyday situations. Even more importantly, I help them discover the love of God and his unique path for their lives. If the blessing of my love is to accomplish the purpose God intended, my children must learn to give it away. This is a deeply biblical principle.

"I will make you into a great nation and I will bless you; I will make your name great, and you will be a blessing...(so that)[1] all peoples on earth will be blessed through you."
—Genesis 12:2,3

Proaction requires diligence to actively teach my children what it means to be a human being created to be a blessing to others. By nurturing their faith, relationships, character, and talents, I help them discover that they are uniquely created by God for a loving relationship with him. I also help my children understand that this relationship with God involves both receiving his blessing, and then bringing blessing to those around them. Even children as young as two years old can begin to understand this, and can learn to bless, or help, other people.

Proaction used to come more naturally for parents. Throughout most of human history, parents' lives were quite visible to their children. Parents didn't have to think so much about how to pass on faith, values, and skills to their children. On farms, in family businesses, and in the context of close-knit community life, children mostly learned from the adults' example. As they grew, children became engaged in the responsibilities and without thought took on the values essential for the family and community to survive and flourish.

I saw an example of this in a primitive village in the northern Philippines. I visited during a week that the men were up in the mountains harvesting rice. Boys of about seven years old and older were with the men, not for some nice father-son time together but because they were *needed.* Back in the village, the mothers and young women prepared and stored the rice as it arrived from the terraces. The remaining children busied themselves caring for the youngest, washing clothes in the stream, or milling the freshly harvested rice with child-sized mortar and pestles. Nearly every community member in this small village had learned important skills that contributed meaningfully to the community's existence.

This is quite a contrast to our fast, modernized, and busy society. As time goes on it seems parents and children often live quite separate lives. So I must be much more purposeful if I am to model and teach faith, values, and skills to my children. After interviewing thousands of parents George Barna concluded, "Most of the parents we've interviewed in recent years have a survival-based philosophy rather than a goal-oriented philosophy... Great parents recognize that from the moment a child leaves the womb until the time he or she leaves the home, they must tirelessly guard and shape the mind, heart, and soul of their child."[2]

Proverbs 22:6 says, **"Train a child in the way he should go and when he is old he will not turn from it."** Josh McDowell reminds us that **"the way he should go"** is not only about God's standards and precepts, as is often taught. It is also about the unique bent of each child. McDowell goes on to share this note for the verse from the Ryrie Study Bible: "'The way he should go' really means 'according to his way'; i.e., the child's habits and interests. The instruction must take into account his individuality and inclinations, his personality, the unique way God created him, and must be in keeping with his physical and mental development."[3]

This sounds like something that requires great attentiveness, engagement, and purposefulness on the part of a parent. This is the work of **Proaction!**

My Foundation for Proaction

What enables me to provide help that is truly helpful?

For **Proaction** to take root in my parenting, I must be on my own journey to know and follow God. As I pay attention to my own growth, I can teach my children what I've learned, and faithfully seek God's guidance for what I still need to learn.

Most parents desire for their children to have strong relationships, a vocation that fulfills them, and a deep faith that enriches their lives. This healthy and God-given desire[4] is what compels **Proaction.** But a problem emerges when parents *need* their children to be successful. If my well-being is dependent on my children's success, then my efforts to encourage them (fill them with courage) and promote their success, may do just the opposite and fill them with *my* anxiety. Lynne recalls this scene:

> The halls rang out with the varied piano music played by young students in private rooms, testing their skills for the judges. Parents waited outside, some nervously attentive, others curiously relaxed. These music contests are always quite a study in parental beliefs and behaviors. I couldn't help but notice one particular dad grimacing each time his son missed a note on a rather difficult piece. At one point he piped, "He hasn't played it that bad in a month!" It was almost as if somehow the dad thought he was the one being judged. When the piece finished he just shook his head.

> The son emerged from the room, also dejected. An expectant glance toward dad was quickly met with a gruff look. Dad turned and walked away. The son followed. His chin descended to his chest and his shoulders slouched. He seemed on the edge of tears. As I observed this, I couldn't help but wonder how the son interpreted his father's disappointment.

Though parents would never say it out loud, what is often communicated at times like this is, "You're loved and valued much more when you succeed (and make me look good)." Even if it is unspoken, children seem to have an innate sense of their parent's anxiety. If I'm anxious that my children's failure might embarrass me, it can put a pressure on them that actually hinders their success. Only when I don't *need* my children to be successful can I freely encourage them toward success. Consider this parent's story:

Dawn began to realize that her anxiety about her daughter Annie's academic challenges was adversely affecting Annie. Because Dawn deeply desired to change this pattern, she began to examine her underlying beliefs. She discovered that fear was behind her efforts to encourage Annie. She feared that Annie was going to struggle through life and that she had failed as a mom for not producing a better student. The thought of watching this struggle, believing she herself was ultimately responsible, was almost unbearable for Dawn. She realized that her anxiety and fear were symptoms of a false core belief that she could be happy only if her daughter was successful on mom's terms.

Once she understood this, Dawn decided to focus on the true belief that God had a special calling for Annie. God's grace would be more than sufficient for Annie to face whatever challenges life would hold. Dawn's *value* of communicating unconditional love for Annie became her *priority.*

Her first opportunity came when Annie asked Dawn to help her study for an upcoming math test. As they began, Dawn looked Annie in the eyes and emphatically stated, "No matter how this test goes for you, I want you to know how much I love you!" Annie burst into tears of relief. Dawn then bought Annie a gift and gave it to her, as a reminder of her unconditional love, *before* the test was graded.

Feelings of anxiety, discouragement, or anger over children's performance can reveal a parent's false core beliefs. These beliefs nearly always somehow link the children's success with the parent's sense of value or emotional well being. To the extent that this link exists, children are often anxious or resentful of their parents' efforts to guide them because of the unspoken pressure it puts on them. They feel responsible for their parents' happiness. It is difficult work for parents to grow in an awareness of their underlying beliefs, but it builds a solid **Foundation** for giving effective **Proaction.** Lynne shares this example:

For years I have struggled with the mess that our lively, spontaneous, creative, frequently disorganized children made at high speed. I used to call it "Trash and Dash." Since their father has somewhat more "relaxed" standards of housekeeping than I do, it was a constant battle in which I felt hurt, alone, and resentful.

I knew it was good to help my children to learn orderliness, but my energy to teach them was fueled by my feelings and beliefs. At times I interpreted every toy, dirty sock, jacket, and backpack left on the floor as a personal attack on me. I believed that everyone thought that keeping the house clean was my job. My anger would easily flare as I engaged with the kids to get them to clean up. Sensing my anger, they would grow angry and resentful in return. One child would complain, "I'm tired of your programs" (of rewards and consequences); another would moan, "I can't stand your nagging." This left me more discouraged, and the cycle continued.

When I started praying about my beliefs and inviting God's truth to define me, I realized that I could be OK, that God loved and valued me even if the house was a disaster and the kids weren't responding well to my training. As I grew to embrace this truth, I began to fully value their spontaneous, creative strengths that contributed to the problem. I was better able to coach my children and hold them accountable in this area for *their* benefit – not for mine. I still get frustrated, but never enraged, a change that has brought freedom and peace. And, of course, the more peaceful I am, the easier it is to help them learn.

As I let go of the need for my children to be successful, the freer I am to value and connect with them as I teach them. This increases their motivation to learn and my joy in teaching, as we engage in this whole process of passing on the values and skills they need for life.

◆◆◆❖◆❖◆◆
**Only when I don't need my children to be successful
can I truly encourage them toward success.**
◆◆◆❖◆❖◆◆

MY RESPONSE...

Is there a skill or character quality which my child has difficulty learning? What emotion do I usually feel when teaching that skill or quality, and what does that tell me about my underlying beliefs?

What truths might help me enjoy my child's learning process? (i.e. God delights in both of us despite our areas of "slow learning," My child's challenges are an opportunity for me to express God's unconditional love to him/her.)

Big-Picture Paradigms

What are my ultimate goals in proactive training?

God's purposes

When talking about teaching kids to be successful, parents often want to jump right to tactical issues like chores, homework, respect, and obedience. These are important issues, and we will get to them. But they are not the most important, because these things ought to flow out of a child's understanding about who they are and why they were created. **Proaction** therefore begins with thoughtful integration of faith and values in the context of daily life.

If the ultimate goal of my instruction is to help my children learn to stand strong as followers of God in today's turbulent world, then I will watch for the uniqueness of each child and capitalize on teachable moments. Here's an example from Lynne regarding messages about what makes people valuable.

We frequently talked with our children about what was truly important in life – a person's heart and character. We looked for creative ways to communicate that they were loved regardless of their performance. We even gave them silly pop "quizzes," such as "Wow, good report card! But does that make you any more valuable?" ("No!") "You look beautiful in that dress. Do you think I love you more?" ("Of course not!")

When Bethany turned eleven, I bought her a teen-girl magazine. I wanted to be ahead of the game in talking about adolescent issues, instead of doing damage control after she absorbed the misguided ideas of her peers! We looked through the articles that were filled with tips on makeup, diets, and catching a boyfriend. We identified the messages communicated by each of the articles about where people get value and what's important, and discussed God's truth.

As a teenager, Bethany now chooses excellent friends, enjoys fashion and makeup occasionally for the fun of it, and feels sorry for kids who are trapped by the need to impress others. She challenged a popular, appearance-conscious friend to try coming to school without makeup. When the girl hesitantly showed her face the next day Bethany announced, "You look beautiful without makeup and we love you just as much!" It occurred to me that her message to this girl was the perspective we had thoughtfully and persistently communicated to her from a young age.

The key messages each child needs will vary somewhat based on age and unique personality. For example, children who struggle with a learning disability may need to loudly and clearly hear the message that God created them in the perfect way for the plans he has, regardless of how school goes for them. Children who are introverts (in our culture that values extroversion) may need to learn that God designed and values their thoughtful, quiet, and sensitive nature. The youngster who loves working with his or her hands but struggles to sit still in class may need extra opportunities to build or fix things. He or she will need to hear that this special gift can be a great blessing to the world.

My Response...

What is my ultimate goal in the Proaction I give to my children?

Picturing each one of my children on Jesus' lap, he looks in their eyes and makes two or three key statements to each child. What would he say?

How can I persistently communicate those messages in everyday situations?

My child's independence

When babies are born they are helpless and dependent on us for everything. It feels good to be needed and in control. However, even before children reach the toddler stage, parents can begin a journey of progressively giving their children independence in certain areas of life. This can be difficult. Instead of embracing the child's journey toward independence, parents often resist this simple reality: It's their life - it's their feelings, their relationships, their responsibilities, and their faith. As a parent it is my job to thoughtfully guide the process by which my children learn to embrace biblical values, make wise choices, and solve their own problems and conflicts.

I'm often tempted to deal with my children in ways that gain immediate results. While this might be gratifying in the moment, it often leads to greater frustration later because I didn't really teach the value behind the behavior. Forced instant compliance tends to leave my children feeling powerless, and maybe angry, and makes it harder the next time I deal with the issue. It is much more helpful to think long-term, focusing on my children's independence. It helps me to ask this question: "What skills and values am I building now, that will guide my child through adolescence and adulthood?" Here's a story we heard from a mom about a long-term approach regarding her nine-year-old son's music, and the values it promoted:

"Seth's friend made a CD for him containing both Christian and secular songs, two of which had swearing and questionable lyrics. I prayed for wisdom because Seth is very sensitive – both easily swayed by his friend and quick to feel guilt or shame when confronted. I knew that demanding that he not listen to the music could drive him toward rebellion. I wanted to be sure to handle this in a way that would encourage his long-term growth, and not just require short-term compliance.

After several days I asked about the CD. He said it was cool. I asked if there were any bad songs on it. He looked defensive, "Well, two of the songs have swear words, but they're really good songs!" I decided, instead of pronouncing judgment, to ask to listen to them together. He obliged. We listened to the songs and talked about the parts we liked. I affirmed that the songs were upbeat and fun. I noticed and commented that Seth really seemed to like the rhythm. Then we talked about the swearing and its impact on our hearts when we hear it repeatedly, and compared that to the verse of Scripture that says **"whatever is good, right, pure, honorable, ...think on these things,"** (Philippians 4:8). I told him it was important for him to learn to make wise decisions on his own and that I wouldn't tell him what to do. He still was struggling with the decision, so he agreed when I suggested we take a few days to pray about it.

I asked the Lord to speak to Seth's heart and give me helpful insight. After a few days we talked about it again. I affirmed my love for him and confidence in him. He hugged me and said he was sorry. I haven't heard those songs since."

This method may not always produce the same results but, regardless of the outcome, I can be peaceful and trust God with my child, knowing I am teaching my child *the process* of gaining wisdom.

Because parents often feel pressure to teach their children right from wrong, and get them to do it, they tend to let that pressure drive them to quick, less thoughtful approaches. Here's how that story might have gone if that pressure had driven Seth's mother:

"When I found out my nine-year-old Seth had a CD with swearing on it, I was quite concerned. As soon as I heard the swearing, I went into his room and demanded an explanation. "It's not that big a deal, Mom! They're good songs." I could see he was a bit ashamed. Believing it would be best for him not to be exposed to such music, I took the CD away. Seth was quite angry at first, but he eventually got over it."

It's a much shorter story now. But that does not mean it was a more effective way to deal with the issue. An approach like this, though it may seem effective in the short run, leaves a child feeling judged and controlled. What the child has likely learned is to keep his mom from finding out about his "bad" music in the future. The opportunity for engaging with the child and discovering a way to help him understand and develop his own convictions is lost.

The following chart shows examples of ways parents either deter or facilitate their children's growth toward healthy independence.

Deter independence	Facilitate independence
Minimize or distract kids from hard feelings when upset.	Help children learn to identify and deal with their own feelings.
Stop conflicts. Separate kids.	Facilitate conflict resolution skills.
Nag to ensure responsibilities are done.	Encourage self-motivated responsibility.
Require children to get involved in church activities.	Nurture authentic, enduring faith.

Many parents place a high priority on their children's *compliance*—on achieving acceptable behavioral outcomes as quickly as possible. Because their methods often result in desired behaviors, these parents believe that all is well with their young children. But the long-term result of such an approach is often anything but compliance. Kids who have been forced into compliance often emerge as overly rebellious adolescents[5]. These kids, driven by anger and resentment built up over the years, begin to learn that they have the power to resist. Because they have had values imposed on them, they must venture out on what is frequently a tumultuous journey to discover their own values. Sometimes they come full circle to the values under which they were raised, and sometimes they do not. As their rebellion unfolds, parents may wonder, "What happened all of a sudden?" But in fact, what happened was a long time brewing.

This perspective compels me to be more thoughtful about my methods and motivation in seeking compliance. In any interaction with my children I must be honest enough to ask myself, "Am I simply obtaining compliance (for the sake of the behavior, and for my satisfaction), or am I equipping them with skills and values for future independence (for the sake of my child)?" More than ever before, today's children are surrounded by hurtful influences and readily available addictive activities. Certainly there are times when I will have to set boundaries that my children won't like or agree with. But I can still work to build the values that support those boundaries.

> ♦♦♦❖◆❖♦♦♦
> **Am I simply obtaining compliance, or am I equipping**
> **my children with skills and values for a lifetime?**
> ♦♦♦❖◆❖♦♦♦

My Response...

What are some ways in which my teaching and training of my children is "long-sighted"?

What are some issues I address simply to gain compliance? How might I address these issues with a more "long-sighted" view?

Kid Connection!

Ask each of your children what they think their life might be like when they are adults. Ask questions to draw out details about family, location, housing, vocation, hobbies, etc. If they are too young for such abstract questions, offer two or three choices for each aspect. Record some of their more significant statements.

Ask each child what he/she needs to learn to prepare for this future life.

Chapter Thirteen

How to T.E.A.C.H. My Child
Principles for Effective PROACTION

"TRAIN A CHILD in the way he should go, and when he is old he will not turn from it" (Proverbs 22:6). Sounds easy enough. Teach them a few basic responsibilities and a few key Bible verses. Send them to church and to school. Everything will work out just fine. Right? If it's so easy, then why, according to numerous studies, are children increasingly at risk?

Perhaps it's not so simple after all. In today's fast-paced world, with kids and parents coming and going at rapid rates, the training of a child is increasingly complex. It is easy to take for granted that my children's needs are being met and they are being well trained in each of the different settings they find themselves. Teachers, coaches, and even peers can become significant "trainers" at a very young age. But do I really know these trainers and the lessons being taught? Can I be sure that others are attentive to "the way he (or she) should go"? Am I confident that the training by others reinforces my hopes for my children to have a productive, purposeful life, intimate relationships, and a resilient faith?

There are many good opportunities for my children to learn and grow beyond the walls of our home and in the context of numerous other relationships. It is important to cultivate these opportunities. It seems almost natural in today's culture to relinquish the training of my children to those more specialized than myself. But it is still my responsibility to be my children's primary teacher – throughout their childhood and well into adolescence. Even when others more knowledgeable are involved in the teaching, it is incumbent on parents to stay engaged with their children's formal (school), informal (extracurricular), and non-formal (day-to-day life) education.

We have developed five principles for effective **Proaction** to guide parents in this monumental role of primary teacher. Some parents will be more structured in this approach and may take more direct responsibility. Others will be more random and may give more of the direct responsibility to others. At either extreme, and everywhere in between, acting on these principles will help parents keep their primary role.

The five principles are an acronym for "**T.E.A.C.H.**" <u>Talk</u> with my children. <u>Exemplify</u> desired practices and values. <u>Affirm</u> character, talents and effort. <u>Create</u> opportunities for success, significance, and service. <u>Help</u>, get in the trenches with them. These principles are the basis for giving **Proaction** in the topics covered in subsequent chapters.

<u>Talk</u> – About Life, Values, Faith

How can I have conversations with my children about deep issues?

> *"Impress [God's commandments] on your children. Talk about them when you sit at home and when you walk along the road, and when you lie down and when you get up."*
> —Deuteronomy 6:7

For most of human history, values and faith have been passed along by the spoken word in the context of one's closest relationships. Telling stories and integrating values into daily conversations was the primary way youngsters learned from their parents. (They also learned by example, which will be discussed next.)

Research on many fronts shows the impact when parents spend time talking to their children about important issues. This research shows dramatic influence related to language development and educational success,[1] faith development,[2] chemical use,[3] and a host of other issues. The bottom line is, if I want to pass my faith and values onto my children, talking about deeper issues with my children becomes a high priority. Paul's philosophy of "parenting" the Thessalonian church is a great picture of passing on core truths through the heartfelt connection of a shared journey.

> *"...we were gentle among you, like a mother caring for her little children. We loved you so much that we were **delighted to share** with you not only the gospel of God but **our lives** as well, because you had become so dear to us."*
> —1 Thessalonians 2:7, 8

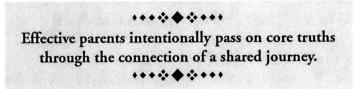

◆◆◇❖◇◆◆
**Effective parents intentionally pass on core truths
through the connection of a shared journey.**
◆◆◇❖◇◆◆

This can easily be done in the context of daily life events. For example, talking while doing chores or preparing meals—even just to explain what I'm doing—can be a great way to communicate the importance of responsibility. Or, if my child comes home talking about the fight on the playground, I might tell a story about my experiences with regard to fighting. This could be a springboard for a short conversation about what things are worth fighting for and what are some hurtful or helpful ways of fighting for what we believe in. For less talkative children, a structured "story time" can provide avenues to either read stories that teach values, or share stories from personal experience. Either way, from my own life or from outside examples, I can look for opportunities to weave in discussions of faith and values—and keep talking!

My Response...

What are two or three significant, untold life events that have influenced my values and perspective in life that I could tell my children?

Particularly as children get older, an important way to pass values is conversations – dialogues filled with the freedom to explore perspectives and ask thoughtful questions about what is important to my child.

One dad enlisted my help to deal with his apparently unmotivated teenager, who was floundering in school. I asked him how he had addressed this so far with his son. He said, "Well, we've had some conversations about it." I noticed his stern expression and tone. "Conversations?" I asked with a slight smile. Before I could ask further, the astute dad said, "Oh, I get it. I've just been talking *at* him." We discussed some ways to have a true conversation with his son about his own goals and desires, and the role of responsibility in achieving these. The dad decided he wanted to ask more questions. Not the kind that set his child up to feel stupid, or to trap his son, but questions sincerely aimed at gaining understanding. This new skill led to an entirely different kind of "conversation" and quite a different result! Through this new approach, the son felt understood and encouraged. Their relationship improved, and ultimately, the son began to do better in school.

Exemplify

What really is the impact of my example?

"Whatever you have learned or received or heard from me, or seen in me – put it into practice. And the God of peace shall be with you."

—Philippians 4:9

This is a bold command to Paul's spiritual children in Philippi. What confidence he must have had in the words and example God had built into him. I am compelled to consider how to be such an example to my own children. "Whatever you have…seen in me – put into practice." Children will most likely follow the examples of the closest people in their lives. Their behaviors are just much less refined than the adults they imitate. It makes me wonder, what do they really see in my example? If I want my children to do well in school, am I regularly learning new things and enthusiastically sharing that with others? If I desire to build respect in our home, what have I said about my neighbors, my colleagues, and those in authority over me? What are my children learning from my example about how to treat my spouse, my friends, and others in my community? Or from how I treat them! Lynne shares her story.

When Daniel and I got into power struggles, I was usually oblivious to my shaming words and tone, but I was keenly aware of how disrespectful he was! With a scowl, pointed finger, and strong tone I would grandly announce, "It is NOT OK to talk like that!" My condescending proclamations were an attempt to feel in charge, but did nothing to calm the conflict. I finally realized that he was basically following my example. The ball was in my court to be the first to change, to learn to be calmer and more respectful. When conflicts would start to escalate I consciously practiced: first take a deep breath and then say something like, "Daniel, I am really angry, and I'm afraid I'm going to be disrespectful to you if we talk about this now. I'm going to take a break, and let's talk about it later." As I learned, Daniel learned from my example. Before long our conflicts became more civil and respectful. Looking back, that was a key step in his journey of learning to calm himself down in conflict.

Parents often overlook the importance of their example. There are many ways in which they intentionally or unintentionally model positive character qualities: self-control, caring, diligence, faithfulness, etc. Tuning in to that modeling makes it easier to do even more often.

MY RESPONSE…

If I step outside my home life and watch my daily existence as though it's a TV show, what have my children seen:
What are some positive qualities that I model for them?

What are there some things I do that are inconsistent with what I would like them to learn?

<u>Affirm</u> – Character, Talents, and Effort

How can I effectively affirm my children, even if they struggle?

"…whatever is true, whatever is honorable, whatever is right, whatever is pure, whatever is lovely, whatever is of good repute – if there is any excellence and if anything worthy of praise – let your mind dwell on these things."

—Philippians 4: 8, NASB

Ricky had just been suspended from school for threatening his teachers – an unusual thing for a fourth grader. I was enlisted to help him and his parents learn new skills for coping with his anger. During our first meeting I asked Ricky, "What are some things you're good at?" He shrugged, unable to give an answer. I probed further, "What are some good things the adults in your life might say about you?" Ricky about hit the roof!

"Are you kiddin'? There's nothin' for them to say because there's nothing good about me! I yell, I swear, I scream, and then I get in trouble!" His intensity surprised me. I'd never seen a child this young so adamant about his perceived failures.

I waited to see if he had more to say. He stared blankly at the floor. "Well," I said, speaking slowly and gently, "I've already noticed some stuff you're good at." I paused. "You interested in what I noticed?"

"Whatever," he said, not looking up.

I waited further and offered, "You let me know if you're interested in knowing, and I'll tell you. Anything else you want to tell me?"

"What did you notice?" he immediately asked, revealing his hunger to be affirmed, but on his terms, not on mine. I proceeded to tell him how I noticed how respectful he'd been with me, a strange adult, during the first part of our meeting. I told him I appreciated the fact that when he got angry, he didn't lash out at me. I even affirmed that he was good at letting me know he was angry. With a half smile, Ricky looked up and said, "Whatever." I knew, however, that he liked hearing what I'd said. This brief but significant interaction paved the way for a season of growth in Ricky's life.

Learning to notice and affirm "whatever is good" is a critically important parenting skill because it helps guide a child "in the way he should go." The starting place for this guidance is my watchful eye as a parent. Developing this "eye" requires studious attention. Then, when I notice something good, I can express it, whatever it is, as I did with Ricky. Unless I express what I notice, it will have no power to shape or encourage my child.

I can affirm my child strongly without creating an insecure "praise junkie." I simply describe what I see: my child's action or attitude; plus the natural result, including the feelings of the people affected. "You shared some of your *favorite* toys with Chris today! The two of you had a lot of fun, and I'll bet he's excited to come back." These descriptions avoid judgments like "good boy," or "great job," and strengthen the values that support the behavior.

When it's hard to find something to affirm I can ask myself, "What negative behavior *didn't* happen?" (i.e., Thanks for letting me talk uninterrupted – that was really helpful!) Or, "What went right, even though some things went wrong?" (i.e., I'm disappointed in what you did, but I'm really glad you told me about it.)

The goal to notice and affirm whatever is excellent or praiseworthy transforms my parenting journey from a maze to a treasure hunt. Instead of simply figuring out the path to managing behavior, parenting becomes a search to find and proclaim the jewels of goodness in my child's life.

> ◆ ◆ ◆ ❖ ◆ ❖ ◆ ◆ ◆
> **The goal to notice and affirm**
> **transforms the maze of parenting into a treasure hunt.**
> ◆ ◆ ◆ ❖ ◆ ❖ ◆ ◆ ◆

MY RESPONSE...

What is an affirmation I can give each child about an easily overlooked behavior, attitude, gift, or character trait?

<u>Create</u> Opportunities – for Success, Significance, Service

How can I set my children up to succeed?

"After this the Lord appointed seventy-two others and sent them two by two ahead of him to every town. ..."

—Luke 10:1-21

Jesus masterfully trained his followers to carry out his mission by creating opportunities for them to learn and grow in the skills they would need to take the gospel to the world. He started with them long before they were ready. In Luke 10 we read where Jesus assigned them small, well-defined tasks. He set them up for success and then rejoiced in the fantastic results, even though the disciples barely knew what they were doing. It seems he wanted them to feel good about practicing some of what they'd learned from him, even though they were far from ready for full independence. By the time he left them on their own, he knew they had learned and experienced what they needed to change the world. What a great model for me to consider as I seek to prepare my children for a life of significance.

Dr. Michael Resnick summarizes extensive research about what it takes to build people's self-esteem:

1. Teach them a skill.
2. Teach them how to use that skill to be of help or service to someone else.[4]

At the heart of this effort is the goal of building into a child a practical sense of purpose, rooted in help and service to others. This is what Jesus did with his followers and it can be done with children. It can be as simple as teaching children to fix one part of a meal for the family. I can help my child learn to draw and then use one of the drawings for a special card for someone. One parent told of his strong-willed nine-year-old, whose desire to take charge frequently resulted in household conflicts. He decided to take her with him to a volunteer program at a nursing home. He hoped she would grow in both her talents and her concern for others. It wasn't long before she was asked to lead the weekly Bingo game!

This perspective of creating opportunities for success adds a new dimension to the ways I involve my children in any variety of tasks. By helping my children have positive and meaningful experiences, I help them grow in the purposes for which God designed them. If they are struggling with learning something, I can rethink how to create a scenario of success – through smaller steps, more encouragement, reminding them of previous succees in a similar situation, etc.

When Bethany was eight, she was still quite shy. When meeting new people she hid behind Lynne or me and used baby talk. Pressure from us to greet people appropriately had only made it worse, so we decided to create opportunities for success. Together we discussed the benefits of being comfortable in this situation, both for her and those people she met. She joined us in deciding how to break the task down into small steps, starting with standing up straight next to us when we introduced her to someone. Each step got gradually closer to looking someone in the eyes, and introducing herself appropriately. We gave her positive encouragement for each small success. In just a few months she enjoyed meeting new people and her true extroverted personality was blossoming.

MY RESPONSE...

What could I do to create an opportunity for my child to experience success in some new way? (This could be learning something new, or teaching something that has been difficult with a new approach.)

**To build self-esteem in my children,
I simply teach them a skill they can use to bless others.**

Help

How can I come alongside, to help my child grow?

> *"I will ask the Father and he will give you another Helper, that he may be with you forever."*
> —John 14:16

"My son is so disobedient," Jeff lamented about his six-year-old son, Andy. "Every time I ask him to clean his room, he starts but doesn't finish. It makes me crazy!"

Most parents want their children to obey their commands and requests quickly. It is good for children to learn obedience. This flows out of the truth that God desires obedience. But God, understanding our inability to fully and perfectly obey, sent Jesus to "become our obedience" (see Romans 6:12 – 23). Jesus then promised to give yet "another helper," the Holy Spirit. The word translated "helper" in John 14:16 is literally "one who comes alongside." What a beautiful picture of how we can best get our children walking on the right path in life. We don't just bark the orders; we walk alongside them.

I talked about these ideas with Jeff and recommended that he do more on the helping side when he expects obedience. He went home intent on "coming alongside" Andy. A few weeks later, Jeff reported the joy he'd experienced in going into Andy's room as a helper instead of a taskmaster. It turns out that Andy was so overwhelmed by the cleaning task, and his dad's negative tone, he just didn't know what to do. Jeff first helped by showing his son what needed to be done. He then made great fun out of giving Andy the power to order Jeff to put things away. Then they did it together a few times, celebrating their success each time. Finally, Jeff watched and encouraged as Andy cleaned the room entirely by himself. As Andy became more independent in this task Jeff learned to let go of his expectation for immediate, perfect compliance. In just a few weeks Andy had gained the ability to obey that request. Jeff says, "It's not perfect. It probably never will be. But it's a lot better."

The extra time this takes is well worth the effort. In the long run, my approach to training my children lays the groundwork for their concept of God either as the One who gives commands and evaluates their performance from a distance, or as the God who is in the trenches with them, helping with guidance, encouragement, and strength.

My Response...

When was a time I came alongside my child to help them learn something? What was the result?

What aspect of T.E.A.C.H. is the most difficult for me? How do I feel and what happens when I implement that principle with my children for an entire day?

Fill in the corresponding principles for the TEACH acronym:

T_____E_____A_____C_____H_____

Kid Connection!

Ask each of your children, "If Jesus were to walk into the room to teach you something you really wanted to learn, what would it be and how would he do it?"

Chapter Fourteen

Nurturing Authentic, Resilient Faith
My Child's Relationship with God

"I have no greater joy than to hear that my children are walking in the truth."

—3 John 1:4

WHAT THE APOSTLE John desired for his spiritual children, most Christian parents desire for their children, to "walk in the truth." Indeed, I have no greater joy than to see my children wrestling with their faith and applying it in their daily lives. It's particularly rewarding to hear words from my children or see actions in them that I have worked so purposefully to model. With the increasing pressures that the world places on each generation, parents must be more thoughtful and intentional about passing on their faith to their children. The good news is that we have access to better resources and programs than we have ever had. The bad news is that in spite of these advantages, children are leaving the faith and faith traditions of their parents in alarming numbers. One prominent study found that between 1970 and 1990 the number of church-going adolescents who reported a personal relationship with Jesus Christ dropped from thirty percent to eleven percent.[1] While new studies suggest the trends are improving slightly, there is still much work to do to effectively pass faith from generation to generation.

The Challenge of Nurturing Faith

What can hinder my child's faith development?

Numerous cultural realities pose themselves as barriers to faith development. The sophistication of an advertising and media industry bent on selling my kids counter-Christian values is mind-boggling. Under the guise of selling toothpaste, soda pop, sneakers, or any other product my children are bombarded with messages about where value comes from: sex appeal, money, power, appearance, etc. Movie and TV characters are usually sexy, aggressive and apparently unbelieving. I can hardly think of a time when a character's value was determined by God's love, or the "bad guy" was defeated or transformed by someone's faith in Christ. It could be easy to point fingers of blame at these and other factors in the outside world. But before looking at these external forces it is critically important to look at myself – the parenting methods I use, the example I set, and the conversations about faith I have with my children.

In my work with high-risk teens, I saw increasing numbers of these troubled kids come from "good" Christian homes. The simplest way I can explain this is that I saw too many parents excessively controlling their kids' behavior, without doing the hard work of lovingly teaching values. Research indicates that children are less likely to develop a strong faith if parents use excessive control in promoting faith or religious behaviors. The greatest rebellion happens within controlling families.[2] In these families, "faith" can become a set of restrictive rules for how to live, rather than a way of life "**rooted and established in love**" (Ephesians 3:17). Further research revealed that children who were directly challenged, lectured, or critiqued by their parents developed little moral reasoning. In fact, the way parents *interacted* with their children was a better predictor of spiritual/moral growth, than was the parents' own level of moral reasoning![3]

Bill was raised in what he called a "model Christian family." His parents put strict emphasis on respect and obedience, and the children learned to perform according to expectations. After eighteen years, the parents proudly delivered their son to his college campus – and freedom. He reports, "I couldn't wait to get away from them. Before their taillights disappeared on the horizon I was drunk. I lived a wild life for quite some time." It took many years, much prayer, and a life crisis to bring him to vital, personal faith in Christ. Many tightly controlled children never return to faith.

In contrast to the controlling spiritual approach is the uninvolved approach. Many parents assume that church attendance will "get the job done." It is easy to relegate teaching of God's ways to professionals and volunteers in today's impressive, high-caliber church programs. George Barna, author and researcher, suggests that eighty-five percent of church-going parents "believe they have the primary responsibility for the moral and spiritual development of their children." Unfortunately, while parents say they believe this, they don't seem to act very well on that belief. Barna goes on to say that of that eighty-five percent, "more than two-thirds of them abdicate that responsibility to their church."[4] This means that the very parents who say they understand how important moral and spiritual teaching is, do little or nothing to purposefully build these teachings into their children's lives. This is tragic! While church programs and pastors can play significant roles in faith building, this abdication by parents may well be impressing upon children that faith isn't really that important after all.

In spite of the increased effort and attention modern churches give to children, one extensive study shows that it is the parents' influence that raises children of strong spiritual fiber. Consider these results: Of church-going families, only twenty-two percent of youth whose parents were not conversational with them about faith were involved themselves in faith activities. When parents openly modeled and discussed faith with their children, the percentage more than doubled to fifty-three percent.[5] In other words, if I am serious about passing faith onto my children, I will talk with them frequently about my faith. Effective discipleship begins when my spiritual life intersects with my every day interactions with my children.

The following section explores practical ways that parents can live out their faith authentically before their children and include the children in their journey. When parents take responsibility for faith development in this way, their own faith is sharpened as they nurture it in their children.

The Intersection of Faith and Life

How can I incorporate faith into everyday life?

"Love the Lord your God with all your heart and with all your soul and with all your strength. These commandments that I give you today are to be upon your hearts. Impress them on your children. Talk about them when you sit at home and when you walk along the road, when you lie down and when you get up. Tie them as symbols on your hands and bind them on your foreheads. Write them on the doorframes of your houses and on your gates."

—Deuteronomy 6:5-9

Remembering Moses' final address to the people of Israel helps me remember the importance of living a life of faith _together_ with my family and community. According to these verses, I am to prioritize my relationship with God, and then share my love for God with my children in everyday life.

This seems easy, but many parents are unsure about how to talk naturally about faith with their children. There are a variety of excellent resources to help parents. _Spiritual Growth of Children_,[6] and _Fun Excuses to Talk About God_,[7] are filled with great ideas for getting started. www.famtime.com also has excellent resources. Some families enjoy regular times for reading a short devotional and praying together. Mealtimes can be a good starting place for this. Bedtime Bible stories can build a long-lasting habit of regularly reading scripture.

A weekly family-time lesson can be as simple as gathering briefly to read the Bible and pray together or as complex as designing a fun mini-lesson for the family. (Kirk Weaver's Family Time resources are very helpful.) Seasonal rituals can be meaningful ways to teach spiritual truths at holidays. The possibilities are endless. These kinds of regular activities can build a lasting value for biblical principles and an increased knowledge of Scripture into both parents and children. They become wonderful opportunities to utilize the children's natural gifts such as acting, singing, or drawing, to increase their interest and reinforce learning.

Some families, including ours, find it difficult to implement regular, structured practices. Our early attempts at family devotions were filled with squirming and squabbling! It is easy to feel discouraged or guilty, and assume I am failing in my responsibility toward my children. John Wimber describes the way he and his wife passed a foundation of faith on to their children.

"I was never any good at family devotions. I read children's Bible stories to my kids; they got bored. Booklets and games didn't do it either. I never fit the mold of a great family devotions leader. But I lived a devoted life. My wife, Carol, and I led friends to Christ in our living room. We served meals, loaned money, and taught Bible studies in our home. Our kids watched and listened. My kids remember a number of instances that served to form their understanding of the Christian life. In their thirties, all indicated to me, in different language, that three things made it possible for them to be believers. First, Carol and I were always the same in public and private. Furthermore, our kids say we always made room for them in whatever we were doing. Lastly, Carol and I were almost together on our various positions or opinions in our household. This seemed to give the family some stability. …Ordinary life and spiritual activities intersected in our home."[8]

Jesus' example brings clarity to the challenge of passing faith to my children. There is no indication that Jesus had a regularly scheduled teaching time with his disciples. We do know, however, that he was very purposeful and persistent about teaching and training his "children." Since he spoke from the overflow of his heart, he naturally and frequently shared scripture with them. He was a master at capturing the events of everyday life and turning them into profound teachable moments. He knew what important life lessons the disciples needed to learn. And he knew it was his responsibility to teach them.

So whether or not a family has regular devotional or teaching practices, carefully and intentionally integrating faith into ordinary life is the ultimate goal. This can mean looking for a natural opportunity to tell my children how I came to embrace faith. I can bring my children into my ministry of others, and talk about the blessing to all involved. At dinner I can read a verse that I enjoyed that day and share how it applies to my life. When relaxing outdoors I can discuss with my children how I see the love of Christ reflected in the beauty of nature. On one camping trip I sent the kids into the woods to look for objects in nature that represented the unique way God created them. They came back eager to share their objects along with their honest opinions and ideas about faith. When finances are tight I have talked to them about God's faithfulness through the years. Lynne and I often tell our children about our conversations with others about faith and, better yet, include them by praying or even inviting them to participate when possible.

MY RESPONSE....

Considering the personalities, ages and needs of my children, what Biblical truths do I want to pass on to them in the next year?

Building on what has worked well in the past (i.e. how I've taught important lessons), how might I teach them these truths?

> ♦ ♦ ♦ ❖ ◆ ❖ ♦ ♦ ♦
> **Whether or not a family has regular devotions,**
> **integrating faith into ordinary life is the ultimate goal.**
> **Effective discipleship begins when my spiritual life intersects**
> **with my everyday interactions with my children.**
> ♦ ♦ ♦ ❖ ◆ ❖ ♦ ♦ ♦

Bringing prayer to life!

Although Jesus often slipped away to pray privately, he also taught his disciples to pray. I can invite my kids to join me or at least contribute to my times of prayer. If they feel uncomfortable praying out loud I can encourage them to pray silently or give them paper and ask them to write or draw their prayer. Most children would be glad to pray, either aloud or silently, for a friend about whom they are concerned. We can talk about things we are each thankful for and pray accordingly. Meals and bedtimes are great times for my family to grow beyond "Thanks for the food," and "Now I lay me down to sleep." *Pray! Kids* magazine and *When Children Pray* by Cheri Fuller are great resources.

As my family becomes more comfortable with various kinds of prayer, we can grow to see that prayer is not so much about asking God for stuff as it is about acknowledging God's work and presence in the daily circumstances of life. This truth compels me to more actively seek to pray anytime and to invite my children to observe or join me. This invitation takes many forms. Sometimes it comes in the form of a spontaneous outburst of praise of gratitude to God for his love or singing a familiar worship song together. Sometimes it's expressing an observation of God's creative genius in nature.

In the difficult circumstances of my life or the lives of others I pray for God's peace, for hearts to be open to his love and comfort, and for God's will to be done. I pray for God's intervention so that God will be glorified. Sometimes I do not know how to pray, so I tell my kids that. Then I confess it to God in their presence. On occasion Lynne and I ask our children to pray for us when either one of us is struggling. This models a natural dependence on God with our emotions and circumstances. I haven't got it figured out, but I continue to work at being more open to bringing my prayer to life in ways that are visible to my family. It's good for me and it's good for them.

MY RESPONSE....

As I think back on the significant events and emotions of my week (for me and my children), what are some little, but natural ways to discuss faith or incorporate prayer into my interactions with my children?

Worshipping and serving together

In the broadest sense, worshipping together simply means living lives oriented toward God – together. It is possible for families to attend church and church programs at the same time, calling it "together," without ever actually being in the same room or program together. That is not *doing* church together or even *going* to church together. That is driving there together.

Having said this I have yet to find a church where families could not truly worship and serve together by making it a priority. Churches that invite whole families to attend the weekly services make it easy to prioritize. Some even have family oriented services. Even if it is not practical for whole families to attend services together, families can worship by serving together.

When a family works together to serve others the children experience the significance of blessing others. Studies show that service matures children in their faith more than even Sunday school, Bible study or worship services.[9] In addition, there are built-in opportunities for children to use their talents in meaningful ways. I capitalize on such opportunities when I find avenues of service within the church where my family can serve together. Almost anything that can be done individually can be done as a family – even if the children are quite young. Possibilities include:

- work in the nursery
- count the offering
- prepare communion
- work on the church grounds

- usher
- make meals for church members in crisis

It's great for families to find ways to serve together at church, but ultimately the purpose of the Church of Jesus Christ is to share its blessings with a world in need. A watchful look beyond my own doorstep reveals endless ways for us to bless and serve others together. In most communities there are numerous ready-made opportunities with seniors, local food-shelf organizations, neighborhood service projects, respite or foster care, etc. One pastor reported, "The best thing that ever happened to our family was doing foster care together."

Serving with other families provides a great opportunity to grow together in community – maybe even with families of your children's friends. In our church several families gather together each month at a local retirement residence to serve meals or help residents with various projects. Not only have the kids learned the value of serving others, but whole families have grown close to each other in relationships that serve to reinforce their faith. One of the most incredible experiences our family has had was a weeklong service trip to an impoverished area along with eight other families from our church.

My Response...

How can I more intentionally worship or serve together with my children? What barriers might I need to overcome? What can I do to involve other families?

Affirming God's work in my children

As God's creation uniquely patterned after him, every child bears the image of God (Genesis 1:27). That image will always seek expression, whether or not the child has yet decided to follow Christ.[10] In addition, Scripture clearly tells us that God is the source of all good things (Mark 10:18, James 1:17). When I help children understand that God is the source of goodness in them, I draw them closer to understanding his character and to the beginning of a real relationship with him. For example when I notice my child being kind, I can affirm the presence of God in her through that kindness by saying, "You were kind just like Jesus."

One morning Noah decided to prepare and serve breakfast. As he set my fried eggs and toast in front of me, Lynne recalled a loose paraphrase of some verses from the Bible: **"For who is greater, the one who is at the table, or the one who serves? Is it not the one who is at the table?"** (She patted my shoulder.) I knew what she was up to and proudly asserted, "Of course!" But Noah knew better - he grinned as she continued. **"But I** (Jesus) **am among you as one who serves,"** (Luke 22:27). Noah soaked up this quick affirmation of his Christ-like actions. We then briefly discussed this as a family. Our prayer before eating focused on the blessing of serving others. Together we thanked God for Noah's gift of service and prayed for Bethany and Daniel's upcoming opportunities to serve others.

When children have professed faith in Christ, parents can strengthen the understanding of the *active presence* of Christ in them. For example when children are generous, I can say, "It seems as if Jesus worked through you to bless (a particular person). How did that feel?" Or, when they have worked hard on a piece of art, "You've worked so hard to create something nice. I can see God's creative heart in you!"

MY RESPONSE...

What are some recent situations in which I can identify the goodness of Christ in my children? How can I express that to my children?

Nurturing an Authentic, Enduring Faith

How can I prepare my children for inevitable faith challenges?

Jesus knew his time with his disciples was limited. The future of the gospel rested on the vitality and endurance of his disciples' faith. He laid a solid foundation in their lives and used them to change the world. By confronting meaningless rituals, challenging conventional thinking, and encouraging those who struggled, Jesus taught and modeled authenticity throughout his ministry.

My time with my children is limited. My focus needs to be on nurturing a faith that takes them beyond the safety of my walls. The following principles help strengthen faith (mine and my children's) for the long haul.

Christ's presence in all things

"...and be content with what you have, because God has said, 'Never will I leave you; never will I forsake you.'"

—Hebrews 13:5

In today's fast-paced world in which parents and children move quickly from one scheduled activity to the next, it is almost natural to view church as just another scheduled activity – the one where God is. A biblical perspective of the Church as the body of Christ, however, never reduces it to a weekly meeting or two. Those who truly embrace the Church understand that it is a way of life. I once had a pastor who emphasized that church meetings were primarily designed to be a celebration of the activity of God in each person's life, and an encouragement to remember and apply that presence in the week to come. He wasn't the greatest preacher and the services were not polished or impressive, but did we celebrate! What a great philosophy!

Indeed, God is with us at all times. It is our awareness of that fact that is sometimes elusive. As I write this, a cold, bitter wind is blowing through the bare treetops outside my office window. It is a subzero morning in Minnesota. The window is covered with frost. Only a small opening in the frost allows me to see outside. I stare through the opening whenever I pause to think about what to write next. I am challenged to put into practice the things I am writing. So I ask myself: "How is it that I am aware of God's presence today?"

At first, I confess, it is hard. I'm busy with a task and I don't want to stop. But I take a deep breath and start looking. It is then that I notice for the first time how intricate and dazzling is the frost formation on the window. I see creative beauty in the stark contrast of the white snow, gray trees, and deep blue sky. I thank God for these things and acknowledge his presence with me in them. But my awareness continues to grow. I look at the books, papers, Post-it notes, and CD's strewn across my desk. These are evidences of my response to the passion God has given me to minister. Even the computer screen filled with these words, is an expression of God's presence within me.

In these few brief moments I am reminded again that God *never* leaves me. When I tell my wife and kids about this experience, I'll invite them to take a breath, and pay attention. For now, I return to writing knowing that in the tasks of my day God is present.

Nurturing this awareness in my children begins with my **Foundation** as I nurture it in myself. Only when I have noticed God's presence this way can I invite my family to recall or recognize it, even in the small, ordinary details of their days.

Faith in trials

Parents often say prayers like this: "God, be with Tyler as he goes off to school today. Keep him safe and help him do well on all his school work." But what if, at school, Tyler gets a "D" on a spelling test and on the way home from school he trips and falls out of the bus, scraping his knee and face. What is Tyler now to conclude about God? Let's see, God was supposed to be with him, but he didn't do well on his test and he had an accident. In his mind, it is reasonable to conclude that his parent's prayer did not "come true."[11] Or maybe he thinks God is punishing him for some other bad thing he did. Either way, he probably thinks God is either not happy with him or has abandoned him altogether. Unfortunately, this kind of thinking and praying is prevalent among Christians.

I know several therapists and spiritual directors who continually address this ingrained thinking with people. One of them wept as he described the vehement rejection of Christ by three recent clients. Each had been convinced of the common but subtle philosophy (fostered by prayers and thinking like Tyler's) that if they lived good Christian lives, the tangible, material blessing of God would flow into their lives. One by one they worked "the plan," only to encounter difficult and painful circumstances. Bitterness toward God festered in them as they followed the formula and it didn't work. Confused and disillusioned, each ultimately and angrily gave up. They concluded that they wanted no part of a God who did not "make life work" for them. These folks clearly never learned to value the presence and work of Christ in trials, and their faith was dashed on the hard rocks of difficulty.

How might Tyler have reasoned differently if his parent prayed, "Father, I am so glad that you will go with Tyler through his day. In the good and the bad, the easy and the difficult, you will be with him. Thank you for the promise that nothing can separate us from your love! Help Tyler to know your presence and your love throughout his day." This kind of prayer would likely help Tyler interpret the events of his day differently. He would understand that it's not God's job to make life go smoothly, but that God is actively present to love and strengthen him even in the rough spots.

Jesus said, **"I have told you these things, so that in me you may have peace. In this world you *will* have trouble. But take heart! I have overcome the world"** (John 16:33). Jesus' promise that we will *all* have trouble in our lives prompts me to do less protecting of my children from trials and more strengthening of them in and for trials. Difficult circumstances are a valuable opportunity to teach my children authentic, enduring faith.

My Response...

What trial has my child faced recently? How could I use it to strengthen my child's understanding of Christ's presence through all things? (I can affirm Jesus' love while validating difficult feelings.)

My example with doubts

While talking about highlights of my faith journey is important, it is vital for me to also appropriately share my struggles regarding faith. This modeling prepares my children to deal with their inevitable faith crises as they grow through life. I can tell them about hard times when I don't have all the answers. Do my kids know what I do to cling to faith in those "desert times" when God seems distant? I can tell them also about the aspects of faith that always seem difficult for me. Lynne relates this experience about sharing a personal struggle with our daughter.

I have long wrestled with the concept of death and heaven. After my grandfather's death when I was five years old, I developed a strong fear of eternity. Even as an adult I sometimes wake up dreading my inevitable death. One day I told my kids about this and described my distorted image of heaven: standing at the back of a large crowd, endlessly singing worship songs toward God's throne in the distance.

Bethany, somewhat surprised by this, grabbed a tablet and drew her impression of this scene - multitudes of people separated from Christ on his throne by yellow police tape, "DO NOT CROSS THIS LINE!" Then she drew her own concept: clusters of people talking and enjoying each other, with a little twinkling asterisk in each group. "What's the little twinkle?" I asked. "Oh, that's Jesus in the middle of everybody."

It was a significant interaction for us. She encouraged me in my faith, articulated her own beliefs, and understood in a deeper way that knowing the fullness of God's love for us is a lifelong journey.

My Response...

What has been a spiritually dark period of my life or a nagging doubt I can't resolve? How have I persevered through it? How can I share that in an age-appropriate way with my children?

◆ ◆ ❖ ◆ ❖ ◆ ◆

**I can embrace every trial (mine or my child's)
as a valuable opportunity to teach authentic, enduring faith.**

◆ ◆ ❖ ◆ ❖ ◆ ◆

My child's doubts, questions, and imagination

A popular Christian web site displays list upon list of steps for achieving spiritual growth and victory. These lists represent what is so often experienced in the American faith community: following prescribed programs guarantees a successful, dynamic Christian life. Lynne and I tend to resist such formulas. Some of what they say may have merit, but these formulas seem to spring more from fear than from faith. Humans have a tendency to quantify spiritual things into a predictable sequence in order to insure success and eliminate uncertainty. Unfortunately, this process often destroys the mystery and wonder of real faith.

Jesus forced people to struggle with faith. His principles were sometimes hidden in parables. He asked difficult questions. He said outrageous things. He refused to be squeezed into a mold or pattern. He is famous for answering questions with questions. A mentor of Lynne's writes, "The Gospels record 183 questions having been asked of Jesus. Amazingly, he only directly answered *three*. And the really amazing thing is that he, in turn, asked 307 questions!"[12] What can I learn from this? Maybe I should tell more stories designed to generate curiosity. Perhaps I could ask more questions and be more thoughtful about how and when to give answers. I could do more to help my children *discover* rather than just hear the answers. If I give quick, easy answers to eliminate or fix their doubts, I rob my children of vital and authentic discoveries on the journey of embracing faith for themselves.

My friend Mike struggled with questions about his faith and lamented what he perceived as his own inadequacy in clearly teaching his daughter the foundations of Christian faith. As she prepared to leave for college, she told him that the greatest gift he had given her was an understanding of how to wrestle honestly with questions and still have faith. What he thought was a poor example, she valued as a model of authenticity and perseverance in pursuing a relationship with Christ.

This perspective about nurturing authentic faith was put to the test when, as a young adolescent, our son struggled with doubts about God. This was unsettling for us, but with Daniel's natural tendency to question authority we were not surprised. Lynne and I both resisted the temptation to try to correct his erroneous thinking or tell him how to deal with his doubts. We empathized with some of his struggle and encouraged him to seek fervently, believing that "you will find God when you seek with your whole heart" (see Jeremiah 29:13). We expressed confidence that his questioning was an important part of his journey. We told him that if he wanted help from us, to let us know. In the meantime, our love was as intense as ever, no matter what he believed. We prayed for him frequently, both privately and together with him. We worked hard to strike a balance between giving him space and staying with him through his struggle. He came through that period with a faith that is truly his own and a passion for Jesus that has amazed and blessed us deeply.

Another opportunity to encourage a vital faith journey occurs when kids question church. One parent reported, "My son says he's not sure why he goes to church; he doesn't get anything out of it." Just days later another added, "My daughter told me church just makes her more depressed." At one point, our youngest son was asking to skip Sunday school and hang out with his friends.

This is a common issue. Many give up and let their kids quit—no questions asked. Other parents require church attendance—end of discussion. Although it may seem that my kids should just go to church and they should like it, to quickly give the right answer may risk invalidating, alienating, and simply not understanding my child.

It could very well be that the best way for me to nurture my child's desire to participate in the life of the church is to listen, learn, and affirm whatever is going on in the child. Through this approach I can affirm my children's desire for an authentic experience that brings them closer to God. I can also affirm their insight to know that something is missing from their experience. Once affirmation is given, parents win the privilege of exploring and discovering together with their child the possibilities for an authentic and valuable church experience. The approach often begins with a question, not an answer, regardless of the issue.

If adults have too high a need to ensure that children believe the right things they will also find it difficult to utilize children's vivid imagination. Young children can probably describe the sights, sounds, and smells that might surround a passage of Scripture with more intensity than I ever could. If I view this strong imagination as a gift from God, I can use it to bring life to their concept of God. Consider this example:

Jill's young son Justin had developed a "relationship" with an imaginary friend during her prolonged business trip. She came to Lynne seeking counsel. Lynne suggested that telling Justin that this friend wasn't real and the fantasy should end might invalidate or discourage the boy and his experience. They discussed how this could be an opportunity to help Justin discover his God-given desire for the constant presence of his friend Jesus.

Jill proceeded to ask (rather than tell) Justin about his friend. She listened carefully to Justin's description, without judging it. She was able to see and help Justin understand the numerous ways in which his friend shared some of Jesus' traits, and revealed Justin's desire to know Jesus. In handling this wisely, she took advantage of a great opportunity to build his understanding of the loving presence of Christ.

KID CONNECTION: (Choose one or more)

- **Ask your children, "If Jesus walked into the room and you could ask him any hard question that bothers you, what would it be?" Discuss it as a family.**
- **Tap into your children's gift of imagination to help them more fully understand God's character and how he relates to us. (Ideas include: help your child create a parable to explain God's love; read a Bible story and have them describe the sights, sounds, smells, etc.; have children imagine what Jesus would be like and what he would do if he lived in your town.)**
- **Create a family flag/banner. When traveling across the wilderness, the Israelite families each camped under a banner that represented their family. Read Numbers 2:34. Discuss with your children what values are important to your family, and what symbols might represent those values. Look for scripture references that support those values. Create a family banner, as simple as a piece of construction paper, or as elaborate as a fabric flag to represent those values.[13]**

Chapter Fifteen

Siblings: From Cell Mates to Soul Mates
(or developing friend/relative relationships for my only child)

OTHER THAN HAVING their kids know and love Jesus, parents want more than anything else for their children to love and enjoy each other. Sibling relationships are potent training grounds for future relationships. Lynne once asked a ninety-five-year-old mother of four, "If you could have one wish, what would it be?" Her response was quick and heartfelt. "That my children would get along." Her children were in their sixties and beyond, and still carried leftover resentments from their childhood relationships. Her wish reflected a lament we hear from many parents; her desires mirrored those of the apostle Paul recorded in Philippians 2:2, **"Make my joy complete by being like-minded, having the same love, being one in spirit and purpose."**

Parents who learn how to nurture strong relationships between their young children prepare them to have strong relationships in the future. Imagine a teenage brother and sister enjoying each other, laughing, playing, and serving together. Not just occasionally, but as a norm. Is this possible? Based on observation and personal experience, I can definitively say YES! But it doesn't happen by accident.

Sibling interaction is a great training ground for building my children's sensitivity to others' needs and feelings. And what a great opportunity to develop conflict resolution skills that will benefit them for a lifetime! If I am proactive and intentional about facilitating connection between my children, I also find that their bickering with each other is significantly decreased.

Note: Parents blessed with an only child can still apply these principles to relationships their child has with a cousin, neighbor, or a close friend. It is important to seek and nurture these relationships so that the child does not miss the opportunities inherent in sibling relationships.

MY RESPONSE… **Parents of only children**

What are some relationships I could facilitate for my child that would provide some of the learning opportunities of children with siblings?

For the rest of the chapters in this section, answer the questions related to your child and his/her closest companion(s).

Creating Opportunities for Connection

How can I facilitate bonds that last a lifetime?

- "Our children just seem to be in separate worlds."
- "I spend so much of my energy dealing with their bickering."
- "Our kids just don't enjoy each other, and you never know when another fight will break out."

At times children naturally enjoy each other. But conflict is inevitable. If parents allow it, isolated conflicts can turn into a persistent rivalry that has the power to dominate their children's relationships with each other.

The starting place for charting a different course is to be purposeful about building connection between siblings. This means I can learn to recognize and intentionally facilitate opportunities for my children to enjoy each other. This can be as simple as setting kids up to go on special outings or complete special projects together. A helpful question to develop ideas for these connecting times is: "What are some treats or privileges the children don't normally get that could be enjoyed together, two at a time?" If I facilitate the kids to come up with their own ideas for special things to do together, they will be even more likely to have a positive experience with each other. (Regardless of how many children are in the family, a special time with two is usually the place to start, since three children conflict much more easily.) The following list of ideas may spark some creativity.

- A privilege enjoyed by young children is a later bedtime. So staying up to watch a video (with popcorn in separate bowls) is usually a no-conflict, fun event if other children are gone for the night.
- Spread out a blanket for children to share a special meal of favorite finger food.
- "Slumber parties" in a different part of the house or in a kid-made blanket fort can be very exciting. When children are older they can set up a tent in the backyard for a night.

- Discover common interests, and create opportunities for children to pursue them together.
- Facilitate a team experience like baking cookies together or making a gift for a friend, sibling, or relative.
- In many families a privilege for older children is going to a restaurant. When children are in a situation requiring grown-up behaviors such as ordering and paying for food, they tend to feel good about themselves and the stage is set for positive interaction.
- To maximize the connection and unity from a special time together, wrap it up by talking about what went well, how each person felt, etc. Cultivate ideas for the next outing.

Restaurant "dates" in our family started at an early age. We don't eat out very often so it became a big deal to help the kids to do it with each other occasionally. I took Bethany and Daniel on their first such date when they were six and eight years old. It was a time in their lives when their tendency to conflict dominated their interactions. But they looked forward to this event. I coached Daniel a bit in some etiquette and made sure he knew the importance of watching out for his little sister. I parked outside to provide some minimal supervision through the windows. I observed no hint of conflict or contention. What a delightful experience to watch them order, laugh, share food, and clean up when they were done.

This became a tradition enjoyed by any combination of our kids, even as adolescents. One time Lynne paid for their meal with the stipulation that they write a list of ten reasons to value and work on their relationship. (Five could be silly, but five had to be legitimate reasons.) They had a great time compiling the list.

In addition to facilitating special dates, here are some other ideas for nurturing sibling connection through everyday activities:

- Join forces with one child to surprise another child in a special way (e.g., make her breakfast in bed, clean up his room for him) and discuss how it feels to do that for a brother or sister.
- Create a memory of special times together with photographs, scrap booking, or journaling.

- Buy or make small presents/posters/cards for each other's birthdays and at Christmas.
- Ask an older child to tuck a younger one in bed and pray for him.
- Comment on children's kindness toward one another and help them to verbalize how it felt.
- Facilitate their affirmation of each other. One family alternates use of the "special person placemat" at dinner. Each person states one positive thing they have noticed

and appreciate about the person using the placemat that night. Giving and receiving affirmation regularly strengthens this dynamic in their relationship.

For years, Lynne and I purposefully, persistently facilitated connection between our children. It is no longer necessary. They have naturally carried a love for connecting with each into their teen years. As parents affirm children and set them up to affirm each other, they will learn to value each other, respect each other, and carry those skills into life.

My Response...

How could I facilitate special outings or activities to build connection between my children?

Building Mutual Understanding

How can I foster empathy?

Building understanding between siblings is a long process. Before a child can understand the feelings of a sibling, he must be able to identify his *own* feelings. This can be hard because some families don't talk much, if at all, about feelings. Difficult feelings get minimized or ignored. In families where this is the case, sadness, disappointment, and other difficult feelings are quickly dismissed. "Buck up," "Get over it," or, "Look on the bright side," are typical phrases in such families. These are not necessarily bad statements. Some kids are quite resilient and can quickly overcome difficult feelings with a positive attitude. But such kids are rare. Most children, when their difficult feelings are not affirmed, learn to hide them. When feelings are hidden, they are bound to return. When they do return, it is much more difficult to understand their source. If kids are frequently crabby, apathetic, angry, or aggressive, it may be that their feelings are not well validated.

Learning to identify and talk honestly about feelings helps to build mutual trust and understanding between family members. When I model a "feelings vocabulary," I help my children learn to express their feelings. I start this process by learning to be aware of my own feelings and then to express them in simple ways to my children. Here are some examples:

> "I'm really discouraged today about…."
> "I feel quite proud about…"
> "I have some anxieties about work…."
> "I'm so relieved that…"

"You seem upset. Can you tell me about that?"

"You look really confident!"

"Your sister said she was disappointed because…"

"You looked so happy when you…"

MY RESPONSE…

How freely are emotions expressed and accepted in our house? Are children able to identify their own feelings easily? Is this an area of strength or potential for growth for our family?

As parents frequently affirm and explore their children's feelings, the children will begin to more naturally understand their own feelings. Once they begin understanding their own feelings, they can learn to empathize with their siblings. I can then foster further understanding by simply saying something like, "Your brother (or sister) is having a tough time today because _____. What do you think we could do to help?" As I teach empathy this way, my children begin to understand for themselves. Consider this simple example:

Daniel was having a hard day. As was often the case those days, Bethany (aged six at the time) became the brunt of his various frustrations. She came to us to report, "I think Daniel is sad because his Lego plane broke." She already understood and empathized, even though she was the victim. This helped her to be less angry at Daniel and more compassionate for him.

When children have difficulty empathizing, parents can describe a hypothetical situation that would result in similar feelings and ask children to identify how they would feel. For example, imagine a bossy daughter playing a game with her little brother. She ignores his input and statements of frustration. Parents normally respond to this type of situation by forcing compliance or an apology. This may communicate the parent's values, but does not actually invite the children's investment in the values. To invite empathy is also to invite investment, or ownership. To do this, a parent might pull the daughter aside and describe a situation in which someone else was bossy to her, and then ask her how she feels in situations like that. Once she identifies some feelings (the parent can give her some examples if necessary), the parent could make an application to her brother by saying "How do you think your brother feels about you not using any of his ideas for the game?"

Nathan the prophet used this method to confront King David about his sin toward another person (2 Samuel 12:1-7). Instead of angrily labeling David an adulterer and murderer, Nathan simply told the king a story. David related emotionally to the injustice done, before he realized he himself was the man in the story. Just as in this scriptural example, the key to telling these empathy stories is a calm, nonjudgmental attitude on the part of the parent. If the child feels *trapped* by the story instead of *taught,* the result will be defensiveness and denial.

MY RESPONSE...

In a typical conflict in our home, what analogy or hypothetical story could I use to help one of my children understand the other's feelings?

Facilitating Conflict Resolution

What do children need to help them resolve their own conflicts?

Parents' efforts to manage and punish disrespectful conflicts often actually fuel the tension by building resentment in the relationship. Conflict is inevitable in a family but it can be a powerful opportunity to teach reconciliation and forgiveness in relationships. When I am both purposeful and persistent, there is much I can do to build conflict resolution skills and true friendships between my children.

When Bethany and Daniel were young, they were like oil and water. (Or more accurately, baking soda and vinegar!) As the intense older brother, Daniel was, very uh… assertive. As a sensitive younger sister, Bethany had a knack for playing the victim role. They had this well scripted: he bossed and hit, she whined and screamed. After many exasperating attempts to stop the conflict, we decided to view the problem as a great opportunity to build skills and hearts for reconciliation. Beneath our desire for them to get along well was (is) a deeper desire for them to establish habits and beliefs about conflict that they could carry into adulthood. Even though we still "blow it" many times in this process we always come back to those guiding principles.

We often wondered if our perspective and efforts were paying off. But over time these two intense, expressive siblings learned the values and skills to respectfully and independently work out their conflicts, even as adolescents. We are hopeful that each will be well equipped for healthy relationships with friends, spouses, and their own children when the time comes.

Core beliefs about conflict

Like one who seizes a dog by the ears is a passer-by who meddles in a quarrel not his own.
                                                                —Proverbs 26:17

This rather entertaining proverb challenges me to ask an important question: "Who owns my children's conflicts with each other – them or me?" Is it their problem or mine, and who is responsible to resolve the problem?

Before I seek to facilitate healthy conflict resolution between my children I've found it helpful to consider my own beliefs about conflict. I sometimes tend to believe that conflict is bad and should be avoided. I may consciously or unconsciously believe it is my responsibility to "keep the peace" in the house. When I don't like the noise, the difficult emotions, and the nasty behaviors that accompany most conflicts, I'm tempted to try to control my children for my own benefit. These beliefs often drive a desire to stop the conflict at all costs.

But unfortunately there *is* a cost to stopping my children's conflicts. If I stop conflicts and impose solutions, I am probably teaching my children to fear and avoid conflict. If I make children quickly say, "I'm sorry," I may also be teaching them to lie to get out of trouble! Such hasty solutions to conflict will likely bury unresolved emotions. The suppressed emotions may percolate for a while and then reappear as general resentment, anger, apathy, sadness, or even depression. These emotional states are much more difficult to work through because their origins are so much more complex.

My Response...

What is the first thing I usually do when my children have conflicts? What feelings emerge? What do these feelings tell me about my beliefs about conflict?

Learning to resolve their own conflicts helps children embrace biblical principles for relationships – particularly the value of reconciliation. Because sibling conflicts provide daily opportunities to build important values and skills, I want to learn to facilitate those conflicts in a way that increases my children's learning. Researchers have discovered that, "Almost universally, the kids who practiced the best conflict-resolution skills at home carried those abilities into the classroom."[1] Nurturing those conflict resolution skills is also one of the most critical gifts I can give my children for their future families—a wedding present in advance—to empower them for true resolution with their spouses and children in their future.

These are examples of helpful messages to communicate to my children as I coach them through their conflicts:

- Your relationships belong to you! (They are not mine to manage.)
- The needs and feelings of others are just as important as yours.
- You can learn to work out the problems in your relationships with some guidance.

- Any difficulty in a relationship is an opportunity for social, emotional, and spiritual growth.
- True reconciliation is God's plan for relationships.

◆◆◆❖◆❖◆◆◆

If I stop conflicts, impose solutions,
or make children say, "I'm sorry,"
I am teaching them to fear and avoid conflict.

◆◆◆❖◆❖◆◆◆

Steps for conflict resolution

When children are evenly matched it is easier for parents to encourage independence in conflict resolution, short of letting the young adversaries duke it out. More often in conflict, however, one child is bigger, older, more assertive, or "all of the above." Parents often feel the only option to protect the more vulnerable child is to intervene and eliminate the conflict. Unfortunately, this is a sure-fire plan to keep that child vulnerable because it does nothing to empower the younger child to express feelings and wishes. Parents can combine skill development with protection by encouraging their children in small steps toward independence.

The following suggestions for working through conflict teach children that they are responsible for their relationships and help them better understand the impact of their behavior on others. They are meant to be a guideline, not a step-by-step prescription. These principles and tactics are effective only if the adult teaching them practices them as well.

Cool hot tempers (Foundation) Successful resolution of a conflict is very difficult when emotions are intense. It's extremely helpful to figure out how to give everyone an opportunity to cool down. This starts with making sure I am cooled down and neutral. I can take some deep breaths while I prayerfully consider what opportunities are present in the situation.

Then I am ready to set the children up for success by expressing caring and confidence in them: "I believe that when you two are ready, you can do a good job of resolving your conflict. It'll be easier if you have a little time to settle down and think things through first." It's helpful to structure children to relax in separate, comfortable areas for a few minutes. This is not punishment; it is preparation for the important work ahead. I can ask if I can pray with them, to ask God for peace and honesty while they talk it out.

Skipping this cool-down phase can make conflict resolution difficult, if not impossible. Consider Lynne's memory of one such time:

Guests were coming, and we were all stressed from cleaning up our messy house. As one child took out frustration on the other, I grew irate with the aggressive behavior. I felt pressed for time and sent them both into one of the bedrooms with a scathing order to quickly resolve the conflict, as I glared at the aggressive child. That child, humiliated by my harsh response, fired a load of hurtful words at the other, resulting in an explosion of tears. When I heard the scream and sobs, my first impulse was to be even angrier, but I knew it was my fault – I allowed my own emotions and time constraints to set them up for failure. My apology to the kids set the stage for true reconciliation between them, which I facilitated while Jim engaged our guests. It was a painful but valuable lesson that served me well in future attempts at conflict-resolution training.

Facilitate resolution (Connection, Proaction) My goal in this step is to provide the minimum support each child needs to negotiate the conflict in a reasonably respectful way. To accomplish this I can be involved at any of a variety of levels: directly involved, starting or supervising the process, or completely staying out of it.

If a child needs my direct involvement I can provide some comforting touch to the younger or more vulnerable child as we talk to his or her sibling. To facilitate respectful listening and responses I can ask simple questions such as, "What do you feel (about what just happened)?" and "What do you want now?" I might give ideas for the children to choose from if they have difficulty answering either question. Two- to three-year-olds can feel safe enough to learn to speak for themselves in this way.

If my children just need supervision I can provide initial instructions such as, "Tell your sister/brother what you feel about what happened and what you want. Remember to listen respectfully." From that point, I should intervene only as necessary to structure more cooling down time or facilitate respectful discussion.

As my children become more capable I may not need to structure their interaction at all. I can express confidence in my children's ability to resolve the conflict when they are ready, then close the door and stay out of it. This demonstrates trust and confidence in them. It also puts them on the same team to resolve the conflict so they can be done with it and go play.

As our children grew into elementary years they got much better at resolving their own conflicts. Once structured to cool down, we'd ask them to go into our bedroom on opposite sides of the bed. They were to work toward resolving the conflict until they felt they could sincerely meet in the middle for a hug. Occasionally, for intense issues, they needed additional assistance. But usually they would emerge harmonious and quite pleased with their accomplishment. Now that they are teenagers we just try to stay out of most conflicts entirely.

Bring closure (Proaction) Perhaps the best way to cement good conflict resolution skills is to review a conflict afterward and affirm any skills the children may have used well to solve it. Children feel good about positive affirmation and will likely begin to apply the affirmed skills in subsequent conflicts. In order to do this, I must first develop an eye to notice what is good and then express it in a way my children can understand. Occasionally I have to be fairly creative about this in order to affirm a less-than-perfect process. Here are some practical ways I might start this conversation:

- "Nice work! Even though you started to get upset again, you didn't do any name calling!"
- "I noticed you stopped interrupting when your sister asked you to. That probably really helped you resolve your conflict."
- "That took a long time and got pretty intense for a while, but you stuck with it. I'll bet you feel really good about solving your own problem."
- "A few minutes ago you both said you were angry, and maybe a little sad. How do you feel now?"

Once I review the conflict, noting even the smallest of successes, I can discuss with my children the joy that comes through forgiveness and reconciliation. A simple illustration Lynne and I created for our young children helped them grasp this at an early age: We held our fists apart, explaining that each represented a person in conflict with the other. We then moved the hands toward each other while explaining, "When people move toward each other in love and forgiveness, they reconcile." We ended by clasping our hands together and affirming the reconciliation our kids were learning.

Many years later our children still remember this hand-clasp illustration and the value of true reconciliation that it taught. Our oldest son recently stated, "I love apologizing, because I can take the wrong I've done, cast it off and be free of it, and have it be forgiven by both God and man. It's beautiful!" Imagine how that value will impact his eventual marriage and parenting!

> ◆◆❖◆❖◆◆
> **Not only is conflict inevitable, it provides a powerful opportunity
> to teach reconciliation and forgiveness in relationships.**
> ◆◆❖◆❖◆◆

Children's understanding of reconciliation in earthly relationships paves the way for them to understand reconciliation with God. Lynne and I modified the hand illustration to show our children how when we sin we move away from God (who does not move away from us) and how we return through forgiveness. Through these conversations we helped our children understand not only the joy of reconciliation in their own conflicts but the ways their reconciliation was a picture of God's love. There are many ways parents can use a child's understanding of conflict resolution to teach spiritual truths, including the following examples.

- "When we reconcile with each other, it also helps us understand God better. God loves reconciliation or 'reconnection;' that's why he sent Jesus, to reconnect us to God when we sin."
- "Did you know that when you forgive each other, you act like Jesus?"
- "How would you describe your relationship with God? Use your hands to show me."

The above ideas are not meant to be delivered as a script; they are simply examples of the possibilities for teaching children true reconciliation. Bringing closure to the conflict this way helps my kids learn and protects them from carrying negative emotions from one conflict to the next. But the bottom line here is that in the daily grind of life, conflict holds a great opportunity. I can either try to manage life comfortably for myself by solving my kids' struggles or I can do the hard work of teaching relational and kingdom values for a lifetime and beyond.

My Response...

What is a frequent conflict between my children? What level of assistance or facilitation would they most likely need at this stage to resolve their own conflicts?

Kid Connection! **Choose one or both of these activities:**

1. **Help your kids come up with an idea for a special treat they'd like to do/have together. Help them make a plan. Then supervise that plan from a distance.**

2. **Work with your children to develop "Rules of Respect" for resolving conflicts.**

Chapter Sixteen

Pals, Peers, Adults and Relatives
Significant Relationships
Outside the Home

THE KIDS SWARMED to the front of the sanctuary, eager to see what the guest preacher was cooking up. I was a little nervous how my object lesson would go in this small, conservative congregation. I got out a ball of yarn, and holding on to the end of the yarn, I tossed it to a particularly eager child, and instructed her to toss it to someone else. The hands waved excitedly as the tossing continued, weaving a web of many strands throughout the group. I explained that the yarn represented connective, supportive relationships between people. These relationships can form a safety net for each member of the community, especially the children. It visibly illustrated an important protective factor for families.

As children grow they form significant relationships with people outside their nuclear families. The influence of these non-family relationships increases as the children grow toward independence. For maximum positive influence, parents can be involved in purposefully facilitating healthy, supportive connections for their children throughout childhood. This can range from inviting trusted others to care for your infant (so they become easily comfortable with others), to lining up various kinds of mentoring opportunities with trusted members of your community, and everywhere between. There is no facet of life where parents cannot intentionally foster connected relationships for their children outside their home.

Relationships with Relatives

How can I maximize the positive impact of extended family?

The importance of extended family has been greatly minimized in today's culture. Over the course of the last century people have become more and more disconnected from their extended families. With the industrial and information ages have grown the tendencies for families to diversify their vocations, uproot, and move away from one another. Connection with extended family can be a challenge in a culture where forty percent of adults plan to move their homes within five years.[1]

We learned something very important by accident. When our children were born they were the first grandchildren on my side of the family. My younger sisters and their new husbands were enamored with our children. They paid lots of attention to them and attended many of the kids' plays, birthday parties, and other special events. Even as they have started families of their own, the connections formed in those early years continue. Our children are now equally enamored with their little cousins.

Once we understood the impact of these positive relationships on our children, we made a commitment to actively facilitate relationships with grandparents, aunts, uncles, and cousins on both sides of the family as often as practical. As we worked to foster these connections, we saw that the children care deeply about their relatives and want to be with them often. This helps them feel a deeper level of accountability and connection to the bonds, values, and faith of their lineage.

Families with this potential for protecting and strengthening family bonds, values, and faith find great reward in nurturing the opportunity to the fullest. Even if relatives are distant, it's worth the hard work to stay in touch through cards, letters, emails, special packages, or phone calls. This work can very much enhance the rare times you are able to be together with family.

Growing bodies of research document the specific benefits of grandparent relationships – to children, parents, and grandparents alike. In this new era, where disconnection is the norm rather than the exception, children need their grandparents more than ever. New organizations have formed in recent years just for the purpose of facilitating connections with grandparents. A few of these are listed in the end notes.[2] Recognizing the importance of grandparents, some families even relocate to get their children nearer to their grandparents.

One of the deep benefits of this connection is the building into my children of a sense of lineage and heritage. The tremendous technological and cultural changes of the last two generations tend to cause children to believe that grandparents, or the older generation in general, are irrelevant and out of touch. This lack of value for their elders and their heritage reinforces the disconnection of children from older adults. Add to this the fact that many families are geographically separate as well, and there is a strong formula for generational disconnect. Combating this has never been more difficult or critical.

In some cases, grandparents and extended family simply will not, or do not provide positive connections. However, to discard as hopeless any effort to reconnect or reconcile difficult family history, the very roots from which a family comes, communicates a value of separation rather than connectedness. Whether those relationships could ever become supportive is less of an issue than whether parents can model a heart of forgiveness and care.

My Response…

What could I do to foster better connections with our extended family?

Relationships with Adults outside the Family

What role do other families play in my children's lives?

Research shows that a significant predictor of healthy youth development is a close relationship with one or more adults outside the immediate family. In his book *Other People's Kids*, noted researcher Dr. Peter Scales asserts that adults have generally assumed that parents and professionals are solely responsible "for reducing problems among young people and preparing them for the future." He goes on to present compelling research to substantiate this conclusion: "Young people need all adults to recognize their own capacity for and role in nurturing the next generation, and then take action to connect with young people in meaningful, sustained relationships."[3]

The Christian community provides a splendid potential for building connections between adults of all ages and children. In this context, purposeful parents can build relationships with children and trusted adults within a community of families. This has been a given through most of human history. It's why an African village could coin the phrase, "It takes a village to raise a child." They understood how the community at large was a significant shaping force in the lives of all the village's children. In modern culture, I have to be more thoughtful and strategic about how I will connect my children to a village of adults and children that will love them and care for them ("raise them") in a manner consistent with my values and faith. These relationships can greatly serve to reinforce the faith and values I seek to teach at home.

This is really a twofold call to purposefully connect my children with other adults and to purposefully connect with other people's children.

◆◆◆❖◆❖◆◆◆
**A significant predictor of healthy youth development
is close relationships with adults outside the immediate family.**
◆◆◆❖◆❖◆◆◆

Connecting my children to other adults

I have regularly invited other men to be involved with our sons. So it was a natural response to advise Steve, concerned about his struggling son, to invite a friend to spend time with John, his struggling teenager. John was deeply troubled by loneliness and anger about his friendships after an out-of-state move. Steve followed the counsel and later that week emailed this report:

> Tom was a huge blessing to my son John. They just went out for a soda. They had a great time and it made quite an impact on John. Not sure exactly of the cause-and-effect, but John chose to go to the football game Friday (he had said before he simply wasn't interested) and spent Friday night and most of the day Saturday with friends. I've been out of town for three days, but my wife says he seems to be doing better. Thanks again for the suggestion. Tom was great about taking the time and it was fabulous.

The reason this connection was fairly easy for Steve to facilitate is that there was some history between the two families. John knew Tom. Steve also knew and trusted him. It did not seem out of the ordinary to John to be invited by Tom to do something together – though they'd never actually been alone together.

The first step to bridging relationships between my children and other adults is to be sure my family is in relationships with other families. The earlier my children get to know to adults I love and trust, the more natural it will be to invite those adults into supportive relationships with my children. The second step is to facilitate special relationships between my children, and the other adults.

Although varied research conclusively shows the importance of such relationships, many people are reluctant to intentionally facilitate connections between their children and other significant adults. In a Search Institute study, fifty-three percent of parents said they NEVER ask other adults for help or to give assistance of any kind in the raising of their children. Thirty-one percent said they regularly turn to family and only twenty percent said they regularly turn to friends.[4] How can the body of Christ be involved in the raising of a generation of faith if we do not seek the participation of its members?

My Response...

Whom could I invite to be more involved in the lives of my children?

Connecting with other people's children

In the same way that it is important for me to invite other adults to connect with my children, it is important for me to connect with other people's kids. Parents often resist this idea because they're already so busy taking care of their own family. It can require creative thinking and a commitment to overcome excessive busyness, but it can be done. Of course it's best if I first earn the trust of a child's parents, so it makes sense to start within the sphere of families I already know, or in settings where I'm already in trusting relationships with others' children. Many parents take advantage of formal structures by volunteering in their children's classes at school or at church, leading a scout troop or coaching, and then looking for one or two children that seem to need special attention.

As simple as these ideas sound, adults typically make little or no effort to become intentionally engaged in the healthy development of children outside their own family. A recent study released by the Search Institute, called *Grading Grown-Ups,* draws this conclusion: "If we were actually giving grades to adults, only five percent of American adults would get an "A" for being actively engaged in young people's lives. Many more might receive a B or C…The majority of adults would receive lower – even failing – grades because they are simply not engaged in kids' lives."[5]

MY RESPONSE…

How do I engage my children's friends? How might I be more purposeful?

Connecting family to family

There are many ways to connect with other people's children and connect my kids with other adults. In the process I foster a closer-knit community, usually simply by altering what I already do. I can:

- Form babysitting co-ops (or connect with families for whom my children babysit), making a point to connect well with both kids and parents in other families.
- Request children to be placed together with their friends on sports teams or for music lessons and share responsibilities with the other parents. I can connect with other parents as we cheer for our own and each other's children.
- Find families within my church whose children are near the same age as mine. I can make a point to meet them and plan a family-to-family activity.
- Look for opportunities to shift my participation in individual ministries to ones that connect families.
- Try the old-fashioned barn-raising approach. I can pair up with one of my children and get work done together with a few members from another family. Or I can invite a whole family to help and follow it with a steak fry as a thank you.

One fun and easy way to foster togetherness with other families is through entertaining, or hospitality. I can ask my children which of their friends' parents they'd like to invite for dinner or a picnic. I can work with them to prepare and serve the meal and possibly plan some activities together. Too many families entertain by having another family over, only to send the kids downstairs or outside to play while the adults spend their whole time hanging out with each other. This is *not* togetherness. We've found great richness in integrating families and children of all ages. Most kids love to play active games with adults, such as Pictionary, Guesstures, or Cranium. Croquet, volleyball (with a beach ball), or kickball are good outdoor activities. Even timid teens can come out of their shells to enjoy such games.

Once this fun and loving environment is established, it becomes natural to add spiritual activities as well. Families can share together, perhaps designate a child to read or say a prayer before the meal, invite simple spiritual questions around the meal table like: "How have you seen God at work lately?" or, "Who has a request for prayer?"

As relationships between them grow stronger, families become the kind of community that can easily and naturally invite others, or reach out with God's love. It seems imperative, in our modern culture, to build community this way – to keep families strong and, from that place of strength, to reach out to a world hungry for that kind of loving, connected community.

My Response...

What could I do (that would not add stress) to connect with other families?

Relationships with Peers

How can I strengthen my child to develop healthy friendships?

Peer relationships carry increasing influence as children grow up. Kids may choose good friends or they may not. Parents, wanting what's best for their kids, have a tendency to over control their children's choices. I was one of those.

As Daniel entered elementary school, he had a friend Lynne and I did not particularly care for. Because they shared common interests, they gravitated toward each other. The fact that the friend was in our neighborhood also made it almost impossible to fully monitor their interaction. We tried to convince Daniel that while this friend needed God's love, we didn't think their friendship was a good idea. But even as a seven year old, he was resistant to our control. We decided that it would be best to guide the relationship rather than to control it. This was hard because we knew that sometimes the influence this friend had on Daniel was not positive. It became our goal to strengthen him for healthy choices.

There are numerous ways to guide or empower my children's friendship choices without controlling them. This approach aligns with the principle stated earlier: It's their life. It's their feelings, their relationships, their responsibilities, and their faith. As a parent it is my job to thoughtfully guide the process by which they learn to make wise choices, solve their own problems and conflicts, and stand before God without me.

Parents often ask, "If it seems to be in their best interest for me to control their friendships, why is that a bad thing?" I answer by asking, "How do you feel when someone controls you, even if they believe it's in your best interest?" Most of the time, they answer by saying, "I feel resentful, misunderstood, or deflated."

When people of any age are controlled, they are also disempowered. Certainly, if a five year old is about to run in front of a car on the street, I will "control" him by yelling or grabbing him. So there may be isolated cases when immediate control of a child is truly necessary for his safety. But most situations do not demand such quick, full control. The question that really is best addressed here is: What is *truly* in their best interest – to be controlled for the near-term, or to be empowered for the long-term?

There are practical ways to guide children to learn to make wise choices in their friendships without controlling them.

Building values early

When children experience deeply connected relationships, respectful conflict resolution, and solid teaching about values at home, they find disrespectful relationships unfamiliar and unappealing. As children grow older their selection of friends becomes more clearly an expression of their values. This is why it is so important to begin the teaching and influence about my children's friends early in their lives. The challenge can be much more difficult when parents wait. Young children are so much more receptive to parents' influence, while teenagers will likely interpret discussions about friendships as an attempt to control them. The older my children are, the more it is likely that control of their friendships will backfire and drive them *to* the very friends I wish they would avoid.

Relaxed curiosity

When my children hang out with kids I don't know or understand, I try to express interest without a judgmental attitude (of course I can do this only if I am sincerely interested rather than judgmental – derived by my **Foundation** work). This approach often provides an opportunity for me to learn about how my children evaluate their friendships. I begin with questions such as, "Tell me about your friend. I'd like to get to know him/her better." "How is your friend similar to you? How is he/she different?" "What do you like about your friendship?" "What's important to you in friendships?" The goal is simply to listen and affirm! This helps them to see me as a resource to their friendships. They will much more likely share their concerns and ask about my perspective. Even if they don't ask for my perspective, the described process gives me a respected place from which to eventually share it.

**Interest without judgment allows me to enter into the process
by which my children evaluate their friendships.**

KID CONNECTION! (Choose one or both of the activities.)

- At dinner this week, decide which family or families you all would like to connect with more. Make a plan that is practical for your schedule.
- Discuss with your kids what "ingredients" make a good friendship. Ask them which of their relationships (with their friends, other adults, or extended family) have those ingredients in them. Record their responses.

    (For younger kids you can use a concrete example – sugar and butter help make good cookies, but ketchup doesn't. What makes a good friendship? Give them choices between ideas; i.e., sharing toys, talking without listening. Help them make a list of things to make a friendship. Then pair each positive quality with a person they know who demonstrates that quality.)

Chapter Seventeen

Raising World-Changers
Developing Gifts and Responsibility

NEARLY EVERY DAY there are clues. Is she always humming? Does he hold the door open for people without being asked? Does he love to build things? Does she like everything to be "just right" when she plays with friends? In life's daily interactions and routines are numerous clues to my children's gifting: their natural talents and inclinations. Learning to pay attention helps me see my child's developing gifts.

This makes me want to learn to see with vision between the lines of life's everyday stresses and tasks. This vision grows out of Ephesians 2:10: **"We are God's workmanship, created in Christ Jesus to do good works, which God prepared in advance for us to do."** This verse clearly declares that everyone is masterfully created by God to do good things. A deeper look at the word workmanship reveals that each person, in Christ, is like a beautiful sculpture or poem. Indeed, each child *is* a masterpiece, created by God for a purpose. I have the incredible privilege and awesome responsibility to affirm my children's gifts and help them discover and walk in that purpose. As I am deeply thoughtful about this process, I can give my children wise guidance in discovering their own calling.

MY RESPONSE...

I can grasp the truth of the above verse (Ephesians 2:10) for *each* of my children as I repeat it slowly and prayerfully:
_____ is God's workmanship, created in Christ Jesus to do good works, which God prepared in advance for <u>him</u>/<u>her</u> to do.

What feelings or thoughts occurred as I read this for each child?

Developing my Child's Gifting

How can I help my child begin to discover God's calling?

Ideally, every parent would identify excitement, eagerness, curiosity, or any host of hopeful emotions by completing the above activity. But this is a scary world and thinking about a child's future can also produce anxiety, confusion, or even fear. For every good possibility there seems to be a bad possibility. Overcoming these fears with faith is critical if I am to "picture a positive future"[1] for my children and give energy to helping them discover it. Acknowledging and prayerfully working through the fears enables me to sincerely identify and call out the "masterpiece" in my child.

Discerning unique talents and interests

It can be quite natural to nurture my children's talents and interests when their bent is similar to mine. They gladly accompany me in favorite activities and learn from my example. They inherently feel affirmed when they show competence in arenas they know are important to me. These areas of common interest provide tremendous opportunities for **Connection** and **Proaction** with my children.

It is a far greater challenge when a child is wired with a very different personality and interests than their parent.[2] Perhaps the following scenario rings familiar: A stoic "nuts and bolts," task-oriented dad frequently devalued his sensitive son's musical, artistic bent. The implied message to the son was, "In order to be valuable, you have to be like me." The son grew up deeply hurt by his father's persistent criticism and subtle efforts to change him. He has forgiven his father and is a great musician, but he still struggles with feelings of inadequacy and shame.

Parents committed to discovering God's special purposes for their children will seize the opportunity to affirm the unique traits and interests God created – even if their children are wired very differently from their parents. These parents notice and encourage what is there. They do not superimpose what is not. This communicates a critical message to the child: "Because you are here to accomplish God's purposes, *not* to meet my needs, I will value your uniqueness." The critical message children cry to their parents is: "Empower me to live life the way God created me to live it rather than tell me *your way* to live it."

I love baseball. Before I ever even thought about marriage, I dreamt about the day I would teach my own children to play baseball. I was elated when I first went into the backyard with three-year-old Daniel to teach him the game. I vividly remember the first time the wildly swinging "fat-bat" connected with my well-timed pitch, sending the ball over the garage and into the alley beyond. His first home run gave way to a wild celebration as he ran randomly around the yard and then jumped on the Frisbee placed as home plate – just the way I'd taught him. My dream was coming true!

The only problem is that as the years went by, in spite of my encouragement, it became clear that Daniel didn't have the patience for baseball, and by age nine his baseball career was over. "This is dumb! I stood in the outfield for four innings and never touched the ball!" I had to let go of my dream and give him the freedom and encouragement to pursue his own dreams.

Since those days, each of our children has grown into his or her own areas of interest. Lynne and I had to first develop eyes to notice their unique bent, accept the fact that some of those interests and skills were beyond our ability or interest to teach, and then do our best to find opportunities for the kids to develop in those areas.

♦ ♦ ♦ ❖ ◆ ❖ ♦ ♦ ♦

"Empower me to live life the way God created me to live it, rather than tell me your way to live it."

♦ ♦ ♦ ❖ ◆ ❖ ♦ ♦ ♦

My Response...

What is a unique gift or interest that each of my children demonstrate? (This would include those I might find difficult to value or invest in.) How could I affirm and nurture each gift?

Providing creative options

One of the downsides of our frenzied culture filled with structured activities is that many children are unable to dream up creative play, entertain themselves for hours with simple toys, or negotiate the rules of a spontaneous group game. TV, video games, computer, internet, etc., can also subtly plunder children's creativity – by comparison, other endeavors that might develop responsibility and God-given gifts often seem slow-paced and boring. Attentive parents, however, can begin nurturing their children's gifts at a very young age. By providing numerous creative options, parents create opportunities for experimentation and discovery in their own home. As my children explore these activities, I can look for an intensity of focus and interest that indicates how a child connects with an activity.

Here are a few practical examples:

- <u>Art/craft supplies,</u> easily accessible.
- <u>Costume box</u> (of garage sale oddities) for impromptu drama.
- <u>Music</u> including exposure to a variety of types of music, simple instruments, etc.
- <u>Odds n' ends box</u> full of interesting household junk, or "treasures" from nature walks, etc., for creative play or projects.
- <u>Games</u> that stimulate quick creative thought, such as Pictionary and Charades.
- <u>Toys</u> carefully selected to facilitate gifts, creativity, and problem-solving: sports equipment, Legos, tools, strategy games, puppets, tape recorder with microphone, old video camera to make movies, etc.
- <u>A variety of books</u> and plenty of reading time with mom and dad.
- <u>Journals or scrapbooks.</u>
- <u>Tolerance for the mess</u> that creativity naturally brings.
- <u>Prioritizing children's discovery</u> over my answers or "right way" of doing things! (i.e., guiding them to form their own conclusions by thoughtful questions instead of giving information.)

Valuing children's discoveries and creativity is a pervasive attitude covering lots of arenas. One morning five-year-old Bethany dressed in quite a unique outfit. Resisting the temptation to pass on a few fashion tips, Lynne said, "My, that flowered shirt and striped pants are an interesting combination." Bethany confidently announced, "Yup. This is the beginning of a lifetime of creative dressing!"

Children who are "movers and shakers" may be uninterested in many of the things listed above. Parents can provide a rough and tumble area filled with pillows, balls, mini-trampoline, empty barrel to ride on or roll in, etc. It's amazing how helpful it can be for children to have a physical outlet. They can invent extremely creative games with such raw materials and a little encouragement. In addition, it provides a healthy alternative for a child that tends to get lost in screen activities. Lynne helped a family with intense 5-year-old twins set up an active movement area in their home – complete with several types of indoor swings and a climbing ladder to interchangeably hang from a hook in the ceiling. (Resources in endnotes.)[3] One of the boys excitedly commented, "Now my brain isn't turning into mush, because I like doing this stuff even more than playing video games!"

My Response...

The above suggestions can be a launching pad to think outside the box as I consider the natural bent of my children. What one or two things could I do to facilitate creativity in our home?

Teaching Godly Perspectives about Gifts

How can my children learn the purpose of their gifts?

Unrelated to personal value

When my children's gifts and talents begin to define their value (and mine) I am tempted to build my life around the development of those gifts. Many parents run themselves ragged providing a well-rounded menu of extracurricular activities to further their children's gifts and interests, including music, dance, Scouts, and a variety of sports. This puts tremendous pressure on children to succeed and can communicate to them that they are the center of the universe, around which life should revolve. And, unfortunately, the current trend is to push children harder and harder at earlier ages.

Newsweek states: "Parents sacrifice their dwindling free time (and their own social lives) to make sure their kids…want for nothing. … They get overly involved in every facet of their kids' lives, stage-managing successes and robbing kids of the opportunity to learn from their failures."[4]

Excessive intensity, management, and positive attention for my children's gifting may breed in them a belief that my love for them is directly related to their achievement. This belief can produce high-achieving children with very low self-esteem. It can also produce fairly intense self-centeredness. A frenetic and child-centered approach to parenting tends to build a sense of entitlement into growing children, so that when they reach their teen years they feel they deserve whatever they want.

I must remember to communicate unconditional love apart from performance, in ways it can't be misunderstood. Jesus modeled this when his "children" (the disciples) returned from their first ministry venture away from him. He had given them gifts of healing and authority over demons, which they used to bless many people. They returned elated! Jesus shared their joy but strongly told them to revel in what was most important – the security of the love of their Father. **"Do not rejoice that the spirits submit to you, but rejoice that your names are written in heaven"** (Luke 10:20). In other words, "Don't get your sense of value from what you have done, get it from God's love for you!"

My Response…

In what ways might my children believe my love for them is related to talents and achievements? How could I communicate to each child that my love is unrelated to his/her most obvious gift/talent?

Given to bless, not impress

Parents can begin facilitating the use of their children's talents in meaningful ways as soon as those talents emerge. Through this effort children can then be taught that God has given them gifts for the purpose of blessing others.

Our son Noah has always loved to draw. At the age of four, during a sermon, he drew a beautiful picture of Jesus inside a heart. When he handed it to Lynne, she said, "Wow! You worked really hard on this. Why don't you ask the Lord if he wants you to give it to someone." He looked carefully around the church, slipped out of his seat, and smiled as he handed it to a familiar man a few rows ahead of us. We watched the man's shoulders began to shake as he cried in heartfelt release of a heavy burden. His business was in danger of failing and he recognized the little drawing as a communication of love and encouragement from Jesus. Noah still remembers that day and loves to give his art to others.

In every child's environment are endless opportunities to foster this mindset. When a child helps prepare a meal for the family he uses his talent to bless his family. When my daughter smiles at a crying baby in the grocery store she acts on God-given compassion. These are simple things. By noticing and affirming them I reinforce them. As my awareness and affirmation increase I can more actively structure activities for my children to use their budding talents to bless others.

MY RESPONSE...

What arenas might be fertile ground in which my children can bless others with their gifts? (With younger children, think of the elderly, relatives, peers, church, home, community, etc.)

Less important than character

Because the expression of talents is so obvious, it is easy to focus on praising the results (i.e.; art projects, musical performance, athletic accomplishment, etc.). It has been shown, however, that focusing on character qualities like perseverance, determination, and self-control go much further toward building confidence in children than to focus on their talents.

One prominent study analyzed the response of two groups of randomly selected children to different types of affirmation while completing test activities. In one group each child was praised for his or her intelligence. In the other group each child's hard work was affirmed.

The group praised for their intelligence gradually took fewer risks (chose easier tasks), used less effort to complete the test activities, and eventually scored lower than on their initial test. In follow-up interviews the researchers discovered the reasons. The children believed that if they were smart they shouldn't have to try hard, and they didn't want to take risks that would reveal they really weren't smart. The group praised for their hard work began to try harder, took on greater challenges, and scored higher with each test.[5]

MY RESPONSE...

What is something one of my children is good at and works hard at? How can I respond in a way that highlights the effort/process and not the gift or end product?

Facilitating Responsibility

How can children develop qualities that support their calling?

For children to flourish in their purposes in life they must value and practice responsibility, not only for using their gifts but also for tending to ordinary, daily tasks. Children naturally avoid such responsibility. As infants they are truly incapable. As toddlers they may be capable of some simple things like turning off lights, picking up small messes, flushing the toilet, or setting flatware at the table. As children grow older their capabilities increase. By the early school years they can be enlisted to help shop for groceries, prepare meals, do laundry, vacuum floors, help in the yard, prepare for guests, and any of a variety of household chores and responsibilities. Whether or not they exercise their capabilities, most teenagers are fully able to care for most of the basic responsibilities of maintaining a household. Unfortunately, many teenagers today actually are given responsibility at the level of toddlers or preschoolers!

This seems to happen for two main reasons. Of course the first reason is that children resist responsibility because they would rather get someone else to do it. Secondly, if that is their goal it usually is just easier for the parent to do the job to avoid requesting, arguing, repeatedly reminding and following up with their children. In the short run it's less painful for everyone. But in the long run this pattern creates dependency and produces children who struggle with responsibility.

These two reasons become a powerful cycle that affects many parents. The more it's repeated, the more deeply it becomes ingrained. Many parents eventually become so frustrated in their efforts to get their teens and pre-teens to take responsibility that they slowly tear down **Connection** with their child. In my experience, the number one need parents of teenagers feel is to get their children to be responsible. The problem is that too many parents wait until their children are teens before really working on this issue. At that point the intense energy they put into changing their child usually leads to further, more emotionally charged resistance.

In *Raising Great Kids,* Drs. Cloud & Townsend state, "The task of parenting is to transform the child's stance from 'My life is my parents' problem' to 'Yikes, my life is *my* problem.'"[6]

They encourage parents to empathize with and have compassion for their children's struggle to develop responsible character. "Their rage, defiance, or whining may be hard to endure. But the child is in lots of pain himself – that's why he is protesting. The child has to give up an entire way of looking at life." [7]

Owning the problem together

Determining the need for a change: So what can I do so my children become motivated toward responsibility instead of resistant to it? Adults that are struggling with motivation and responsibility at work like to be involved in solving the problem, not simply told by their boss what consequences will be imposed. Children are no different. Our three kids used to roll their eyes and say, "Oh great, another one of mom's programs" (of rewards and consequences). It was a helpful change when we began to view the situation not as a parent's problem but as our whole family's problem, and to involve our children in solving it. No one likes a cycle of mess, nagging, and conflict. The difficult feelings involved can be a motivation to the whole family to change the cycle. The discussion to solve the problem can involve everyone or just one child, whether the issue is homework, chores, bedtime, clean up, etc. Even young children can contribute ideas.

I remember one such conversation with Noah that invited his ownership of a family problem. At a young age, he became enamored with Legos. By age seven, he had so many that his bedroom floor, dresser tops, and every nook and cranny in the room could easily be covered with a colorful mess. Lynne and I first took the nagging approach with these messes. After numerous ineffective reminders, I'd finally blurt in frustration, "Noah, pick those up or you'll lose them!" He lost many Legos, but it seemed this approach was not effectively teaching him anything. Lynne and I decided to have a conversation with him. "Noah, how do you feel about your Lego messes?"

"They don't bother me."

"Well, they have become a problem for us because we can't come into your room without stepping on them. Do you ever step on them?

"Sometimes."

"Does that bother you?"

"Sometimes." (Noah has never been very talkative at times like this, and is prone to giving the shortest answer he can.)

"And then, do you ever have trouble finding certain Legos?"

"Sometimes."

"Does that bother you?"

"Yeah."

"So, it bothers you that you step on them sometimes, and that you can't find what you're looking for."

"Yeah."

At this point, we had helped Noah to see that there was a problem and that the problem bothered him. We also helped him identify that he didn't like repeated reminders or the constant fear of losing his Legos. At this point, he was ready for some problem solving.

Brainstorming ideas: Once Noah admitted the parts of this problem that he didn't like, he was open to talking about possible ways to solve it. We asked, "What ideas do you have about solving this?"

"I don't know." (A classic answer – trying to give the responsibility back to us.)

"Well, should we just keep it the same?"

"No."

"Should we just take all the Legos away?"

"No."

"Can you think of other ways we organize things around here?"

(Based on his experience in our home, this was a rather leading question. Lynne is quite good at keeping small items organized throughout the house, from photographs, to recipes, to small hardware, to storage systems for dishes in a small kitchen. Noah is well aware of these systems and has been shown their benefits.)

"Hmmm. Maybe like the little drawers for stuff in the workshop."

"Great idea, Noah! How can we help?"

We made a plan and got some small drawers and bins for his Legos. He and Lynne worked hard and felt quite a sense of satisfaction when the huge project was all done. On a grander scale we believe this process contributed greatly to Noah's emerging desire and ability to organize other aspects of his life, like school folders, other toys, and his desk and locker. We're still working on his clothes drawers.

Other questions that can be asked in such an interaction might be:

- How could we keep better track of your responsibilities?
- What rewards and consequences would be helpful motivation?
- How could everyone work together to make the responsibility easier or more fun?
- How could I be more encouraging?

Modifying the plan: Once Noah saw and experienced the benefits of a new system, he stayed quite motivated to manage his Lego mess. But as his Lego collection grows and spreads to other parts of the house, we continue to build on those early conversations to make adjustments. One aspect of the plan is the continued understanding that leaving his Legos in common areas of the house could result in their confiscation. It is just a rationally established piece of the plan to keep him responsible.

Once plans are established there is a baseline for parents to initiate new conversations when the plan does not seem to be working. It's important to reenlist the child in a conversation to modify the plan as needed. If modified too often, however, the child can construe even this idea as a form of nagging. So I try to find additional ways to nurture my children's responsibility.

Everyday opportunities to teach

Implementing these ideas early in a child's life helps build life-long habits for responsibility. Equally important are the habits parents can form as teachers rather than naggers. In everyday life are numerous opportunities. As I become more attentive to them, the more effectively I can teach responsibility. I can capitalize on the natural independence drive of a two-year-old ("I can do it MYSELF!") and teach him to take responsibility for his things: to hang up towels and jackets, put laundry into basket/clothes chute, flush toilets, clear dishes, turn off lights, etc. Building responsibility is a long process that benefits greatly from daily "come alongside" help and training.

My Response...

What area of responsibility causes stress in my home? How could I help my children to "own the problem" and reach a solution, considering their ages and personalities?

I can nurture my children's gifting, affirm their hard work, and facilitate the responsibility needed to use their gifts. Then I can savor the possibilities of how it will all be used for God's purposes. When I express confidence that God has a purpose for my children and a plan to use the gifts he's given them, I can encourage *them* to wonder and dream about the details of that calling.

Kid Connection!

At dinner ask each child (depending on age and memory), "What was the favorite thing you did today... or this week?" As a family, discuss the gift beneath the activity and imagine ways it could be used some day to benefit a church you attend. Older children might enjoy the same question related to assisting an overseas mission to impoverished people. List the most significant idea for each child.

For example, children who enjoyed playing with pets or dolls could use their gift of nurturing in the children's ministry, kids who had fun with Legos could use their mechanical skills to help with the planning or construction of a church or mission building, a computer game fan might help with the ministry's technology needs.

Chapter Eighteen

Swimming Against the Current
Clear Teaching about Right and Wrong
-in a Confusing Culture!

"...let us throw off everything that hinders and the sin that so easily entangles, and let us run with perseverance the race marked out for us."

—Hebrews 12:1

A GROUP OF four-year-olds in a Stanford University study were each given a marshmallow. They were promised a second one IF they could wait for several minutes without eating the first one while the examiner left the room to get the second marshmallow. This was a concrete measure of the preschoolers' ability to delay gratification. Some children quickly grabbed and ate the first marshmallow, while others waited eagerly for their bonus of two. The study then assessed the impact of their ability to delay gratification in their lives as they grew.

Fourteen years later, as high school seniors, those who had been the 'grabbers' had low self-esteem, and were perceived by others as easily frustrated, stubborn, and prone to envy and conflict. The 'waiters' were more trustworthy, dependable, and socially competent, coped better with stress and frustration, and got better grades.[1] Those children able to delay gratification even scored about 210 points higher on their SAT tests![2]

Instant gratification has become a hallmark of our culture. Only 34 percent of parents believe they've succeeded in teaching their kids self-control and self-discipline – that is, the ability to wait, to think before acting and to understand potential consequences of their actions.[3] Dr. David Walsh, national expert on media and cultural influences, has coined a term for what he believes is a widespread problem among young people today: DDD – Discipline Deficit Disorder, resulting from our culture of "more, easy, fast, and fun."[4] He describes the symptoms of Discipline Deficit Disorder as ranging from impatience, a lack of respect, and a need for instant gratification, to inflated expectations, a sense of entitlement, selfishness, and falling test scores. Clearly these are not the kinds of characteristics that will help a child walk in God's purposes for his or her life.

Because of my career working with troubled youth, I was given a stark look at these trends of instant gratification and immorality that could potentially threaten my children. Lynne and I decided early to do our best to train our children to have a solid biblical perspective of the cultural trends, so they could be **"in the world but not of the world"** (see John 17:14, 15). Jesus courageously proclaims, **"the *truth*** (of my gospel and principles for living that flow from it) **will set you free"** (John 8:32b). In other words, my family and I do not have to be bound by these societal trends and their hurtful consequences.

The Cultural Climate

What trends threaten to undermine my children's values?

"...A large majority of parents say American society is an inhospitable climate for raising children, where parents can never let down their guard..."[5] Research substantiates this. When we compare our country to other nations, we find that "children in immigrant families are (emotionally) healthier than U.S.-born children," an advantage which declines the longer the immigrant children are in the U.S.[6]

Here are prevalent messages in our "more, easy, fast, and fun" culture that powerfully impact my children:

If it tastes good, eat it!

- Between sixteen and thirty-three percent of children and adolescents are obese[7]
- The prevalence of obesity has nearly *tripled* for adolescents in the past two decades.[8]
- Teenagers average almost two cans of soda a day.[9]
- The type of diabetes closely linked to obesity (previously considered an adult disease) has increased dramatically in children and adolescents. [10]

If you like it, buy it!

- Americans keep building bigger and more expensive houses: "The average mortgage today requires over one hundred hours of factory labor a month to pay, compared to forty hours two decades ago."[11]
- Americans' average credit card debt is now $8400 per household.[12]

The Federal Reserve reports that:

- More than forty percent of American families spend more than they earn.

The seemingly insatiable desire to buy things drives not only spending habits, but earning habits as well. And while we have long considered affluence a blessing, the misuse of affluence seems to have considerable effects on true reliance on God and belief in his Word. One study clearly shows the relationship between wealth and belief. Of those with incomes under $20,000, seventy-five percent of people believe that "The Bible is very important." Of those with incomes in excess of $60,000, only thirty-five percent agree.[13]

If it feels good, do it!

- Nearly seventy percent of college students are sexually active.[14]
- Nearly forty percent of college students have had six or more sexual partners.[15]
- Between 1965 and 1974, about ten percent of all marriages were preceded by cohabitation.[16] By 2005, over two-thirds of married couples reported cohabiting before marriage.[17]
- More than fifty percent of all married men and women – some surveys give figures as high as sixty-six percent - have had an affair (the rates for men and women are now virtually identical).[18]

If it's entertaining, watch it....endlessly!

- "Children, ages 8 to 18, spend more time (44.5 hours per week) in front of computer, television, and game screens than any other activity in their lives except sleeping."[19]
- Half of parents say their child has a TV in their room.[20]
- Watching approximately 3 ½ hours of television every day, the average American child may view as many as 40,000 commercials every year.[21]
- School age children average less than 5 minutes/day in recreational reading.[22]

The consequences:

These beliefs, and the consequences of acting on them, now permeate American culture. We are reaping what we have sown. The Scriptures teach that doing whatever I want, when I want sooner or later brings bondage and pain from sin. King Solomon vividly described people who make hurtful, self-destructive choices: **"They ambush their own lives"** (Proverbs 1:18b NASB). Research shows this principle at work:

- Obesity: Excess weight and a sedentary lifestyle cause at least 300,000 premature deaths and more than $90 billion in health care costs each year.[23]
- Materialism: The majority of parents list finances as the top stressor in their family.[24]
- Morality: One of the strongest predictors of divorce is sexual behavior prior to marriage. "Marriages preceded by a spell of cohabitation are as much as fifty percent more likely to end in divorce…than marriages not preceded by cohabitation."[25]
- Media: As entertainment screen time increases, so do ADHD symptoms,[26] low grades,[27] low self-esteem,[28] obesity,[29] and aggression.[30]

These trends are bad news! Helping my children learn to "throw off the sin that so easily entangles" (see Hebrews 12:1) means I daily figure out how to incorporate spiritual truth into my life and the lives of my children. This is not just a matter of saying, "Yes" to the gospel. It is a commitment to a lifestyle that flows from a belief that the gospel is really true. The primary reason for thoughtful, proactive teaching of character and wise choices is that my children might experience the life of freedom and fulfillment for which they were created and become lights in a dark world.

Godly Character and Wise Choices

How can I most effectively teach right from wrong?

In the context of this confusing culture, helping my children understand and embrace godly character and wise choices is a challenging but important aspect of parenting. According to Josh McDowell, youth in the church are losing their ability to determine right from wrong because they have been taught the "whats" without the "whys." They often get the rules, without any explanation of how the rules are connected to God's character and desires for his beloved children. The youth culture that surrounds our children generally believes, "If I think it's right for me, it is." This sets kids up to be thoughtless about the nature of their behavior. To counter this, children must learn the *whys* of right and wrong behavior—the reasons or consequences of poor choices and good choices.

In other words when I tell my children it's wrong to lie, I must also tell them what is right about the truth, as well as the underlying principles that motivate truth-telling. Truth is right because it grows out of God's character and it builds trust. Lying is wrong because it hurts other people, it breaks down trust, it places self before others, and is opposed to God's character. Right and wrong are thus ultimately rooted in the person and character of God. Careful thought, study and prayer will equip parents to understand and explain rules, expectations and right and wrong behaviors in this light.[31]

Developing this consistent approach to setting and explaining family rules helps me better understand my rationale for our family rules. Then, even if the "whys" are not that important to my children at first, as they understand them, they begin to slowly embrace them. Even if they never do at least I have respectfully laid out a rationale.

MY RESPONSE...

What two issues cause one or more of my children to struggle? (Possibilities include: Disobedience. Stealing. Cheating. Gossiping. Disrespect/bullying.)
How can I help them discover (at an age-appropriate level) what is right and wrong, and why?

KID CONNECTION!

Have fun with some of the wisdom sections of the Bible with your children. Read through the Proverbs and find verses that portray scriptural values in a creative way.

Possible references to discuss: Proverbs 3:5-7; 6:10-11; 8:17-19; 9:7-9; 12:4; 14:12; 16:9; 18:7,8; 20:1, 29; 21:20, 24:26, 25:28; 26:2, 28:19,20; 29:25; 31:30.

After you read the verse, you can discuss questions like:

- What is the value or character quality this verse talks about?
- What might be some natural results of living in this way?
- What "proverb" might TV shows, movies, or magazines write on this topic?

Chapter Nineteen

Media, Materialism, Meals (picky eaters)

Media: The Stranger in Our House

How can I help my child learn wise and balanced screen habits?

WHEN "HAPPY DAYS" star Fonzie got a library card, he enthusiastically told his buddy, "Hey Ritchie, you can get a library card, and they're *free*!!" After that episode in which Fonzie discovered the wonders of libraries, the number of library cards issued went up 500 percent in the U.S.[1] Media is a powerful molder of values! It has great potential for benefit - educational television has been shown to teach positive attitudes, academic skills, and emotional insight.[2] Unfortunately however, research shows that "diets of typical television tend to teach... sexist and aggressive attitudes, fear, and consumer behavior."[3]

It's no surprise that violent content in video games (even in games with combat between cute cartoon characters) increases aggressive behavior. "Practicing intentional harm is what matters, even if the game looks cute and harmless," concludes an Oxford University study.[4] The media ideal of sex appeal and "perfect bodies" also takes a toll on children's self esteem. One study discovered that the amount of time adolescents watch soaps, movies and music videos is directly related to their level of dissatisfaction with their body.[5] Watching commercials depicting women who were unrealistically thin caused adolescent girls to feel less confident, more angry, and more dissatisfied with their weight and appearance.[6]

Imagine allowing a stranger to come into your house for hours every day. He sits down next to your child, and subtly whispers messages of sexuality, violence and materialism into that impressionable mind. No parent in their right mind would stand for it! Unfortunately, the media explosion is a new frontier and most of us are ill-equipped to combat the pervasive values "whispered" during screen activities. In addition, as the bar keeps getting raised higher on realism, shock, and excitement, these activities become increasingly addictive. With the average 8 – 18 year old engaged in entertainment screens for 44.5 hours per week, it can be a daunting task to try to "swim against the cultural current" in this issue.

The children who fight the hardest about screen time limitations and guidance are usually the ones with the most potential for obsession or addiction. Children with ADHD and sensory sensitivities tend to be more intent about screen time than other children. If they have a tendency for over-stimulation in their environment, whatever screen they are watching makes the environment "disappear" and helps them feel focused and less overwhelmed. Many parents report their most difficult time each day is getting a child off the video game or computer. A minority of children can choose appropriate content, can balance their screen time wisely and should be allowed to do so, but most need persistent guidance. (Excellent, practical resources to help parents can be found at *www.mediafamily.org*.)

Michelle was frustrated by the conflicts about TV time at her house. "It was the same hassle almost every night. The kids seemed to put down roots in front of the TV, and the negotiations for more time were exasperating! We decided to limit screen time to the weekends, except for an occasional weeknight show that we all watch together. It was a little adjustment, but after a week or two with no TV, our house was so much more peaceful! The kids often get up and read in the mornings or go outside and play instead of turning on the TV. I'm lovin' that!" Michelle's approach fits well with the research that says that school performance is significantly hindered by weekday screen time, but not by screen time on the weekend.[7]

Certainly children often need concrete, clear limitations, but if I stand over my child with my hands on my hips and proclaim the ills of his or her screen activity, I am sure to draw the lines of battle and strengthen my child's determination to stay glued to the screen. Part of Michelle's success was a kind but firm approach based in her conviction that this would truly help her children.

I have the best shot at helping my child engage wisely in screen activities if I determine to strengthen our connection, rather than letting the conflict erode our love for each other. Josh McDowell said, "Rules – relationship = rebellion. Rules + relationship = positive response. If young people perceive that you are more concerned about the rules than you are about them, they will likely be tempted to disregard your rules. But when they know that they are more important to you than the rules – that you love them no matter what they do or don't do – they are much more likely to follow your guidelines."[8]

Neither Lynne nor I particularly enjoy computer games. Our two sons were crazy about them, and our efforts to encourage more creative pursuits had not yet had a significant impact. Realizing that I was rejecting what was important to them, I decided to find out what one of those games was all about. The boys eagerly became my teachers. My desire to connect with them on their level helped me endure my incompetence. They watched and instructed, telling me all their little secrets for success. After nearly an hour of laughter, failure, and defeat at the hands of a far superior computer program, I gave up the joystick and returned to my routine.

Later, our oldest told Lynne, "I know Dad decided to learn our computer game just to be interested in our stuff and be with us. I want to learn about something that he is interested in." Now certainly, this "Walt Disney" ending doesn't happen every time parents engage with their children's interests, but I strengthen my platform to influence my children about their time use, when I non-judgmentally join them in their activities.

MY RESPONSE...

What impact do media and screen activities have on our family's values and relationships?

Screen time (particularly before completing responsibilities) was the source of the most difficult on-going conflict with our oldest son for years. Working through this problem with Daniel took determination, a team effort as parents, and a relentless perspective that he was called to important things in God's kingdom.

Many times it seemed we were getting nowhere, and we wondered if the struggle was worth it. The conflict had so suffocated Lynne's relationship with him that they decided to reconnect through a road trip to someplace hot and exciting. Their adventures in Mexico and the sheer determination to nurture their relationship turned the corner on their pattern of frequent conflict.

In this challenging arena of guiding balanced and purposeful screen time, it's also very helpful if I sincerely believe my child has a God-given calling to make a difference in the world, and if I persistently nurture that belief in him or her. 1 Thessalonians 2:11-13 expresses the heart of this approach, **"For you know that we dealt with each of you as a father deals with his own children, encouraging, comforting and urging you to live lives worthy of God, who calls you into his kingdom and glory."** Research shows that children that truly connect with the love of God and are involved in serving others are at much lower risk for unhealthy behaviors.[9]

Children need persistent guidance and a positive focus on developing purposeful, alternative interests that are a fit for their unique gifting. It takes time and sensitivity to find out what it is that they love about their screen activities, and how I could help them give those desires expression in the three-dimensional world.

We had many discussions with Daniel about how to balance his screen time with creative alternatives that were a fit for his unique bent. He gradually understood that screen time was "dessert for the brain," and he needed a real world "healthy diet" to thrive in life. We paid the price both literally and figuratively, as we bought a camcorder, a digital camera, tree fort supplies, golf lessons, etc. These things provided three-dimensional real life fulfillment of the adventure, creativity and conquest that he was seeking in his computer games. Each of those activities required parent involvement – I worked on his tree fort and coached his golf team – but it was well worth it. And his current photography business is helping to pay for college!

As a philosophical young adult, Daniel recently reflected on the impact of his previous screen habits, "When you have to stop playing your video game, *it takes awhile for real life to regain its relevance.*" No wonder it's so tough to get children away from the electric entertainment which creates an exciting false world. This led him to conclude, "Single player video games are like a soul drain!"

> ◆◆◆❖◆❖◆◆◆
> **I have the best shot at helping my children engage wisely in screen activities if I determine to strengthen our connection and nurture their sense of God's purposes for their lives.**
> ◆◆◆❖◆❖◆◆◆

No matter what the parenting issue is, our challenge is greatly reduced when we meet our children's deep needs for unconditional acceptance, belonging, and significance.

MY RESPONSE...

How could I be better informed about my child's media/screen activities?

How might I help my child evaluate the potential benefits and detriments of their screen activities?

Materialism –Rising above our "Want it, Gotta Have it" Culture

How can I pass on wise, biblical perspectives on money?

"I really want that new Lego attack robot. I saw it on TV and it's soooo cool! It even shoots little missiles! Billy has three of them in different colors. Please Daddy, pleeeeeze!!!"

"Mom, I can't believe you won't buy me those jeans! Do you really expect me to go to school in these things? Are you trying to murder my social life?!"

Regardless of the age or gender of the child, kids' intense desire for stuff is propelled by powerful cultural forces. A typical American child views approximately 40,000 advertisements each year![10] One expert writes, "Youths...shape the buying patterns of their families. From vacation choices to car purchases to meal selections, they exert a tremendous power over the family pocketbook."[11]

The starting place for dealing with this challenging "cultural current" of materialism is the **Foundation** question, "What's going on inside of me?" Am I swept along by it as well? Is my own interest in new gadgets, fashions, adventures, or experiences getting out of balance? Am I even paying attention? Do I tend to "buy first, think later?" Am I anxious about not falling behind the standard of living of my friends? Or, am I thoughtful about my values of self-control and generosity? This is clearly an area where children learn by watching!

Sometimes what's going on inside of parents isn't materialism, but rather a fear of that problem developing in their child. This can result in an over-reaction to a child's developmentally typical desire for "stuff." Lynne remembers an over-anxious response to Bethany's case of the "gimme's."

Glitzy displays and tempting toys packed the isles. My children felt like millionaires, each with a budget of $20 from my mother for Christmas. Bethany chattered excitedly about all the toys, and wanted far more than what she could purchase with her $20. My anxiety escalated my irritation – surely she would grow into a materialistic teenager! As a fashion-challenged garage sale enthusiast, I couldn't stomach the prospect of buying designer clothes. That fear fed irrationally critical, controlling responses to her. "Bethany, stop it right now! This is ridiculous! You can't have everything in the store!" She started to cry at my harsh words. Fortunately my mother smiled peacefully and calmed both of us with a much wiser perspective on the situation.

MY RESPONSE...

What is going on inside of me related to our family's spending habits:
In what ways do I "buy first, think later?" or, how do I model moderation and generosity?

In what ways might I be anxious about my child's materialistic/selfish desires?

In addition to understanding my *own* attitudes and actions about spending and materialism, there's a lot I can do to help my children if they are preoccupied with getting the latest, greatest toys, clothes, electronics and other trendy items.

Two university researchers discovered that materialistic attitudes go hand in hand with low self-esteem, and both of these characteristics are the most intense between the ages of 13 and 18. The researchers hypothesized that children "use...material possessions as a coping strategy for feelings of low self-worth." (Hmm... I wonder if a few of us adults do that too.) The study also revealed that children valued material possessions *less* after they received affirmation for qualities that others appreciated in them![12]

Interesting research, but how does that affect my parenting? First – I don't hit the panic button if my teen seems to be struggling with materialism. It's pretty common, and odds are it'll get better. Second and more important: As usual, it's the underlying need (in this case, for self-esteem) that is most important. Whether I have toddlers or teens, the fastest way to drive my child toward more materialistic values is to batter their self-esteem with criticism for being selfish or materialistic!

The bottom line is – my children need *me* and my encouragement more than they need stuff! And it bears asking, "How can I express love to my children, whether or not they are struggling with a case of the "gimme's"?

From a strong **Foundation** of self-awareness (what's going on inside me?) and a solid **Connection** with my child, I can focus on **Proaction**: "How can I mentor success and teach/train character?" A great way to teach my children how to set priorities and delay gratification is to bring them into my financial decisions.

Most children are aware of when their parent buys something, but are not aware when their parent saves or gives money. Let's consider the example of getting a new TV. If one day I announce, "It's time for a new TV," and later that day I come home with one. "Hmm," observes my child, "Daddy wanted it, so he got it." Lacking any other explanation, of course the child's logical conclusion is "If I want something, I should get it."

To use this purchase as a teaching opportunity with a young child I might simply say, "I chose to spend some of the money I earned to buy us a new TV. The rest of the money got saved in the bank, paid for the house and our groceries, and we gave some to the church."

An older child benefits from involvement in basic elements of my financial planning process. He or she can help me prioritize how our family's disposable income will be spent. What are the essentials in our budget? What do we need to save? What is left over for our "wish list?" What things on the wish list are most important and how can we plan to get them? Involvement in this process helps my child feel responsible and effectively passes on values about money.

MY RESPONSE...

What is a significant purchase I may make in the next few months? How might I capitalize on the opportunity to teach my children some financial perspective?

Once my children participate in my process of determining family priorities and saving for important items, they are ready to experience it for themselves. I can help my child build an understanding about the difference between their needs and wants with simple questions like, "In 6 months (or even 1 month) will you still be glad you spent this money?" or, "Is there something else you could use instead, that you already have?" I can encourage my child to write the item down and think about it for a while before purchasing.

Once my child decides to buy something, earning the money for it develops both responsibility and delay of gratification. Even a young child can do extra jobs around the house to earn money for a new toy. Older children can also enter into discussions about saving and spending – it's a great opportunity to discuss what's important to them and why. When a desired item is finally purchased, I can help my child feel good about the growth in character and the ability to work toward a goal. "Wow, now you've got a new dolly (Lego kit, guitar, or iPod...) and you did the hard work of saving for it yourself! How's that feel?!"

MY RESPONSE...

What item might my child(ren) really want *and* need, for which they could work toward saving money?

Whose money is it, anyway?

> *"The earth is the Lord's, and everything in it, the world, and all who live in it."*
>
> —Psalm 24:1

> *"You open your hand and satisfy the desires of every living thing."*
>
> —Psalm 145:16

Lynne and I recently had the privilege of being with a family on the day their new grand piano arrived. What a joy it was to circle around the beautiful instrument with the family and thank God for the blessing of the resources to buy the piano, and then to dedicate the piano to God's purposes to grow and use the musical talents in that family to bless others. In the months since, we have gathered around that piano with neighbors, friends and family numerous times to sing God's praises and share the blessing of music.

Once I understand that money, and even the stuff it can purchase, really belongs to God, I can consider with my family, "How might this item be a blessing to someone else?" This question puts into perspective the idea that possessions can be used to bless others and raises the importance of using our possessions to reach people with Jesus' love. It's amazing to see what asking this question does to influence children's use of even ordinary items like PlayStations, video cameras, Legos, and dolls or action figures.

When I give money away I can invite my children to join in that process as well. I can tell them about my thinking and my excitement. It's a great opportunity to explore together what the Bible says about giving. 2 Corinthians 9:7 says, **"Each man should give what he has decided in his heart to give, not reluctantly or under compulsion, for God loves a cheerful giver."** "The real opposite of materialism is spirituality," says Dr. Paul Coleman, family therapist and author. "Try to do something with your child that's focused on giving to others in a way that he can see."[13]

The 2004 Tsunami disaster provided such an opportunity. As we realized the enormity of this disaster, it became hard to sit at our family table feeling so blessed and seemingly so immune from the kind of pain and suffering such an event produces. While discussing the event we asked the children to consider what we might do to help. Based on all reports the biggest need was financial. It gave a reason to discuss our giving patterns and the specifics of our gifts so far that year. The kids decided we should sacrifice beyond the norm. We invited them to do some research, and then we all shared in the decision to pool our resources for a generous contribution.

Just Say "No"

No matter how much we model, teach, and encourage thoughtful decisions, there will be times our children simply need us to say "no!" to their requests. These can be unpopular decisions, but can be an opportunity to teach contentment and the ability to cope with disappointment. A parent's boundary setting re: materialism can even start with turning off the TV! Research shows that when parents denied children's requests for products, children who were heavy TV viewers argued about the purchase 21 percent of the time, while light viewers argued only 9 percent of the time![14] Whew, another good reason to "tame the tube" in my house!

Mealtime: Passing the Peas in Peace

How can I encourage healthy eating without power struggles?

As the statistics in the last chapter suggest, America is getting more obese and sicker by the day. In five years, the national cost of treating obesity related sickness more than doubled.[15] Advertisers get better than ever at making people believe they "need" their products. In spite of widespread concern over obesity trends, the sales of soft drinks and other non-nutritious foods continue to rise. Most parents are not well equipped to fight these trends. To guide my children in making wise eating choices, I need to understand what approaches are truly helpful and which ones are potentially hurtful.

The approach that is the most hurtful seems to be that of over controlling children's food choices. A Duke University study revealed that the more parents controlled and restricted their children's food intake, the more obese the children were.[16] Researchers also concluded that "children had poorer diets when their family tried too hard to control their behavior in general, not just their eating."[17]

What about the challenge of picky eaters who refuse to eat? Again, research clearly shows the detriment to children when parents attempt to nag, trick, bribe, threaten, or otherwise manipulate children into eating healthy food choices. A study of preschoolers revealed that children who were rewarded for eating a new food were *less likely* to eat it the next time it was served than were children who were simply presented the food on two occasions.[18] The children may have concluded, "If an adult has to work to get me to eat this, there must be something wrong with it." So what can a parent do to encourage children to eat reasonable amounts of healthy food?

Ellen Satyr, noted nutritionist and author, answers this question in a simple guideline. "Parents are responsible for what is presented and the manner in which it is presented. Children are responsible for how much and even whether they eat."[19] This guideline dovetails well with basic principles for **Proaction.** I am responsible for proactive modeling, teaching, and training, and for setting appropriate boundaries. Within these boundaries my children are responsible for their own choices.

My responsibilities

As with any area of **Proaction,** guiding my children into healthy, moderate eating requires that I draw from my **Foundation**. Does this type of eating come easily for me? Why or why not? What experiences and beliefs affect how I relate to food? Do my children see me growing in trying new foods and improving my own eating habits? These are questions I can address to help me get in touch with my attitudes and the ways I may be influencing my children.

From this awareness I can more effectively guide my children. This includes proactively teaching them (at age-appropriate levels) how the food they eat affects their bodies, health, and strength. It is also quite helpful to involve children in meal planning and preparation as soon as they are old enough.

Modeling healthy eating, an important **Proaction** element, has much more impact if I serve one or two of my children's food choices at each meal. If I eat a small amount of food they enjoy, they are more likely to try foods I enjoy. Including a food my child enjoys at each meal also decreases demands and power struggles over food choices. One mother told Lynne this suggestion from her was sufficient to dramatically improve her son's eating selection and the tone of their family mealtimes. Her son had even recently tried Sushi!

Setting appropriate boundaries about the food I serve (being responsible for *what* is presented) can be challenging, and again draws on my **Foundation** as I remember that parenting is not a popularity contest. If I focus on my ultimate goal of my children's well being and not their approval, I can kindly but firmly say no to excessive demands for unhealthy food. (They can't eat what I don't buy them.) It takes persistence to provide repeated exposure to a variety of healthy food. My child may need numerous exposures before even tasting a new food. Studies have shown that people have to try food on an average of ten different occasions before they know if they like it or not.[20]

Being responsible for *the manner* in which food is presented involves providing it at regular family meals, which has a direct impact on children's nutrition. "Children… who have more regular dinners with their families have more healthful dietary patterns, including more fruits and vegetables, less saturated and trans fat, fewer fried foods and sodas, and more vitamins and other micronutrients."[21]

My child's responsibility

When I focus on my responsibility, it is easier to keep myself from doing what is *not* my responsibility – namely, making my children's choices. Children need to understand that eating is for their own nourishment and enjoyment, not to please anyone else. Lynne's family had a helpful mealtime mantra: "You don't have to eat it, but don't complain about it." (More positively stated, this could be, "Eat what you want, but respect the cook!") I can express confidence in my children, "You can try a bite." If they protest I can simply respond, "You can when you're ready," and then respect my children's choices. As with any area of **Proaction,** it is important for me to consistently communicate my love for my child regardless of his or her choices. I must let my kids know I love and enjoy them regardless of what they eat or weigh!

Lynne tells this story of a family with strong challenges related to eating:

When Josh's parents came into the clinic, they were at their wits' end. Their five-year-old son's previous medical problems had made eating difficult and even painful. His well-intentioned parents were desperate to get food in him and even though the medical issues were resolved, a pattern was ingrained. He survived on pop, candy and a very limited diet, mostly of other carbohydrates. Family mealtime was a nightmare! The intense power struggle between mom and son would often end in Josh throwing up at the dinner table, and both of them in tears. This conflict tainted his whole relationship with his mother.

For several months I worked with his parents to help them overcome this challenge. I taught them in detail the principles for how to do their responsibility related to meals and to let Josh do his. They slowly learned to focus on providing a variety of healthy food, making mealtimes pleasant for all, and letting him make his own choices. At our last session, his mom was beaming, "He eats everything I serve at meals." The most rewarding part for me was to see how the tension in their relationship was gone. [22]

MY RESPONSE...

Which is most true of my family?
- My family is on a journey of learning healthy eating; our mealtimes are pleasant.
- My children's intake of healthy food is quite limited, and I "special order cook" to keep them happy at meals.
- I try to control/strongly influence my children's choices.

How can I be more proactive with my children related to healthy eating and give them more freedom in appropriate choices?

KID CONNECTION! (Choose One or More Activities.)

1. MEDIA: Ask your children to list the things they love about their screen activities. Add your own observations to the list. i.e. a love for drama, excitement, problem-solving, competition, social connection, etc. Then ask your children, "What are some things we could do to experience those things without watching TV – in real life experiences? (Examples: One family with young children uses the plot of the shows their children watch to spark imaginative play and dress-up drama. You could encourage a MySpace or Facebook enthusiast to plan a party with friends. Many families have found that participating in martial arts together meets a need for excitement and competition.)

2. MONEY/MATERIALISM: Try this activity with each of your children. Make it fun! Give them a chance to ask questions.

   (a) Get a pile of coins and invite your children to sit with you to learn some things about money. Tell them that the pile of coins represents the money your family gets in a year. Ask them how they think you get the money. Discuss briefly.

   (b) Then split the coins into piles that approximately represent how much you save, spend, and give away. Explain each pile and break them into smaller piles to represent subcategories.

(c) When you finish, ask the child, "Now that you see all these piles, whom do you think the money really belongs to?" Encourage them regardless of their answer, and then remind them that all the money belongs to God (Psalm 24:1). He gives it to us to care for, so we should remember where it came from.

(d) Use this activity to discuss your kid's money. Do what you can to encourage their healthy choices.

3. MEALTIME: Next time you are preparing dinner with one or more of your children, ask why they think God created our bodies to need food. (There are lots of answers, possibly including: so we trust God for our "daily bread," for the fellowship of shared meals, to prepare us for the feast of heaven, etc.)

Chapter Twenty

Talking about S – E – X
with K – I – D – S

Guidance for Sexual Choices

How can I help my children embrace God's plan for sexuality?

IT WAS BY far the largest pair of breasts I'd ever seen. When you enlarge to billboard size, the torso of a voluptuous model with a very low neckline leaning toward the camera, it's quite a sight to behold. "Turn on Howard" (Stern), her pouty lips said. I wished that it were more unusual – I was dismayed, but not surprised. At least it was the fuel for a lively discussion with my children!

American culture is more sexually charged than at any other time in history. Sex is no longer valued by the general population as an intimate expression of love and commitment to be shared only between a husband and a wife. It is viewed instead as a normal part of growing up. Many adolescents consider themselves "ready" for it whenever the juices first start to flow. What a tragedy! When the act God designed as the ultimate expression of intimacy and commitment is corrupted, it greatly damages one's ability to be intimate with others and with God. Sexual activity outside of marriage seems to build an inner sense of opposition to the ways of God. **"Everyone who does evil hates the light, and will not come into the light for fear that his deeds will be exposed,"** John 3:20. Certainly the sexual values of our day are among the most dangerous currents of our culture that will damage children emotionally, physically, and spiritually.

Kids can only be protected for so long from the influence of culture. For children to stand strong they need parents who will communicate more clearly and strongly than the culture. This is no small task!

Understanding _my_ beliefs

Some parents find it awkward or shameful to be affectionate in front of their children or to talk appropriately and openly about sexuality with them. This is fairly typical. Only a generation or two ago, parents felt no need to talk about the private parts of their lives. But the power of today's trends no longer allows a parent's silent example to have the impact it once did. So it is time to learn to break the silence—before the opportunity for influence is gone.

Some parents are embarrassed or just don't know what to say. Some are ashamed of personal experience with the negative consequences of sexual sin. Many parents experience tension about sex in their marriage relationship, even to the point of marital breakdown. These all contribute to the difficulties parents have about talking with their children. If it's hard to talk about sex with my kids, it's time to start thinking, praying, and talking about why this is difficult. It may be helpful to think through (on my own or with professional help) the impact of how my parents related sexually, and how they explained or modeled sexuality to me. I could privately journal a sexual "autobiography," or read a book on sexuality for Christian couples and discuss it in a small group with some trusted friends.

Modeling intimacy and affection

Children first begin learning about interaction with the opposite gender by watching their parents. Whether they see parents hugging, kissing, offering "silent treatment," or fighting passionately, the children are getting impressions from the parents about what it means to a man or a woman. The way parents respond in these interactions teaches their children about boundaries – whether healthy or unhealthy.

For children to have a healthy view of marriage and sexuality, it is essential to protect and nurture the marriage relationship. Children ought to see parents talking and connecting regularly. You can let kids know that there are times when you are going to enjoy conversation together and cannot be interrupted. Regular "connection time," date nights, and getting away for longer periods alone without kids, communicate that marriage is an enjoyable, fulfilling relationship.

Most younger teenagers believe that sex between married people is not only boring, but gross. To counteract this false belief, even though it may be awkward for some parents, it is healthy to model appropriate romantic affection. Statements like, "Someday, if you get married, you'll have someone to snuggle with like this," communicate to even young children that intimacy is a blessing reserved for marriage.

In our home we have made a priority of giving kids little hints about the fact that mom and dad actually do make love. We occasionally make light-hearted references to "power-snuggling," or "late night fun." During such references at mealtime, Daniel would respond, "You guys are gross." Bethany would often join his protest, "I didn't need to know that." Noah generally pretended he didn't hear us.

One might think we were inappropriately transparent, but the funny thing is, they'd have little grins on their faces as they protested, and Daniel in particular began to encourage our "playfulness." We've even heard them brag to their friends about how open and affectionate we are. The true fruit of this approach is evident as we watch them hold strong convictions and encourage their friends to do so: they value sexual intimacy in marriage and understand the consequences of premature sexual experiences.

If you are a single parent, do not lose heart. While we speak to the ideal of marriage, we have seen many single parents adapt these principles to their reality. They work hard to discuss these issues with their children and highlight the principles in the context of their current community relationships. While it can be very difficult, we strongly encourage that you find ways to stay connected to a community of grace-filled people that will both accept and minister to your family and model healthy marriage and family values for your children.

My Response...

What are my feelings about this topic of sexual intimacy, and the example I am setting for my children? (It may help to share these feelings with your spouse or a close friend.)

Their earliest and clearest teacher

When parents truly believe sex is a beautiful gift from God, it is natural to want to give their children an understanding of that gift. Certainly a parent's example is critical. What my children witness in my marriage relationship will have some influence on them. But in a climate where peers, advertisers, TV and movie heroes, music stars, and even teachers are talking daily to my kids about sex, I'd better figure out how to be the clearest, strongest voice! (www.4parents.gov is a resource for parents to help their child, pre-teen, or teen make healthy sexual choices, including deciding to wait until marriage to have sex.)

If I stay silent about sexuality, my children most likely won't talk with me when they begin to have questions or feel sensations. This "no talk" approach reinforces the secrecy and shame that often accompanies sexual development. Worse yet, it allows the bold, loud, and misguided culture to be their primary teacher. Breaking the silence about these things with teens or preteens can be quite intimidating. If that's their age, it's better late than never to try to start talking. But clearly, it makes sense to start with children as soon as possible, in the simplest of terms.

For example, if a parent notices her three-year-old exploring his or her genitals, there's no need for panic. It's very normal for kids to explore their bodies. Remember when they first discovered their hands or feet? There is a fascination with each new discovery. This is a perfect opportunity to affirm their exploration and begin to affirm God's purpose and plan. To say, "You're discovering your penis or vagina," is a natural, non-judging way to begin. Parents could go on to ask, "Did you know that's one of the ways God made boys and girls different and special?"

Opportunities for parents to talk with their children occur even when kids begin to experiment with each other. The following is a composite of several stories from parents I've coached through this issue, when other kids have been involved.

One mom discovered her preschool son playing "doctor" with a neighbor girl the same age. Her impulse was to scold them. That's what the mom had done before, but it didn't seem to curb the behavior. She wisely remembered to take a breath and get some perspective. Her resulting thought was, "Don't panic, this may not be such a big deal. Come to think of it, I played this way sometimes when I was his age." This allowed her to calmly say, "Kids, whatcha doin'?"

The kids were obviously ashamed, because they already had some sense that this was not appropriate. She peacefully asked them to put their clothes back on, which they quickly did. She then invited them to the living room for a conversation.

"You know, kids," she slowly began, "God made everyone's bodies very special. You kids are each very special. Did you know that?" They both nodded. She smiled and asked, "Are you sure?" The kids smiled a little and nodded again. "Good!" She continued in an affirming tone, "Did you know that your bodies are so special that you really shouldn't share them with someone else that way until you're married?" The kids had no response. "So from now on, when one of you gets asked to play like that, you can say 'No!' It's just not good for you." Knowing the kids still felt ashamed, and wanting to make sure they knew she still loved and valued them, she joyfully offered, "Let's go downstairs and build a really cool fort."

In the above scenario are some important principles for dealing with such potentially volatile situations. First, the mom checked her own emotions (**Foundation**) and kept her cool. Because she had calmed herself, she was able to offer quick, calm, and clear teaching (**Proaction**) about what is and isn't OK, and how to act in the future. She then immediately and sincerely **Connected** with the children by making a plan to play with them. When it was over, the kids had at once been allowed to feel bad about their behavior, been taught, and been affirmed.

Following this event the mom kept a keen eye on her son's play with other children. She took great care to set him up for success and to energetically affirm her son's appropriate behavior. Her son and his friend did do some more experimenting. A couple of times she calmly asked the girl to go home and gave her son a "time-out" from their friendship (**Correction**) saying, "It looks like you kids are having a hard time learning, so I'm going to separate you for a couple of days." Over time, her strategy of a graceful approach, informing and coaching the girl's mom, and giving consistent affirmation eventually helped the children learn appropriate boundaries for how to play together.

Sometimes a child's persistence in inappropriate sexual play may be a signal that more than the simple, graceful approach described is needed. Children may act out sexually when they are experiencing ongoing anxiety, anger, or shame. Some children have sensory imbalances that create an increased "skin hunger." When the touch that children are receiving is insufficient for their particular level of need, they will either seek others for touch, or spend more time self-soothing (masturbation). Increasing the appropriate physical connection with your child can go a long way to energizing them to make healthy choices.

Sometimes, a child's acting out sexually is a form of imitation, meaning that he or she is doing what has been observed or experienced. If indeed this is the case, it is important to remain low key, find out all you can, and determine a graceful, sensible course of action.

Regardless of what factors may be contributing to a child's sexual acting out, if a parent's best efforts do not seem to effectively curb or address the issue, it's best to seek some professional guidance.

As children approach adolescence, they become highly aware of both the external sexual climate and their internal responses (sensations) to the stimulus. For boys, this tends to be physically based. For girls, this is more emotionally based, (although in our sex-crazed culture it is becoming increasingly physical for girls also.) Some parents would prefer it if their kids never had thoughts or "urges" until they were married. But they do. So did the parents when they were young. The difference is, even a generation ago most teens knew that pursuing their urges was wrong. Today's youth culture has normalized adolescent sexual behavior to the degree that right and wrong is no longer defined. So if parents aren't talking, the kids will listen elsewhere.

But what will we talk about? How do I break the ice? Empathy is a great place to start. Remembering my own sexual feelings from my youth gives me a way to begin relating to my child. Imagine this conversation at the mall between a dad and his twelve-year-old son:

Dad: (lightly) I noticed you checking out those Victoria Secret posters back there.
Son: (unfazed) Whatever.
Dad: (after a pause) Yeah, I remember.
Son: (defensive) Remember what?
Dad: (slowly, generating curiosity) I remember Jackie.
Son: (off guard) Jackie who?
Dad: (glad son responded, but still wanting to build curiosity) Oh, Jackie from when I was a kid.
Son: What about her?
Dad: Well, I'm not totally comfortable saying it, but let's go over to the coffee shop and I'll tell you about it (**Connection**).

(At the coffee shop, after some small talk)

Dad: I was gonna tell you about Jackie. She was one of the original Charlie's Angels. I first saw her on a poster not so different from the Victoria Secret one. She had on a few more clothes than those models – or, at least, bigger clothes. But you still didn't need much imagination to wonder what was under them.

Son: They had posters like that back then?

Dad: Oh yeah! I remember feeling a little strange looking at that poster. On the one hand I really liked it. On the other hand I felt like I didn't want to get caught. Like there was something wrong about what I was doing. (pause – hoping son will confess to the same experience. Nothing.) You ever feel that way?

Son: (pensive) Not really.

Dad: (resisting the temptation to tell his son he should feel that way) Well, it took me a long time to figure it out, and I made some mistakes along the way, but I finally realized that those mixed feelings were both about how God made me (pause again, giving permission for son to ask questions or change subjects).

Son: Whaddya mean?

Dad: (glad he asked, but still careful to not over lecture) On the one hand, God made me to be attracted to women, after all, that's how you came along (nervous laugh). On the other hand, he made me to feel bad when I do stuff, or am tempted to do stuff that goes against his desires and plans for me. Looking at the poster wasn't necessarily bad, but when I started to want more than just the poster, I did what the Bible calls lust – or wanting something that God didn't intend for me to have. Do you get it?

Son: (ready to be done) Yeah, Dad. Can we go to the arcade?

Dad: (reluctant to stop when he's on a roll, but wanting to respect his son's discomfort) Sure, son, for one quick game before we go.

This is one of a myriad of possible ways to address sexuality with children as they approach or enter adolescence. The basic principles in the above example are to stay relaxed, take small steps, and look for ways to comfortably introduce the topic. Remembering the basics can help me effectively initiate these important conversations.

MY RESPONSE…

On a scale of 1 (not at all) to 10 (extremely), how comfortable am I discussing sex? Then, on the same scale, in my opinion how important is it to talk about sex?

What can I conclude from these answers?

When teens struggle

Pornography is rampant in today's high-tech, quick access world. It is virtually impossible to fully protect our children from the onslaught of sexual imagery and messages prevalent in everything from commercials, TV shows and movies, to video games, and blatant internet depiction of perverted sexuality. As a result, parents regularly call us for help about what to do when they catch their teens or pre-teens dabbling or immersed in pornography.

A common interaction with a young teen describes what we believe teens need when they become caught in this struggle.

Dave's parents caught him looking at internet pornography. Over the course of a few months they discovered him exploring a few times. Each time they did the best they knew how to address it, but their efforts were beginning to erode their relationship with Dave. Wanting to do something different, but not knowing what, they called for help.

This was a constructive choice. Many parents believe that if they just "tighten the clamps" hard enough, they can control and eliminate the behavior. Unfortunately, this tends to drive their teen's behavior further "underground."

When Dave saw me he spoke words similar to what we hear nearly every teen say about this. "My parents freaked out at me. There was no talking about it. First they took away my computer access, then my phone, then they wouldn't leave me alone about it, always reminding me that they couldn't trust me. I felt really bad, but it was like a hunger for sugar – you know it's bad for you but you just keep eating it. Then you feel awful afterward. The strange thing is, the more my parents did to punish me, the more my hunger grew. Every time I saw a billboard with a good looking woman, or a sexy TV commercial, I wanted so bad to see more. I kept finding ways to sneak around the password when my parents weren't around and started looking at the stuff more than ever. They caught me again and really went crazy on me. That's when they called you."

It was clear to me that Dave felt bad about what he'd done, and that he wanted help dealing with it. It was also clear that his parents' well-intentioned approach of control and consequences not only didn't help, but seemed to make matters worse. I asked Dave what he thought he needed in order to start getting over this. He gave what we believe is the answer that parents need to hear.

"I need them to not freak out. It just makes me feel worse, and it keeps me from ever feeling like I can talk about it."

"I need them to quit reminding me of all my failures. I already feel really ashamed, and then I get angry. And when I'm angry I just want to get away with it more!"

"I need them to appreciate it when I'm honest about it. The only time I tried telling them the truth about what I'd done, they just yelled more. So even though I want to talk to them, if they just keep yelling there's no way I'll tell them anything."

"I need them to start trusting me again, or I'll never be ready to go out on my own. I know I don't deserve much trust, but even if they give me some little trust and then help me feel good about doing the right thing, I think it will help."

Pornographers and advertisers grow more sophisticated by the day in their ability to either blatantly or subtly break through to seduce our children. We would all do well to heed Dave's wisdom about what kids need so that they can stay connected to their parents and work through this challenge together.

Exposing the "media madness"

Once I've taught kids some basic truths about the joy of intimate marriage, I can actually take *advantage* of distorted sexual messages in the media. I do this by using them as the source of good discussions for exposing the false and harmful messages. I have no shortage of examples to choose from. Most grocery store checkout lines have an ample supply of spicy magazine covers. Nearly ninety percent of the time sexual intercourse is discussed or implied on primetime TV it is between unmarried people.[1] And, of course, these unwed partners experience little to no consequences for their actions. Even most PG-rated movies provide opportunities to address this.

When our children were in elementary school, we chose to watch Tootsie with them. It's a movie from the early 80s that I remembered as quite funny and fully appropriate for the kids to watch. I forgot about the scene where Dustin Hoffman ends up having sex with one of his acting students. When the scene started (the sex was mostly implied) I immediately shut off the movie and said, "Oops – I forgot about that scene. But since it's pretty obvious what happened, let's talk about it for a minute. Why do you suppose that happened?" I asked. The kids threw out a few quick answers – "He was just thinking about what would feel good....They didn't know the Bible says we shouldn't do that....She was weak and couldn't say no." They gave some answers that grew out of previous discussions we'd had with them.

Then I asked, "What does this movie seem to tell us about unmarried people having sex?" They answered, "That it's OK...That we should just be in love...That it's fun."

I responded, "And what's God's view of that?" "Bad idea!...It messes us up...He wants us to wait to be married," they replied. "Can we finish the movie now?" I added a sentence about the loving wisdom of God's guidance and clicked the movie back on.

Some would argue that I should have done my homework, or should never have shown a movie about a lonely cross-dressing actor to my children. The argument has merit. But in this instance, it was too late. I was watching the movie with them and, since I was, I could either find ways to talk about the reality that would confront my kids through the media, or ignore it. I chose to talk.

Whether in movies, magazines, TV shows, on billboards, or on the radio, there are endless ways in which my children will be confronted daily with messages I cannot control. So I figure the best thing I can do is keep talking openly and inviting my children to think and talk too.

> ♦ ♦ ❖ ◆ ❖ ♦ ♦
> **Peers, advertisers, TV and movie heroes, music stars,
> and even teachers are talking daily to my kids about sex.
> I'd better be the clearest, strongest voice!**
> ♦ ♦ ❖ ◆ ❖ ♦ ♦

Proactively teaching boundaries

In addition to talking with children about sexuality, the way parents interact with them will greatly impact their response to a sexually charged culture. I decided early on to prepare my daughter, Bethany, to stand strong when confronted by aggressive efforts to get her to say "yes."

Most dads with daughters, having lived through adolescence themselves, are irrationally suspicious of testosterone-saturated adolescent boys. One dad even joked, "I figured if I shot the first one, word would get around." While I shared this typical fatherly suspicion, I wanted to give my daughter more confidence to recognize manipulation and stand up for herself. At an early age I began to playfully train Bethany by trying to manipulate her into giving me a kiss. "Bethany, if you love me, you'll give me a kiss!" I then taught her to look me in the eye and say with gusto and a grin, "Daddy, that's not the way it works!"

I have played this game with all the kids over the years, in different ways. "If you love me, you'll cook my dinner," or "If you love me, you'll come shopping with me." They have learned that they can love me and not give in to manipulation to do what I want. The application to resisting sexual pressure is obvious – not to mention confident boundary-setting in general.

MY RESPONSE...

What have my children learned from me so far about sexuality and sexual intercourse? (I can ask them a few questions to find out.)

Parents who know the wisdom of God's principles have been given marvelous truth for life. With thoughtful, proactive modeling and teaching of this truth, children can experience the freedom and fulfillment for which they were created, and become lights in a dark world.

KID CONNECTION!

Watch a favorite TV show with your children. Be aware of character and choices that are depicted, including but not limited to sexual choices. Ask your kids what they saw. Invite a discussion. What did you learn from each other?

Chapter Twenty-One

Grace-filled, Biblical Correction
The What, Why and
How of Corrective Discipline

"I CALLED FOR help with my son's out of control behavior. I don't have time for any more of your psycho-babble!" Click. Dial tone. I had struggled to ask the angry dad the kind of questions that would help him look at his relationship with his son in a broad perspective – ...in what ways do you still enjoy each other? ("We can't stand being with each other!") ...how are you working to affirm whatever he might be doing right? ("There's nothing he's doing right these days!") ...what are you doing to strengthen yourself for this challenge? (I'm not calling you about *me*!) He simply wasn't interested in anything but strategies for punishment and control.

"Correction." "Discipline," and "Setting Limits" are the seminar subjects that consistently produce our biggest audiences. When things aren't working, parents feel the greatest need for help. The help they want is for fixing their children's misbehavior. It certainly is important to know what to do when children act up. But the chapters about **Correction** are at the end of the book for a good reason: We've found time and time again that when parents do a good job of implementing the first three principles of the framework (**Foundation, Connection,** and **Proaction**), there is far less need for the effort called **Correction**.

It is important before parents work hard on correcting misbehavior, that they have first put great effort into building a strong **Foundation**. This is built on the cornerstones of:

- Faith (God's love is present no matter how intense our conflict.)
- Purpose (Wise discipline is an important way to build character in my child.)
- Community (It's important to get the help I need when things get tough.)
- Insight (What am I believing about this situation? What is God's truth?)

From that solid starting place it is easier to build a strong **Connection** of unconditional love and enjoyment with their children. From there parents can learn how to give the kind of **Proaction** that empowers children to discover and grow in God's purposes for their lives.

Do not mistake this to mean that there should never be a need for correction. All children, some more frequently than others, certainly need correction. They get off track. They sin. The Bible gives me some instructions about this. This section is about bringing the principles of **Foundation, Connection,** and **Proaction** into the equally important arena of **Correction**.

Consider this typical scenario: Dad has just arrived home from work, tired and crabby because things didn't go so well today. The beeping oven timer and the faint aroma of something burning in the oven greets him. Mom is in the basement, chatting with a friend on the phone, while sorting the last load of laundry. She is exhausted from a full day of managing the high-energy kids and all the various needs of the household. She's a bit lost in this mini-retreat from monitoring the kids, who have spread their Legos all over the living room on the main floor. They've not yet cleaned up the last mess they left in the basement family room, but Mom didn't say anything, so they moved on to more toys, in another room.

"Honey! I'm home," Dad calls expectantly. Mom quickly says good-bye to her friend and shows up at the bottom of the stairs, with the overflowing laundry basket in one arm. "Boy, am I glad you're home! I need you to take over dinner for me while I take a breather," she states.

"Are you kidding?" he snaps. "I just had one of my hardest days in months. I have to put my feet up. What's burning anyway?"

Mom smells the burning lasagna, drops the laundry, and races up from the basement to the kitchen. "Why didn't you check the oven when you smelled that?" she yells, feeling frustrated and somewhat hurt that he didn't offer to help out. "Did your stress deaden your senses?" she adds sarcastically.

Ignoring the comment for fear of making matters worse, Dad walks into the living room, stepping on Legos as he rounds the corner. "What the…. Oh no!" The kids look up at him, with fear in their eyes. "Honey!" he calls, "Did you tell the kids they could play here?"

"No!" she snaps, on the edge of her patience.

Dad snaps, "How many times have you been told not to bring your Legos in here? Clean them up this instant. Then give me the pail because you're grounded from them!" In fear, the kids quickly throw the Legos in their pail. "All right, now go to your rooms until dinner. You should know better than this!" The kids quietly head for their rooms.

As the kids leave, Mom looks sadly at the dad, nestling into his easy chair. "What are we going to do?" She pauses to see how or if he'll respond. Nervous about the possibilities, she quickly continues, "It seems they never listen."

My Response...

What behaviors and attitudes in the above scenario are in need of correction?

It's clear in the above scenario that the children's behavior is not the only problem needing attention. The parents have missed the mark as well. The vast majority of calls I receive asking for help with correcting behavior troubles in children are from parents who are in need of some correction themselves. It is difficult to help parents until they can agree that they often contribute to their children's misbehavior.

The Bible states it clearly: **"all have sinned and fall short of the glory of God"** (Romans 3:23). That is the problem – not just with children, but with parents as well. All too often parents want to correct the sins of their children without taking responsibility for their own sins or their own selfishness in the parenting journey. This selfishness is actually what often drives parental efforts to correct.

Therefore, *effective* discipline requires that I prayerfully examine the strong emotions involved and the beliefs that produce them—first in me, and then in my children. Once I understand this I am ready for a discussion about how to effectively address my children's misbehavior.

The <u>What</u> of Correction

What is biblical "discipline"/"correction?"

In the broadest sense, **Correction** is the comprehensive effort parents make to raise children to love God and follow his calling on their lives. The word "discipline" is used in many different ways in the Bible. In some places it generally describes the various methods of training to walk in God's purpose and plan. Some have called these the "spiritual disciplines." In other passages discipline refers to correction when people have "missed the mark" or sinned. Discipline may also include modeling desired behavior, offering firm rebuke or chastisement, gentle reproach, rewards, consequences or punishment, or any variety of other approaches.

For the purposes of this section, however, when I refer to *either* correction or discipline, I refer specifically to "corrective discipline"— parents' attempts to deal with misbehavior and "correct" a wrong turn when their children have gotten off track.

The <u>Why</u> of Correction

What is the purpose of correction?

To respond to the problem of sin

People need correction because of sin. The book of Romans describes in detail the classic conflict between the spirit and the flesh, or the inclination to sin as opposed to the inclination to do good: **"I do not understand what I do. For what I want to do I do not do, but what I hate I do"** (Romans 7:15). The capacity to choose to do good or to sin is a struggle for everyone.

My children, if left to their own devices, will never walk in the full pleasure of a life God has planned for them. It is only with Christ in them that they can learn to live right and good lives. In a theological sense, nothing *I* do can truly correct the sinful nature of my child – any more than I can become sinless myself by my own effort. Yes, I can employ various techniques and strategies to influence their behavior. Those methods may (or may not) reflect something about God's nature and influence the heart of my child, but the ultimate correction is left to the work of Christ on the cross. He corrected my inability (and my children's) by redeeming us. He then left the Holy Spirit to be my teacher (and my children's). This perspective helps me to let go of the need to get an immediate desired response to my discipline efforts. God is in charge of transforming my children. My part is to be faithful to discipline with wisdom and love.

As a vital expression of love

Much has been written about how to discipline. Unfortunately, most recommended methods are limited in their ability to apply to every situation. Rather than focusing on a particular method of correction, I want to keep evaluating and adjusting so that whatever method I choose is implemented in a context of grounded (**Foundation**), connected love. It can be hard work. It can often be unpleasant. What was effective one day may not be effective the next, so constant energy and adjustment may be necessary. It takes faith to view discipline as part of my calling as a parent.

The bottom line: It is on the strength of my connected relationships with my children that disciplinary or corrective measures gain power and effectiveness. There is a profound relationship between connected parental love and effective, loving correction. Hebrews 12 speaks to this: **"The Lord disciplines those *he loves*"** (v.6). **"If you are not disciplined…then you are… not true sons"** (v.8).

We are at a time in history when kids are largely disconnected from their most significant adults and this disconnection hinders discipline from these adults. Many call this permissive parenting. These parents allow their children to blatantly misbehave with little or no effort to correct them. A selfish need for peace at all costs may cause parents to avoid discipline. They fear the difficult emotions and even rejection by their child, or wish to avoid the intense effort of corrective encounters.

At the other extreme, a parent's need for control may lead to excessive use of power (authoritarian discipline) to gain compliance or eliminate undesirable behavior. The Bible tells parents, **"Fathers, do not exasperate your children; instead, bring them up in the training and instruction of the Lord"** (Ephesians 6:4).

"Authoritarian parents characteristically impose many limits and expect strict obedience without giving children explanations."[1] In a study by Search Institute forty percent of parents leaned toward this approach. In the extreme it is characterized by statements such as, "I will not allow my child to question the rules I make," or "I expect my child to believe I am always right."[2] This approach is exasperating for children. Children parented this way frequently become susceptible to peer pressure because they learn to rely on external control rather than self-control.[3] The greatest amount of rebellion is also seen in these families.[4]

My Response...

Do I have a tendency for either permissive or authoritarian parenting? What would those close to me say? What are some helpful truths that I can remember in discipline situations?

For my child's benefit and growth

Whether permissively avoiding difficult emotions or authoritatively seeking control, both discipline styles (especially at their extremes) communicate a subtle rejection of the child. The message to the child is: "My needs as a parent are more important than yours."

If I am to follow God's model, my children's needs (not my convenience or emotions) must drive my discipline. **"God disciplines us *for our good*"** (Hebrews 12:10). Effective discipline asks, "What corrective action will most benefit my child in the big picture of life?" Hebrews 12:10, 11 further clarifies the goal of God's discipline: **"that we may share in his holiness."** Understanding this truth makes me deeply desire the **"harvest of righteousness and peace"** that godly discipline can bring to my children.

Although situations and methods vary greatly, the purpose of correction does not change: to get children back on a good path in life, their path. With this in mind, even when my children misbehave, I can be more thoughtful to remind them of what's true about them (rather than always point out their faults). I can reinforce the truth that they are loved unconditionally and they have a divinely-fashioned purpose.

◆ ◆ ❖ ◆ ❖ ◆ ◆
**Effective discipline asks, "What corrective action
will most benefit my child in the big picture of life?"**
◆ ◆ ❖ ◆ ❖ ◆ ◆

My Response…

After reading through Hebrews 12:6-11 prayerfully several times, what stands out to me personally about receiving or giving discipline?

The <u>How</u> of Correction

How can I most effectively provide correction?

Filled with grace

The Bible lets us in on how God feels when we sin. In the midst of a long list of serious relational sins to avoid – stealing, unwholesome talk, bitterness, rage, anger, brawling, slander, and every form of malice, the apostle Paul implores us – **"Do not *grieve* the Holy Spirit"** (Ephesians 4:30). Grief is a response to loss. It seems the Holy Spirit loves us so much that he grieves when we wound each other and lose the joyous intimacy with God and "abundant life" that Jesus came to bring (John 10:10, NASB).

It is interesting also that Paul does *not* say do not *anger* the Holy Spirit. The New Testament tells us that God's wrath does not fall on his children, but only on those who don't know him, who have not received his forgiveness. **"Like the rest** [those who are dead in their sins] **we were by nature objects of wrath. But because of his great love for us, God, who is rich in mercy, made us alive with Christ…"** (Ephesians 2:3-5). Jesus took God's wrath for our sin—once and for all!

Understanding Christ's forgiveness of *my* misbehavior (sin) can drastically change how I feel when my children misbehave and need correction. **"Be kind and compassionate to one another, forgiving each other, just as in Christ God forgave you"** (Ephesians 4:32). As I soak up the riches of God's grace for myself, I can begin to let go of the anger toward my children that is driven by my own sin. I can even begin to catch a glimpse of the godly desire for them to rise to a fuller experience of the life Jesus bought for them. It is through this lens that I am able to see the *opportunity* that is imbedded in each difficult situation to remind children of God's love and purposes for them.

MY RESPONSE...

What is a situation in which I really blew it as a parent? As I remember the riches of Christ's mercy, I can imagine him communicating his love and forgiveness to my spirit for my attitude and actions. What might he say to me?

What blessing does my child miss out on when he or she has done the thing that exasperates me the most? Does this change my perspective from anger to sadness?

Given these perspectives, how might I respond to my child in this situation?

By principle, not method

Certainly there *are* various methods that can be used to effectively shape a child's behavior. But it is quite limiting to suggest that if a child does that, then the parent should do this – every time, without exception. At best, relying on methods alone to shape behavior does nothing more than, well, shape behavior. But that IS NOT the ultimate goal of correction.

Even after hearing or reading this, parents frequently ask, "So what should I do when my child _____?" The blank represents any variety of inappropriate or unacceptable behaviors. Most are hoping for a formula or method that will eliminate the misbehaviors in whatever situation they might occur. Jesus' relationships are a rich example of parenting, but those who are looking for a prescription or formula will find there is none. Jesus understood and modeled well the importance of looking beyond behavior into the hearts of his disciples and followers.

Consider Jesus' confrontations of greediness. When confronting the money changers in the temple, he overturned their tables and scattered their coins (John 2:14-16), an immediate act of strong **Correction**, no discussion. He instructed the rich young ruler to sell all that he had and give to the poor (Luke 18:18-25), challenging him to deeper character and faith (**Proaction**). But with Zacchaeus, a wealthy tax collector suspected of swindling, he simply announced he would stay at his house. His act of **Connection** to a greedy man (rejected by most of society) brought repentance and salvation (Luke 19:1-9).

We also see Jesus with three different people caught in the sin of adultery (See John 4:7, Luke 7:37, and John 8:3). In each case he dealt gently and wisely with the adulterer, but with widely varying responses based on the unique circumstances of the encounters. Jesus' goal in any corrective situation was not to force proper behavior, but to ask questions and choose actions that looked past the overt sin and penetrated the hearts of those he addressed. His goal was *always* changed hearts.

Jesus' consistency was not in his methods, but that he consistently operated from a **Foundation** of oneness with the Father. He was driven by a compassionate love for those people (**Connection**) and constantly pointed them to the eternal purpose of loving God and others (**Proaction**). On occasion he used purposeful, righteous **Correction** to respond to sin. The following chapters explore discipline using these four *principles* that are transferable to any situation, age, or personality of a child.

♦ ♦ ❖ ◆ ❖ ♦ ♦

**Jesus' goal was not to force proper behavior,
but to penetrate hearts.**

♦ ♦ ❖ ◆ ❖ ♦ ♦

KID CONNECTION!

Find out how your children perceive the goals behind your discipline. Choose a frequent misbehavior for each of your children and ask why they think you discipline them. Note their responses and the insight you gain.

Chapter Twenty-Two

Stop before Starting
Gaining the Insight to Discipline Wisely

"I HATE YOU, Mommy!!" Carrie was at the end of her rope with her 5 year old. "Alex is always an intense kid, but he seems so angry and defiant these days. What do I do when he says 'I hate you!!'? I've punished him a few different ways because it really hurts my feelings, but he doesn't seem to care." Lynne shared a phrase she'd learned that "a misbehaving child is a discouraged child."*

As they talked more about this, Carrie considered what might be discouraging Alex. His 3 year old brother Zach was now staying dry through the night, loudly celebrating this achievement every morning. This seemed to bother Alex (who still needed Pull-ups at night), but he didn't say much about it. We discussed how she could gently approach the issue and reassure Alex of her love for him. She realized it was possible that he was venting some hurt or discouragement at her because he felt very safe with her.

That night Carrie decided to tell a story about two brothers. An older brother who still sometimes wet the bed, and a younger brother who was for the first time staying dry at night. She asked Alex how he thought the older brother felt about all the attention the younger brother was getting. His response was, "Really, really BAD!!!" He exploded into a long flood of tears. She held him and told him over and over again how much she loved him. She affirmed that whether or not he misbehaves, she will love and delight in him no matter what! She later observed, "He's so different. It breaks my heart to think of how he was feeling all that time – and that I missed it! She determined to interpret any future "I hate you" declarations as a cry for help instead of an attempt to hurt.

Sometimes our kids misbehave because they are tired, hungry, or sick. Sometimes it's because it is developmentally appropriate for them to test the strength of their will and their attempts at this are misguided. Sometimes they feel overwhelmed and are struggling to gain some sense of control in life. Sometimes it's because children have a mistaken belief about how to attain attention, affection and significance. And sometimes it's simply because we misbehaved first and they are following our example.

When children misbehave, parents often look for a formula or method that will eliminate the misbehavior as quickly as possible. If the goal in discipline situations, however, is a big picture goal to shape the heart of our child (instead of just change a behavior) it requires a different approach. Outward behavior is often a smokescreen that disguises what's really going on with a child, so it can be helpful to start by noticing circumstances or relationships that might be affecting their emotions and behavior.

If a misbehaving child is indeed a discouraged child, I may find that my child's misbehavior does not require discipline at all, but is a symptom that he feels left out, unloved, inferior or insignificant. Addressing those feelings allows me to connect with my child's heart, meet whatever deep needs he might have for reassurance and encouragement, and convince him of my love – even when he struggles.

Parents need discernment when their child struggles, not a one-size-fits-all approach to discipline. Sometimes, as in the illustration above, a child needs only heartfelt **Connection.** Just guiding the child into an appropriate response (**Proaction**) might be a great approach. Other times a simple, unemotional consequence is helpful (**Correction**). Often, a combination of all three principles is the most effective.

The ability to implement wisely each of the principles of **Connection, Proaction,** and **Correction** as needed in a particular situation is directly related to the strength of a parent's **Foundation.** The hard thing is that at any moment any parent can experience weakness and forget to apply these principles. The goal of growth is not to get it right all the time, but to continue in my **Foundation** to thoughtfully and prayerfully reflect about the principles and ways to implement them in my parenting experience. Here's a practical and familiar real-life example of forgetting:

Four-year-old Billy was transfixed by the toy display at a fast-food restaurant. Tricia, his mom, was finishing her burger a few tables away. She quickly got up, threw away her trash, and approached her son. "It's time to go." She said. He did not respond. Tricia raised her voice. "I said it's time to go!"

"I don't wanna!" Billy lazily replied, his gaze fixed on the display. Tricia paused, presumably to figure out some way to end this quickly. "Honey, I'm running late, and I need you to come RIGHT NOW!" Her voice was firm. He ignored her again. She grew visibly angry.

"If you don't come right now, I'll leave without you," Tricia lied. She headed for the door. Once in the vestibule, she turned around to find Billy unfazed by the empty threat. She waited a moment. Her head and shoulders slouched as she marched back to the toy display. Without a word, she swooped Billy up and headed for the car. He instantly started screaming and kicking, making it hard to get through the doors. Once outside, she dashed to her car, whisked him into the back seat, and raced out of the parking lot.

My Response...

Relying on the principles I have already learned, I can place myself in this scenario and rethink it. (If my children are older, it can apply to similar defiance about leaving a favorite place.) What might I have done differently, remembering the framework's principles as my guide?

Foundation: What's going on inside me? How could I have been more peaceful?

Connection: How could I have connected with my challenging child?

Proaction: What teaching opportunities were imbedded in this challenge? What gifts might have inadvertently driven my child's misbehavior?

Correction: What consequence might have been appropriate and helpful?

If Tricia had known and remembered the framework's principles, this event may have gone altogether differently. Perhaps if Tricia had paused to gain perspective, she would have done a better job anticipating Billy's responses **(Foundation)**. She might then have taken some time to tell Billy her expectations **(Proaction)**. At his first resistance she could have squatted down at his level and spent a few seconds affirming Billy and his interests **(Connection/Proaction)**. Then, even if he continued to resist, she could have spelled out his options. For example, "Come on Billy, it's time to go now. Do you want to go by yourself or hold my hand?" He may choose to go or he may still resist. Upon further resistance, Tricia would thoughtfully **(Foundation)** confront Billy **(Correction)**, "You're disobeying me," and give him two viable choices **(Proaction)**, "Billy, you can come on your own or I'll carry you." He may come, or he may not. If not, Tricia would calmly **(Foundation)** follow through by carrying Billy to the car. At that point she would decide and follow through on any other consequences she thinks are important **(Correction)**. She would then be sure to warmly affirm her love for Billy, even when he disobeys **(Connection)**.

This seems so easy when I'm objective and a step removed from the volatile emotions a situation like this evokes. I can think it through and form more rational conclusions. But when kids misbehave, most parents quickly go into "fight" mode. They lower their horns and don't give up until they've conquered the situation. Lost is the objectivity and awareness needed to determine the contributing factors – including the parent's own bad thinking. Behind this energy is an almost instinctual question: "What should I do right now to fix this?" All the parent's faculties go into gaining immediate resolution. When danger is imminent or when time is of the essence, this is necessary. In most cases it is not only unnecessary, it is ultimately counterproductive.

Insight: The Impact of My Responses

How do my emotions and responses affect my child?

Parents sometimes say to me, "So what if I get upset when my kids misbehave? That's normal and they should know they are out of line!" It's true that when kids act this way, it is appropriate, even necessary, to correct them. And there may be times when intense expressions of anger effectively help parents meet their long-term goals. But, in most cases, it may curb behaviors in the near-term while increasing a child's anger, fear, and resentment of the parent.

Jeannette has just arrived home from a long day with customers. She's a bit late so the babysitter has to leave at once. She has a few fresh thoughts she needs to get out in emails before she gives full attention to the family. Tyler, her six year old, is glad to see her. She greets him warmly with a hug and a kiss and explains her need to wrap things up before she can spend more time with him. Before long he is singing at the top of his lungs. Jeannette tries to ignore him, but it's no use. "Quiet down!" she says. "I need to concentrate on these emails for just a few minutes." She gets up, wanting to briefly connect again. "Why don't you draw me a picture of something fun you did today. Then we can talk about it when I finish." She sends him off and heads for her computer.

Two minutes later Tyler is singing again. Only this time, he's singing loudly in the den doorway. "Tyler!" She shouts, "I told you to draw for me! Now I'll have to give you a time out." She grabs his hand and leads him away, lecturing about respect and obedience.

Tyler, like most kids, craves intense connection. If he can't get it one way, he'll seek to get it another. In this case he clearly needed some intense connection with his mom. When he didn't get it appropriately he misbehaved in order to get his need met. Jeanette may have inadvertently reinforced his misbehavior by the way she handled the situation, because his antics got such an energized response from her.

Her yelling and shouting is actually a mild form of "psychological aggression." Researchers have shown the negative effects of such approaches, including yelling/screaming, empty threats of spankings, and generally demeaning discipline techniques. These methods are statistically associated with higher rates of delinquency and psychological problems as children mature.[1] Knowing this motivates me to more closely consider my responses to my children's misbehavior. It also prompts me to reflect on the needs beneath my children's misbehavior.

The more intensely wired my children are the more they need intense connection. They desire my direct eye contact. They crave my excited responses. They yearn for expressive interactions. Unfortunately many kids get this kind of energized engagement from their parents only when they misbehave. Consider this explanation:

"The energy, reactivity and animation that we radiate when we are pleased (can be) relatively flat compared to our verbal and nonverbal responses to behaviors that cause us displeasure, frustration or anger. ... The sensitive, needy or intense child can easily become convinced that the 'payoff' for not doing what a parent wants is much greater than the 'payoff' for complying or behaving nicely."[2] A simple analogy for this is that when we think our angry responses will be the "weed killer" to eliminate our child's misbehavior, what we actually are applying to the behavior is "fertilizer!"

When parents can learn to give their most expressive, energized responses to their children when the children are NOT misbehaving, they often find that the children will not misbehave so much. It is helpful to remember –"Our challenging children are not out to get us. They are out to get our energy."[3]

My Response...

What was a recent time I expressed strong anger toward my child? How did they respond?

What was a recent time when I responded with patience and grace? How did my child respond?

To avoid the hurtful results of losing control of my emotions during discipline requires an ongoing effort to build my **Foundation** for effective correction. This process allows me to stay more objective, rational, and ultimately respectful to my children as I focus on what is best for them. Although this may seem much easier said than done, there are practical ways I can learn to approach discipline situations in this way. Understanding why I act the way I do sometimes, particularly in challenging corrective situations, is the starting place.

Insight: My State of Mind

How does my own mental state affect my response?

I was already a bit anxious, running late for an appointment while trying to get a simple breakfast for the kids before I left. Lynne was downstairs exercising. The kids were arguing, and I was nagging them to stop. The later it got the more my anxiety increased and my efforts to correct the kids grew harsher. At one point Bethany confronted me, saying, "Daddy, you're being mean!" I yelled angrily, "I wouldn't be so angry if you kids would shape up!" She burst into tears and Daniel sarcastically confronted me, saying, "Nice job, Ogre." I gave him a time out for talking to me that way, slammed their oatmeal and fruit on the table, and yelled good-bye down the stairs to Lynne. In my wake I left a wife who didn't have a clue about what had just happened, a justifiably angry and crying daughter, a son on the time-out bench (whose defiance arguably had good merit), and a mess in the kitchen. I reflected as I drove away, realizing that I had not practiced what I preach. I knew that I had some responsibility to take for this and that I needed to reconcile with everyone, which I later did.

Upon further reflection I reviewed my feelings, thoughts, and actions. I had been anxious to begin with. In that state, I was easily irritated by other circumstances. I kept thinking that I just wanted to get out of there. I was worried about the consequences of my lateness. As the circumstances quickly cascaded, I did nothing to step away and think more deeply about what was happening. I made thoughtless choices. I had to confess to myself, to God, and eventually to the children, that my selfishness and need to be in control were the driving forces behind my actions.

Many parents let this kind of thing happen without ever giving thought to why it happened. Learning the following simple analogy has helped me understand and be more aware of what's going on inside me at such times:

My brain stores information according to emotional states, kind of like information stored in the files of a computer. In the "relaxed" file are all the memories, skills, and information obtained when I have been relaxed. These memories and skills are most readily accessible when I am feeling relaxed. Likewise, in the "anxious" file, is the information I have obtained while feeling anxious. It is very difficult for my brain to access the information in the "relaxed" file when I am feeling anxious, and vice versa. (A classic example is the inability to access test information learned in a calm state, when I'm anxiously taking the test.) So, in the 'test of parenting,' when I'm feeling anxious about one thing (being late) and that "anxious file" is already open, peaceful responses are simply not very accessible. I'm much more likely to respond anxiously to other stimuli (like noisy kids) and so the problem escalates.

In my "relaxed file" I have stored concern for others, creative thinking, problem solving, and emotional insight and connection. The very things I needed to effectively address and correct my children that day! But, if I allow myself to grow frustrated and upset when correction is called for, my "angry file" pops open. In it are probably a variety of aggressive or defensive memories and responses. In this angry state of mind, it is easy to recall my child's previous offenses (when I felt this way before), while almost impossible to access feelings of love, or thoughtful rational options.

The prospects for successfully resolving a conflict are dim if both my child and I are operating in anger/defense mode. It serves to reason that one of the most important things I can do in corrective situations is to find a way to calm myself and facilitate that for my children as well. It's truly amazing to see how effectively I can deal with conflict when I buy a little time to get truly calmed down.

This reminds me of the popular adage for what to do if my clothes catch on fire. Every school child learns this: "Stop, drop, & roll!" I've never known a person whose clothes have caught on fire. I've known many, including myself, whose emotions have "caught on fire." For that situation, Lynne and I have coined this phrase: "Stop, breathe, and get perspective!" These are practical steps to putting out the emotional fires that so often burn:

Stop the charge into conflict. A variety of practical ideas may help: take a step back instead forward; sit down instead of towering over your child; or go to a different room for a few minutes. Getting space from the situation definitely helps a parent calm down. Research shows that after a fifteen-minute break from an intense discussion, people are able to resolve conflicts much more calmly and effectively.[4]

Breathe deeply. This helps reduce stress symptoms or excess emotional energy in my body. This step can be as brief as a few deep breaths or as long as a walk around the block. We know a day care provider who carries a small bottle of hand lotion in her pocket. Whenever she can, she takes time to rub some into her hands before dealing with highly charged situations.

Get Perspective by thinking about my options, praying for wisdom, or both. I can pray something like, "God, give me wisdom." Or, "Give me your heart for my child." Helpful questions I can ask myself are, "What am I believing about this?" and "What is the opportunity here?" (i.e., how can I connect or teach through this situation?) In most cases, it's both safe and helpful to wait until I have insight before dealing with situations.

Linda was working on learning to stop, breathe and get perspective before handling discipline situations. When she encountered an explosive conflict between her three young boys, she stopped her impulse to angrily intervene, and instead counted to ten loudly. Still angry she counted again, and then one more time. By the end of her third repetition of ten, she and her boys were laughing and able to resolve the situation well. The next day her middle son coached her youngest who was revving up for a good tantrum, "Don't get upset, remember to count to ten!"

We call this ability to stop, breathe, and get perspective a "Sabbath mentality." The original Sabbath was about comfort, rest, and focus on God. Practicing this process empowers me to step away from life's chaotic circumstances and into a deeper awareness of myself, the realities of my circumstances, and God's presence. It can be done in a matter of seconds or, if the situation allows, several minutes. Once I begin to practice it, I can explain to my children what I'm doing and why.

Learning to stop, breathe, and get perspective helps give me the wisdom to avoid thoughtless, hurtful words. Dr. John Gottman concurs. After years of family research, he succinctly states, "A harsh startup simply dooms (me) to failure."[5] A Stop – Breathe – Get Perspective start, however, enables me to assume the attitude of a coach, objectively encouraging and training my children. I can be a helpful observer rather than a participant in a power struggle. Learning to seek God's wisdom, truth, and grace for corrective situations gives me confidence to discipline with love.

◆ ◆ ◆ ❖ ◆ ❖ ◆ ◆ ◆
STOP – get space, take some time.
BREATHE – physically calm down.
GET PERSPECTIVE – seek God's wisdom.
◆ ◆ ◆ ❖ ◆ ❖ ◆ ◆ ◆

I taught these principles one morning at a family camp. Later that day I was in the recreation hall, standing in a doorway watching some of the kids at the camp play billiards. My son and one of the other boys got into a heated squabble. As they wrestled to grab the pool cue, I felt a surge of anger. No kid of mine was going to act this way and make me look bad - after all, I was the parenting speaker that week.

Almost instinctively (actually a behavior learned through years of trial and error) I stepped back, leaned against the doorframe, and took a deep breath. I've done this so many times I was hardly conscious of it. In that brief moment I was able to relax, think clearly, and walk slowly over to the boys as they neared blows. I then helped them identify their feelings, got them talking to each other, and helped them figure out a solution. Within minutes, they had joined forces to help some of the other kids in the hall learn to play pool.

I would never have remembered to write this story had it not been for a dad in the back corner of the room. Unknown to me, he was watching to see how I would handle the situation. Later, he announced to the whole group, "This stuff works! I watched him step back, take a breath, and then calmly deal with those kids. I would have blown up, but he had them reconciled and friendly in just a few minutes!"

My Response...

Picturing a recent challenge with one of my children, at what point during the progression of the conflict could I have practiced "stop, breathe, get perspective"?

From that starting place what might I then have done differently in resolving the situation?

Insight: Underlying False Beliefs

What core beliefs often affect my discipline responses?

When I continue to struggle with intense, negative responses to my children's misbehavior, it can be a reminder to examine the core beliefs in my Foundation. When I stop, breathe, and get perspective I can get the space I need to think and pray through my negative feelings and actions. There are two fairly common pitfalls that frequently keep parents stuck in their responses.

Pitfall #1: "Extreme thinking"

Most parents have endured one of those days when everything goes wrong. If at the end of such a day a parent concludes that life is dreary, the children are chronic problems, and he or she is incompetent, that parent is exhibiting a tendency known as "extreme thinking." Extreme thinking forms black and white judgments about the moment (one part of the picture) – and uses those judgments to define the whole picture.

This tendency is fueled by the principle of "folders" from the last chapter. Because the brain doesn't easily access memories and feelings from a different emotional state, it is natural to form pervasive conclusions and opinions based on temporary situations. A scene from the movie *Parenthood* contains a comic example of this.

Steve Martin plays the worried father of an insecure son. During one scene he is coaching his son's Little League team. Despite the protests of the parents and players, he sends his son to play second base with the game hanging in the balance. As his son runs onto the field, the dad gets lost in a daydream in which his son becomes the game's hero. His dream then jumps into the future to his son's speech as Harvard's valedictorian, "I'd like to thank the greatest guy in the world, my Dad, for making this all possible. His belief in me during a little league game turned my life around. Thanks Dad!"

Crowd noise snaps Martin back to reality as his son drops a pop fly and his team loses the game. Martin returns to a different daydream - his desperate son is now in the Harvard bell tower with a rifle. Students and parents scramble from an onslaught of bullets. "It's all your fault, Dad!" he screams. "If you hadn't made me play second base that day, none of this would have ever happened!"

This clip is an extreme example of "extreme thinking" - viewing specific, temporary behaviors as pervasive and permanent. The humor of it comes from the tendency that we all relate to as parents to exaggerate the significance of our child's behaviors.

Extreme thinking may lead parents to believe false messages such as, "He's *always* done this and *always* will." Focusing on the negative future may fuel thoughts like, "She's gonna be just like ____ when she grows up." "The teenage years will be horrible!" "This kid will never make it in life." Parents caught in these kinds of thoughts then subtly or overtly communicate these negative expectations to their children. The subtle evidence of these thoughts may be found in a parent's exasperated sigh that precedes a corrective interaction with a child, or in the simple tendency to always assume the worst when entering corrective situations. A more overt clue may be found in the words parents use. "What's wrong with you now?" "You're never going to amount to anything," "I'm so sick of your behavior!"

The way out of extreme thinking is to learn to keep negative situations in a proper perspective. When I can view and treat such situations as *temporary*, and full of *opportunities*, I can help my kids to learn and grow through them, rather than be defined by them.

MY RESPONSE...

What subtle anxieties do I feel about my child's struggles and their implications for the future? How do they affect my responses to my child?

What are some true statements about these struggles? How can I remind myself about these truths when I need them?

Extreme thinking forms black and white judgments about the moment and uses those judgments to define the whole picture.

Pitfall #2: Taking it personally

Another pattern of thinking that increases my emotional stress and excessive responses during corrective situations is taking my child's behavior personally. "If my child behaves well, I am a good parent. If my child misbehaves, I am a bad parent." Stated so bluntly, it's obviously not true, but it is still a powerful and subtle belief for nearly all parents. This belief can cause parents to change their perspective (and therefore their mood) quickly based on their children's behavior. That inevitable wild outburst in a store becomes a great embarrassment because it's about the parent's failure. This drives the parent to overreact in order to get the child under control. The overreaction then leads the parent to make further conclusions about being a bad parent. Defining parenting by a child's behavior puts tremendous pressure on him/her to "get it right." This usually has very negative results for the child and for the parent as they both ride an emotional roller coaster together, overreacting to the normal ups and downs of children's behavior.

The day Noah got caught lighting matches in the church provided a good test of my ability to not take his behavior personally. Apparently he and some friends had gathered in the corner of a crowded hall between services, and Noah was lighting farmer matches, spreading that distinct sulfuric odor throughout the area. I was quite embarrassed when I heard about it from of all people, the pastor's wife. Lynne and I are our church's endorsed parent educators. My credibility was at stake! "How could he do this - and in front of so many people?" was my thought. My first impulse was to find him and punish him. I learned long ago, however, that my first impulse is very rarely "for my child's own good." So I took time to stop, breathe, and get perspective.

I was able to think more clearly after I settled down a bit. I could acknowledge that his behavior was not at all about me. I even said out loud, "Even parent-educators' kids misbehave." I could then focus on how to help him learn from this, not on reducing my embarrassment. When I found him, he was laughing with some friends. I stopped when I saw him, and waited to catch his eye. When I did, I subtly motioned for him to come to me. He came, and we started walking away from the crowd. As we walked I calmly told him I'd heard about his antics. It was clear he already felt bad. I acknowledged this by saying, "It looks like you feel bad about this." He nodded. Since I wasn't sure if he felt bad about what he'd done, or just about getting caught I asked, "What do you think might be a consequence that could help you learn never to do this again?" "I don't know," he replied.

Because I'd been thinking about the question, and even anticipated his answer, I instructed him to find the church custodian and confess what he'd done. We found him, Noah explained his actions, and the custodian took the time to firmly but graciously explain the dangers. I could see that Noah was listening. Since to my knowledge this was the first time this had happened, I decided the consequence of removing him from his friends and taking him to the custodian would be enough. I told him he was forgiven and sent him happily on his way. He never lit matches in the church again.

Without taking time to stop, breathe, and get perspective, my corrective actions would have been driven primarily by taking his misbehavior personally. Rewinding the scenario, it probably would have finished like this instead: When the pastor's wife informed me that Noah had been lighting matches, I quickly apologized to her and told her I'd take care of it right away. I set out immediately to find and punish him. I wondered as I searched if the pastor's wife would tell her husband and what impact that might have on my role as the church's parent- educator. I wondered who else had seen him and what I might do to protect my reputation.

When I found Noah, he was laughing with his friends. I was conscious of numerous onlookers, so I decided to hold the scolding for later. "Noah, come with me right now!" I firmly demanded. It was clear he was embarrassed and he came immediately, wanting to avoid further humiliation in front of his friends. When we rounded the corner away from the crowd he snapped at me, "What are you doing?" "Are you kidding?" I replied. "Why in the world would you light matches – in here of all places? You've embarrassed me in front of half the church. I'm grounding you for the next week!" Noah did not argue. He knew what he'd done was wrong. But he remained angrily quiet for the rest of the afternoon.

My Response...

When was a time that embarrassment drove my correction responses to my child? How did my child respond?

I've followed that second course of action (parenting by taking my child's misbehavior personally) on numerous occasions. I'm grateful to have learned some things that keep me from getting stuck there. I know that working to be aware of my own motivations helps me to parent with my child's best interest in mind.

Insight: Thinking the Truth in Love

How can I change my responses through truthful core beliefs?

The simple truth regarding these pitfalls is:

> #1—Present experience does not define my child.
> #2—My child's behavior does not define me.

As I grow to understand this I can more effectively open myself to the truth that God's love and purposes for my children and me are what ultimately define us. If my perspective does not fluctuate every time my children either excel or struggle, I can parent with freedom and stability. Lynne shares her journey with these principles.

Much of my early parenting experience was filled with conflict with my children, and with many stressful, dark moments and thoughts. I beat myself up with extreme thinking patterns and blaming myself for our struggles. These thoughts were sometimes like a loop tape that kept playing over and over in my head, especially when I would butt heads with my oldest son. I resented him because, of all my children, he made me feel like a failure as a mother. My most memorable false belief was, "I'm an angry mom, raising an angry child; when he gets to be a teenager, it's gonna be horrible!" This type of thinking fueled my frequent discouragement and angry responses. It also made me more determined to control his behavior immediately, so the scenario I feared didn't happen. Nip it in the bud before he's a juvenile delinquent!

I gradually disciplined myself to think the truth in love (to paraphrase Ephesians 4:15). I consciously practiced a different "loop tape," which was, "I'm an intense mom raising an intense child. We butt heads, but we love each other!" I also developed some statements of faith to refresh my perspective during times of struggle:

- God created and gave me this specific child as a gift, for His perfect purposes.
- God has also chosen me as a gift to my child.
- We are on a good journey despite our ups and downs.
- Christ has promised to bring His work in us to completion.

As I learned to look at the big picture of our relationship through the lenses of faith and hope, I realized that raising this child was a hilarious adventure. Today he is a teenager with strong character who loves Jesus and loves people; he is intense, witty, occasionally exasperating, very endearing. By the grace of God he is nothing like what I had dreaded!

When parents can view their children with faith and hope, they are freed to love them for who they are, not for who the parents need or would like them to be. Instead of simply asking, "What should I do right now to fix this?" parents are able to ask the most important corrective questions: "What does my child need?" "What is the opportunity here?"

Understanding how discipline of my children flows out of my **Foundation** is work that will be helpful – for as long as I am a parent.

◆ ◆ ❖ ◆ ❖ ◆ ◆
**From a perspective of faith and hope,
parents are able to ask important questions:
"What does my child need?"
"What is the opportunity here?"**
◆ ◆ ❖ ◆ ❖ ◆ ◆

KID CONNECTION!

1. The next time you begin to get upset with one of your kids, verbalize to that child your process of taking a break to get perspective; i.e., "I'm really angry right now! I'm going to take a break so I can calm down and think clearly." What happened in the situation?
2. Together with one or more of your children (with whom you experience some challenges), develop a sentence or an analogy to describe your relationship truthfully, but with faith, hope, and love. (Or develop this thought yourself prayerfully, and discuss it with your child.)
   Remind yourself and your child of this thought when things get difficult.

   What impact does it have on your correction?

Chapter Twenty-Three

Don't Waste a Good Crisis!
Connection, Proaction, and
Correction —Working Together

"BUT WHAT DO I do when my son disobeys?" Or, "How should I handle my daughter's refusal to clean her room?" Of course at some point, the parenting journey brings all of us to these questions. The principles of this framework of **Connection**, **Proaction**, and **Correction** work together in everyday, real-life corrective situations. This is not a prescriptive formula but a flexible guideline to help parents navigate challenges. This means that at some point, as I review corrective situations with my children, I will be able to look back and see each of the principles in action.

Connection in Correction

Why and how should I connect with my child during discipline?

It is remarkable to listen to reports from parents who simply and strongly learn to connect in the midst of corrective situations. One such parent had just been in a class session covering "**Connection** before **Correction**."

Andy was addressing his son Mike's resistance to a particularly stressful math homework assignment. Tired of his son's complaining, Andy tried to ease the situation by offering to help. But Mike's discouragement was relentless. He seemed determined to fail. As Andy's irritation grew, he was tempted to follow his standard approach by saying something like, "I don't care if you do your math, but if you want any privileges this weekend, you'd better get this done!"

Instead he remembered the importance of connection that he'd learned in class earlier that week. He took time to "stop, breathe, and get perspective." This calmed him and helped him make a different decision. He got down on his son's level, held him by the shoulders, looked him in the eyes, and with sincere affection said, "I love you!" To his surprise, the son quickly relaxed, quit complaining, and they calmly worked on the homework together. Several months later the dad reported that his son's complaints about math were greatly diminished.

Sometimes connection in correction strongly impacts the child. But not always. Sometimes the one most changed is the parent! Years ago, Melanie came into class with the label "angry mom" etched by the scowl lines on her face. She lost no time in telling us about her daughter's difficult behaviors. A few weeks later she came in glowing, and eager to share her story.

Her daughter Anna had disobeyed by playing with a soccer ball in the living room...near the antique family heirloom lamp that was absolutely her mom's most prized possession. As the soccer ball ricocheted into the fragile antique, it exploded into "lamp shrapnel" all over the floor. Melanie rushed into the living room, to see her daughter shivering in fear of her anger. Just as she was about to grab Anna and scream at her, she remembered that "connection in correction" was a valuable opportunity to communicate unconditional love. She dropped to her knees, gathered up her daughter into her arms and said, "That lamp was really special to me, but I love you *so much more* than that lamp!" Relief poured out in Anna's deep sobs, as her mom held and rocked her...problem-solving about what to do about the lamp could wait.

Seven years later we ran into Melanie again, a vibrant, joyful parent. "That was absolutely a turning point in my life that changed a lot more than just my relationship with Anna," she shared. "It changed me!"

The point of these stories is, when inclined to give corrective energy, try giving connective energy first. When my goal is to convince my children of my love no matter how difficult their behaviors, an entirely different corrective tone and interaction is set in motion.

Dr. John Gottman notes that, "in Chinese, the ideogram representing 'opportunity' is encompassed in the ideogram for 'crisis'. Nowhere is the linking of these two concepts more apt than in our role as parents."[1] In times of crisis I have a tremendous opportunity to train and teach. If I look for the opportunity for connection within the crises of parenting—through support, empathy, encouragement, humor, affectionate touch, and, most importantly, forgiveness and reconciliation—I can achieve a far deeper level of intimacy and influence with my children.

There are no guarantees that connective expressions will automatically result in proper behavior from children. But it is amazing how often and to what degree simple connection can take the stress and fighting out of everyday struggles and pave the way for rational problem solving. (Expressions of love should *never* be given as a means to gain a behavior. If the expression is used for the purpose of gaining a particular behavior, it is nothing more than manipulation. There are few things more confusing and even damaging to young children.)

MY RESPONSE...

How could I have added an element of connection into a recent corrective situation?

**The goal of convincing my children of my love,
no matter how difficult their behaviors,
puts in motion an entirely different corrective tone and interaction.**

Proaction in Correction

What are the opportunities in correction for teaching and training?

Clarifying rules and rationale

Not every misbehavior is filled with bad intentions. In some cases, my child simply doesn't know the rules yet. Children are likely to feel confused, hurt, and angry when given consequences, even logical ones, if they are unclear about the expectations in the first place. God gave his children a clear list of rules, some of which are in the Ten Commandments. In the same way, children need to know what's expected of them. It is also helpful to think through and communicate explanations for the rules. So if a household rule is, "No hitting," it should be stated clearly and with an explanation such as, "We don't hit because it hurts other people. Using our words instead of our hands helps us be gentle and respectful with others." As children grow older, they can be asked to give input into the rules and explanations. It is an excellent way to teach them the family values and help them to internalize those values.

The following is a simple list of examples of possible rules, each with its rationale. These are appropriate for kids as young as two years old and can be effective through the growing years.

Sample Rules	Rationale
Clean up toys in common areas.	It keeps toys and people safe, which is a way of caring for others.
We all help clean up after meals.	Each person is a necessary part of the family team. It is respectful to share the work.
No loud noises or screaming in the car.	The car isn't safe if the driver is distracted. The small space makes noises hurt people's ears.

♦ ♦ ❖ ◆ ❖ ♦ ♦
**Developing rules together as a family is an excellent way
for children to internalize their family's values.**
♦ ♦ ❖ ◆ ❖ ♦ ♦

Children need to know what the rules are and need to be confident that they are able to follow the rules. Once household rules are established and communicated, I work to make sure that I give at least as much energy to my children's successes as to their failures to follow the rules: "Wow! I see you cleaned up your toys." Or, "I noticed how hard you worked at clearing the table. Nice work!" These statements serve to reinforce the behaviors.

Encouraging positive behavior

Replacing "No" with "Yes." If a child is stuck in repetitive behavioral challenges, it is probably a clue that the child could benefit from more proactive training instead of repeated correction. Such a challenge provides a good opportunity to think about what skill or positive behavior the child needs to replace a negative behavior. This means teaching children respectful phrases to replace hurtful phrases. It took us *many* repetitions to teach our children to say, "This is not your issue," instead of "Shut up," to a sibling who jumps into an argument. Whenever I tell a child "no!" it's very helpful to quickly find a "yes" (an appropriate behavior) to replace the "no." For example, if my child complains about dinner, I can tell her that it's disrespectful to complain during meals, but I will involve her in meal planning and preparation.

At age five, Daniel loved to discover creative ways to harass his younger siblings. One of his tactics was to roar in their faces to scare them. This got him a delightfully intense reaction with no incriminating blood or bruises. ("But Daddy, I was just playing!") The harder we tried to stop the behavior, the more powerful it seemed and the more entrenched it became. We decided to try channeling his energy in a positive direction, so I talked with him about ways in which roaring could be both fun and appropriate. I played a silly roaring game with him, and then told him, "When you want to roar at Bethany, you can ask mom or dad to play "roaring lion" instead. It'll be lots of fun and then Bethany won't be mad at you!" It took only a few roaring games until the problem was resolved. It worked so much better to tell him what he could do instead of punishing him for what he shouldn't do.

Replacing "Can you...?" with "You can...!" Parents use many different ways to get children to comply with requested behaviors. Often the request is phrased as a question, such as "Can you put your shoes on now?" This actually implies doubt in my child's abilities, and all he or she has to do is say, "No, I can't." (Hmm. I asked a question and got an answer. Now what?)

Another common approach is to *command* children to complete a desired behavior. Commands like "Put your shoes on!" almost invite a power struggle starting with my child's immediate "No!" (OK, now I've made this into a bigger issue than it needed to be, but since my child is defiant I now have to deal with that response.)

A simple change in wording can make a huge difference. In her work with highly challenging children, Lynne has helped many parents avoid power struggles by setting their kids up to feel *confident* instead of *controlled*.

> One of the most valuable things I've learned and taught parents is to express confidence in children through the words, "You can ...(desired behavior)."[2] For example, "You can put your shoes on before we go." If a child responds in a negative way to a "You can ..." statement, simply responding with, "You can when you're ready," is usually enough to encourage the behavior.

> It is particularly helpful to give a child two reasonable "You can..." choices. "You can put your shoes on here, or you can carry them and put them on in the car. It's OK to put them on in the car, but since the garage floor is dirty it would feel better to put them on now." As I develop a habit of offering "You can..." choices, it teaches my children to look for the possibilities in challenging situations. Of course some things are non-negotiable and I still clearly *tell* my children to do certain things, but many power struggles are avoided if I limit my demands to truly essential behaviors.

> This "You can..." phrase, particularly when included in two choices, has been so helpful in the clinic that I found all sorts of good uses for it at home with my own kids. It took months to train myself to use it. When I would forget and issue a command or a "Can you...?" question, I'd just repeat the sentence in a "You can..." phrase. Which leads me to pass on to other parents, "*You can* learn to use this helpful phrase also." But even more important than learning this phrase of "You can...," is for parents to develop a "you can attitude" toward their child, of confidence in their child's ability to make wise choices.

My Response...

What are several persistent behavior challenges in our home? What positive training might I do to reduce or eliminate the need for correction? (Possibilities include clarifying rules and rationale, teaching appropriate alternate behaviors, using a "You can_____" approach with my child.)

Discerning gifts in misbehavior (discovering a "Gift Gone Awry")

Believing that my children are created in God's image gives a basis for not just correcting misbehavior but for working to find and give expression to any gift that might be beneath the misbehavior. For example, most parents deal with young children who draw with crayons on the walls. It is not OK to draw on most walls. Children should be taught not to do it. They should be taught to respect a home's décor. When the only goal in a parent's mind is to keep their child from drawing on the wall, there are numerous possible corrective actions a parent could take. The parent will likely explain why it is wrong to draw on the wall. They may take the crayons away. They may punish the child with a time-out. Some parents might spank. Other parents may enlist the child's help in cleaning up or repainting the wall. Any of these approaches may effectively prevent children from drawing on the wall.

But what if alongside the goal of teaching right from wrong, there is a goal to identify and affirm whatever gift or need is behind the child's behavior. One couple's innovative approach to wall coloring accomplished both goals. When their son first drew on the walls, they clearly told him this was not OK and implemented consequences to reinforce the teaching. But as the problem continued, they recognized some God-given desire in his behavior. In fact, the art on the wall was pretty good for a five-year-old. So they affirmed their child's love of color and artistic expression. They went so far as to fill a small, unused room in their basement with art supplies. In that room, it was now OK to draw and paint his "Michelangelo murals" all over the walls. It's one of the child's favorite activities, and he has not drawn on other walls since they set him up in this room. Imagine what might have happened if this couple only punished the behavior without giving their son an opportunity to act on his desire and talent to draw big, colorful, expressive pictures.

Well-meaning parents whose only goal is to correct misbehavior without first seeking to discover what potential is behind it often squelch children's talents and traits. One example of this is found in strong-willed children. Most strong leaders are strong-willed. Surely at some point, their strong wills have gotten them into trouble. How many potentially great leaders have been stifled by discipline techniques that focused only on punishing inappropriate strong-willed behavior? When I think of the alternative....would I rather have a weak-willed child? That perspective helps me value and develop my child's strong will appropriately.

Then there are the creative people. Most of them are easily bored with routine. In their boredom, they often seek excitement by misbehaving. How much creativity is lost because it was punished rather than recognized and given expression? Great communicators sometimes can't stay quiet. They blurt answers out of turn, or simply talk when they shouldn't. Their gifts frequently drive their misbehavior. How many potentially great communicators were never affirmed, and their voices are now silent? Lynne had such an experience with Daniel:

Daniel and I were driving to one of his school activities, having an intense discussion about unfinished chores. He vividly described feeling nagged, "Mom, you're like a little dog, yapping at my heels!" What did he say?!! My face turned red and my knuckles were white as I gripped the wheel of the car. I was so furious, I knew that opening my mouth was a really bad idea! So I zipped it shut and prayed, "OK God, what could be something good behind this lovely statement?!" Discerning a response to my son took some time.

"Why are you so quiet?" he asked. I answered carefully. "I'm disappointed that our time for connection on the way to your concert has turned into a conflict. But I was able to realize that you have a gift for powerful language and vivid word pictures. I believe God will really use that gift someday to help people understand his love for them. It's just not very helpful right now." He paused, "I'm disappointed too; I'm sorry Mom." It was several years later that he used this gift to speak powerfully to the students at his Christian high school about the passionate, intimate love of Christ for each one of them!

Any God-given quality or gift when tainted by sin can go awry and fuel misbehavior. For example, one of the first full-blown misbehaviors children exhibit is to say "No!" to their parents' many requests to clean up, go to bed, get dressed, come to dinner, brush teeth, etc. Behind the will to say no may be any number of God-given inclinations such as pleasure with activity, desire for connection with parents or siblings, a developmentally appropriate drive for independence, a particular intensity of interest, or simply a strength of will. Taint these desires with sin, and there's sure to be misbehavior. To punish the misbehavior without affirming the quality behind it may both reinforce the child's identification with the sin (I'm bad!) and stifle or weaken the trait. It is therefore critical when correcting a child's misbehavior to also affirm and find a positive use of the gift that fueled it.

MY RESPONSE...

What specific challenge or misbehavior does my child consistently present? What strengths may contribute to the behavior? (Think of as many as possible.)

◆ ◆ ❖ ◆ ❖ ◆ ◆
**Any God-given quality or gift, when tainted by sin,
can fuel misbehavior. To punish the misbehavior without affirming
the quality behind it may reinforce the child's identification
with the sin (I'm bad!) and stifle or weaken the trait.**
◆ ◆ ❖ ◆ ❖ ◆ ◆

Time for Correction

What discipline tools effectively shape behavior and hearts?

Through effective use of the three principles of **Foundation**, **Connection**, and **Proaction**, much misbehavior is either prevented or redirected. But children will misbehave. When they get off track, children need effective discipline, or **Correction**, to help get them back "on track." The following are a few **Correction** tools that have proven to effectively help parents to "discipline those they love, for their own good."[3] They are general principles for consideration and by no means intended to be *the* formula for getting kids to behave. Even the best correction methods are ineffective if used insensitively or selfishly.

Natural consequences

Many consequences for misbehavior such as disrespectfulness or irresponsibility occur naturally *without the intervention of an adult.* If a child is disrespectful to friends or siblings they may not want to play with that child anymore. If a child has a messy room she can't find her shoes in the morning before school. If a child tells a lie people won't be as likely to trust him. These are examples of natural consequences. Oftentimes helping my child to understand and experience these consequences is the best way to help them learn, because these are the consequences that will follow him/her into life beyond the walls of our home. Helping children learn from natural consequences requires two important ingredients.

Avoid protecting children from natural consequences. Because it's hard to watch my children struggle, it is tempting to protect them from the natural, immediate results of their misbehavior. When I protect them now, I may well be setting them up for greater challenges later on. This means I avoid the temptation to help my children find their missing objects if their room is a mess. I don't rush in to patch up their broken relationships. I encourage their teachers to make them redo lost homework. It can be difficult to watch them struggle with problems I could easily fix, but natural consequences are powerful learning tools because they help children learn that their problems are *theirs,* not mine.

Facilitate awareness and understanding of natural consequences and rewards. Children can only learn from a natural consequence if they stop to think about it and form practical conclusions. Parents can help assure they don't miss valuable lessons. An example of this occurred at the local supermarket. At age seven Noah was frustrated that he didn't have the money to buy Legos. He whined and begged for me to buy him some. I started to lecture him about whining when I remembered this principle about facilitating awareness of natural consequences. I stopped and empathized a bit. "I know it's frustrating when you can't get what you want." I then used the opportunity to teach. "Your frustration is the natural consequence of spending your allowance too fast. I'll bet next time you'll work harder to save."

Feelings are strong natural consequences. As an adult, I rarely have other adults give me consequences for my behavior. Instead, I tend to feel frustrated, sad, or remorseful when I've "misbehaved." Being aware of these feelings helps motivate me to change. For my children to learn to pay attention to their feelings and be internally motivated to change, I must learn to impose consequences less quickly when they misbehave. Teaching my children to listen to those feelings prepares them for life. Here's an example from an interaction with my young nephews.

"How are you feeling right now?" I asked four-year-old Sam who, along with his younger brother, was in my care for the weekend. He had just hit his younger brother. "Mad and sad," he quickly responded, his head drooping. "Do you like how you feel right now?" I asked. "No," he shook his head. I continued, "How do you think your brother feels?" "Sad too," he said, the natural consequences of his actions seeming to sink in. "What could make you each feel better?" He thought for a minute, smiled, and said, "Say sorry!" I took him by the hand and walked over to his still-pouting brother. He said he was sorry and they hugged.

It would have been very easy in this situation to give immediate corrective energy or force my nephew to say he was sorry—even if he wasn't really sorry. However, that would almost certainly eliminate any awareness of how his actions impact his feelings and the feelings of others. If I had immediately punished my nephew the focus of his feelings would have switched from his brother to the punishment and his anger at me. I might have controlled his behavior, but I would have missed the opportunity to help him understand the real impact of his misbehavior.

MY RESPONSE...

What misbehaviors cause my child to have negative or unpleasant emotions? How can I facilitate awareness and problem solving regarding those emotions?

Logical consequences

When children are not motivated by natural consequences, they may need more concrete consequences to help them learn. A logical consequence is simply an enforced consequence that is related as closely as possible to the misbehavior. This could include losing a related privilege, or requiring the child to fix what they broke. Losing the privilege is a common Biblical pattern for consequences. When Adam and Eve misused the fruit in the garden they lost the privilege of being there. Moses' disobedience and poor leadership caused him to lose the privilege of leading the people into the Promised Land. David's sin of adultery cost him the honor of building God's holy temple. When Jonah defied God, he was "assisted" in doing what he had been asked to do.

Dr. Jane Nelsen, author of *Positive Discipline,* suggests three principles to insure that consequences are both logical and helpful.[4] Consider the example of a child who comes in from playing outside and tracks mud onto the carpet after being told to put his boots on the mat by the door.

Related – The consequence is related to the misbehavior. In this case, a related consequence would be to have the child clean the carpet where he walked. If he is too young to do this alone, I could either use the opportunity to teach him or at least help him do the cleaning. This not only lets children know they are responsible for their actions, it provides a positive interaction for learning further skills and responsibilities. It is far more helpful than taking away some unrelated privilege (like their favorite toy, or withholding dessert).

Reasonable – The consequence must be appropriate to the age of the child and the severity of the behavior. Scrubbing the floor where he tracked is a reasonable consequence. It is not reasonable to have the child clean all the spots on the carpet or to forbid him to play outside for three days.

Respectful – The consequence must be spoken and enforced respectfully. Adding humiliation to a consequence makes it hurtful instead of helpful. Simply and kindly explain, "Tracking mud in the house is not OK because it damages the carpet and makes extra work to clean it up." A simple explanation of the consequence diffuses negative emotions and enlists cooperation. Also, do this as soon after the infraction as possible. Waiting to implement consequences may extend the problem beyond the memory of the child.

Let's return to the list of three rules in the section on clear expectations, and explore a consequence for breaking each rule.

Infraction	Logical Consequence
Toys are left out in a common area.	After child gets one request to clean up, the toys get a "time out" (one week?).
Child makes a brief effort at mealtime responsibility, then heads off to play.	You'll receive an additional job, in order to practice responsibility.
Force/aggression is used in an argument.	You'll be removed from people until you are ready to truly reconcile.

MY RESPONSE...

What are some key rules in our home? What could be some natural and logical consequences for breaking those rules?

Restitution consequences

A form of logical consequences that is particularly helpful is called "restitution consequences." These are consequences administered when a child has mistreated another person. If I keep in mind the goal of building character in my child and maintaining connection in the relationship, I can find ways to help the offender "right the wrongs" while restoring the victim and the relationship. Punishing the offender usually breeds resentment and therefore more and craftier aggression toward the unpunished child. Restitution consequences encourage personal responsibility and usually end with one child feeling cared for and the other feeling caring. The message to the child is: "Your relationships are valuable. When you mess them up, it's important to do your best to reconnect."

This does not mean quickly forcing children to "say you're sorry." Forced apologies give the appearance of restitution without any real connection between people. The child might conclude, "Say whatever you need to get out of trouble." A key ingredient to any correction that involves conflict is to set the children up for sincere reconciliation. I don't have to force my children through the process, but I can put certain privileges on hold until the restitution is done. On more than one occasion in our family we have applied this to child-parent relationships also. Either one or both people involved (depending on who is at fault) reconcile the offense by doing a specific kindness for the other, such as helpfulness, making a little gift or card, planning a special time of connection, etc.

As young parents, we would often spank Daniel when he was aggressive toward his younger siblings, particularly his sister. No matter how we did it, this seemed to be a contradiction – you hit her so I'll spank you. So we tried other corrective strategies like time-outs, separation, and lectures. It seemed each of the approaches did little to change his behavior or shape his heart. So we decided to try a different approach. We encouraged him to comfort her with kindness after hurting her. This oriented him immediately toward her, and her toward him. We watched to be sure he wasn't manipulating the approach in order to get away with hurting her. We saw an immediate reduction in aggressive incidents and felt that they both were learning true reconciliation when conflicts occurred (they still practice this approach as teens).

We have fond memories of some of our children's early restitution consequences. On many occasions Daniel would choose to make chocolate milk for Bethany as his "love gift" for her after aggression or roughness. (She would sometimes even choose to share a few sips with him.) By the end they would both be beaming – Bethany because she loved chocolate milk and loved being treated like a princess, and Daniel because he had switched from "boy in trouble" to "knight in shining armor." They often played together wonderfully after that.

Because children often enjoy the creativity and connection that happens during this type of reconciliation, they will probably begin to implement it on their own. After an argument over a Scrabble game, with no prompting Noah spelled out, "I'M SORRY BETHANY" on the Scrabble board. She quickly found the letters for "I FORGIVE YOU."

Name-calling between children is a challenge for many families. It is said that it takes four kind statements to "undo" one unkind statement. With this in mind, our family implemented a "four kind and true" policy. Each time one of the kids said something unkind and/or untrue (i.e., "You're STUPID!"), they completed a restitution consequence of four kind and true statements before resuming privileges. ("You're NOT stupid, you're really good at reading, I'm glad you shared your Legos with me, you're fun to play with.") This policy set a wonderful tone of reconciliation in our family. Adding a discussion of Ephesians 4:15, about **speaking the truth in love,** has helped cement the biblical nature of this activity.

The approach described in this section flows from a perspective that it is much more helpful to train than to punish. It is interesting to note that the child in our family who most often needed to complete "four kind and trues" has become the strongest affirmer of others. This morning we found a note Daniel wrote spontaneously to his little brother. "Dear Noah, Thanks for being a neat, fun, little guy who defuses conflicts wisely and says funny things all the time and is smart like crazy, who makes me a proud big brother." (Wow, even more than four!) With the intense personalities in our family, conflict will never be eliminated, but the blessing of this approach is that we easily return to a place of connection and joy.

◆ ◆ ◆ ❖ ◆ ❖ ◆ ◆ ◆

**"Your relationships are valuable. When you mess them up,
it's important to do your best to reconnect."**

◆ ◆ ◆ ❖ ◆ ❖ ◆ ◆ ◆

To spank or not to spank?

Using the "rod of correction" (see Proverbs 22:15) is clearly a biblical idea. What is far less clear is the nature and use of the rod. Christians are divided about this issue. At one end of the spectrum are those who suggest that spanking children is a biblical mandate for any disobedience. At the other end are those who teach that since Jesus never used physical punishment, neither should parents. Most are somewhere in between. With no clear consensus about this, I am led to do my best to seek the wisdom of Scripture and the counsel of others, and prayerfully decide what is best for each of my unique children. Here's what I've found:

The rod spoken of in Proverbs is translated from two different words, one meaning a rod that demonstrates spiritual power and authority, and the other word a tool used by a shepherd.

This tool was used with the least amount of force necessary to guide and herd the sheep. Psalm 23:4 describes the Lord as a shepherd – his rod and staff protect and comfort. Grace Chou, author of *Disciplining Children with Confidence*, writes, "The more I studied, the more it became obvious to me that using the rod meant using my authority over my children to protect, warn, comfort, guide, correct, and examine their hearts."[5] Ultimately this is a personal and prayerful decision made between both parents.

Whatever my choices about correction I am challenged to be a learner, to humbly admit to God and others when I don't do the right thing, and to keep growing toward God's desires. Only from this place of humility can I let go of my own desires and truly correct with my child's best interest in mind and in heart. This dependence on God is my most powerful correction tool. I will take strength in his power to do the best I can to love the children he has entrusted to my care. I will take the same strength in his power to forgive myself when I fail.

KIDS CONNECTION!

Choose one or both of the following activities and journal below:

1. **Discuss common misbehaviors that occur in your home. Ask the children what they think some helpful consequences might be.**

2. **Discuss with your children the importance of true reconciliation after a conflict.**
   - **List their ideas about the difference between what happens in people's hearts in a forced or superficial "sorry," and in a true re-connection. (For younger children, you can use age-appropriate terms and a visual to illustrate. A construction paper heart can represent the love that gets ripped in a fight. Use different lengths and types of tape to represent different ways to reconnect the love. Note: a quick fix with a short piece of tape leaves the paper vulnerable to tears again, but a heart carefully repaired with masking tape is stronger than the original paper.)**
   - **List your children's ideas about ways to strengthen their relationships after offenses.**

Chapter Twenty-Four

So What Do l Do When...!?
Practical Correction Scenarios

AS LONG AS there are children on this earth, there will be parents asking: "But what do I do when _____?" When learning to naturally integrate these principles of **Foundation, Connection, Proaction, and Correction**, it is helpful to imagine some scenarios of challenging situations. Some of the following scenarios may seem quite familiar. Others may not. Use the space provided to write about how a parent might give each of the four energies to their child in the described situation. Work through all of them, because sometimes it is easier to learn the principles in unfamiliar situations than in familiar ones.

When Kids Whine

Four-year-old Elisa has been told numerous times that it's not OK to whine, but she is persistent. She sees the candy in the grocery store aisle and begins again, "Daddy, I want some candy." "No honey," Dad responds. She gets louder: "I want candy, I want candy!" Dad feels the eyes of other shoppers looking his way. He snaps quickly. "I said no!" Elisa continues. Dad feels constrained by the many witnesses. Finally, in his exasperation, he offers, "If you're quiet until we're done, I'll get you a pack of gum."

Think through the principles:

Foundation (What's going on inside me?)
- What might the dad be believing (about the behavior, about his daughter, about his own value or competence)?

- What objective perspectives or truths might Dad recognize if he were to become peaceful?
- What is needed for the dad to become peaceful even though his daughter is whining?

Connection (How can I connect with my child no matter what?)
How might her dad connect through:
- Words?
- Touch?
- Empathy? (Does Dad know what it feels like to want something really bad but not be able to have it?)

Proaction (How can I mentor success and teach/train character?)
- Which of Elisa's gifts or traits can be affirmed – even in the misbehavior?
- How could the gifts or traits that contributed to the misbehavior be redirected toward proper behavior?
- How might Dad teach about proper asking?
- How might the proper behavior be reinforced or taught proactively in other settings?

Correction (How can I calmly use logical, reasonable boundaries/consequences?)
- What did Elisa learn from the way her dad handled this situation?
- What natural consequences (the consequences or results that happen regardless of adult intervention) of Elisa's behavior could Dad discuss with her?
- What are some possible logical consequences (related, reasonable, and respectful) the dad could communicate and enforce?

Author's perspective

Parents are often worn down by a child's amazing ability to be relentless. Although relentless whining may drive you crazy, your child's persistence can be a marvelous trait in life. Beneath the discomfort of the whining is often a child with a strong will and determination to achieve his or her goals – even if the goal is not the stated object of the whining. The child may want satisfaction, comfort, attention, power, or any variety of physical or emotional desires. The discerning parent can more easily teach a child how to cope with the answer "no," when the parent understands the needs, desires, or wiring which might be behind the whining.

It can also be helpful to you and your child to explain the principles by which you parent: "I love you just as much when you whine." (When spoken in a kind tone with eye contact, this is **Connection**.) "…But it is my job to teach you that whining isn't a good way to get what you want" (**Proaction**). Laying those cards on the table holds the parent accountable to work toward a positive goal and helps the child understand and cooperate.

Helpful aspects of **Proaction** may include teaching a child how to make respectful, non-whining requests, an important skill in life. Don't assume that your child understands how to do this – it may require some modeling and explanation by the parent. (You can have fun demonstrating whining for a Mocha and then asking for it respectfully. Children love to play the parent and tell you "no" when you whine.)

It is often helpful to ask the question, "How would Jesus parent?" Most Christians can point to times of "whining" or "tantrums" before God when life didn't go their way. (David sure did that in some of the Psalms he wrote.) It's helpful to imagine God's typical response to this behavior based on his character: Doesn't faze his love for us. Doesn't change his plans for us. And at some point, he'll work to teach us a better way. One thing for sure – he doesn't work up a lather in a power struggle to get us to quit whining.

Negative School Report

Johnny is a first grader. He has just come home with his first progress report. His mother wells up with pride as she scans the first couple of classes and sees that he is excelling. Her countenance changes, however, as she reads further down the page to discover that he is struggling in most of the others. She is particularly troubled by the behavior comments at the bottom of the page:

- often speaks out of turn.
- sometimes is disrespectful to other students.
- has trouble keeping his hands to himself.
- frequently does not follow instructions.

Her mood has changed dramatically. A grimace replaces her grin. She begins shaking her head. She doesn't know how to respond. Her impulse is to scold Johnny for the behavior problems, and poor performance in some classes, but she doesn't want to overlook the good classes. Clearly some correction is needed for the behavioral issues.

Think through the principles:

Foundation (What's going on inside me?)
- Why might the mom's moods be so readily affected by this report? (i.e. What might the mom be believing – about her son, about her own value or competence?)

- What is an objective perspective or truth this mom might recognize if she were to become peaceful?
- What is needed for the mom to become peaceful even though her son is not doing so well at school?

Connection (How can I connect with my child no matter what?)
How might Mom connect through:

- Words?
- Touch?
- Empathy? (Does Mom know what it's like to have a hard time sitting still?)

Proaction (How can I mentor success and teach/train character?)
- Which of Johnny's gifts or traits can be affirmed – even in the misbehavior?
- How could the gifts or traits that contributed to the misbehavior be redirected toward proper behavior?
- How might the proper behavior be reinforced or taught proactively in other settings?

Correction (How can I calmly use logical, reasonable boundaries/consequences?)
- What natural consequences (the consequences or results that happen regardless of teacher or parental intervention) of Johnny's behavior could Mom discuss with him?
- What are some possible logical consequences (related, reasonable, and respectful) the mom could discuss with the teacher, or possibly enforce at home in cooperation with the teacher?
- If Johnny is disruptive this way at school, he is likely to be disruptive at home as well. What might be some rules and consequences to clearly communicate to Johnny about this behavior?

Author's perspective

School performance can be one of the more complex issues parents face. On the one hand, this is your child and your responsibility. On the other hand, you want to help him to learn to be responsible for himself and learn to face whatever consequences the real world has to offer him. On top of that you want to honor the child's relationships with teachers, while doing your best to keep informed about progress or lack thereof. Though poor school performance is ultimately the child's responsibility, the schools often blame parents for their child's struggles.

These dynamics tend to reinforce for parents the belief that their own worth and value is dependent on how their kids do in school.

If there is one thing we would like to convince parents about their children's school performance, it is this: Your children are NOT your report card. If they struggle, love them anyway; be sure they know it. Help them, but do not take responsibility for their success. We have seen far too many children eventually rebel because of the parents' need for their child's success (academic or otherwise) and resulting pressure to do well so the parent can look good.

So whether the issue is poor grades or misbehavior at school, the starting place is for a child to feel truly loved and understood (**Connection**) by his parent, who as an adult has had plenty of opportunities to know what it is to struggle in life. If you can communicate your love and understanding in a way your child truly receives it, his defenses will drop and you can help him talk about how he really feels about school – probably discouraged. At that point, you can problem solve together what he needs to support his best performance or behavior. (Identifying feelings and problem solving are elements of **Proaction**.)

If the issue is grades, it might be a quiet study area, tutoring, rules about what privileges are reserved for after homework is done, organizational strategies, etc. If the issue is misbehavior, the teacher ought to be the primary enforcer of consequences for misbehavior at school, while the parent deals with misbehavior at home. It is helpful to remember, however, "Misbehaving children are *discouraged* children, who have mistaken ideas on how to achieve their primary goal – to belong."[1] One of our sons changed dramatically when transferred from a school behavior program that kept track of everything he did wrong, to a system in which he earned points for everything he did right. A united, positive focused approach at school and home is very helpful. Parents could even explain principles from **Connection** and **Proaction** to school staff to help them develop a positive approach. (Note: Some children may be almost unable to control impulsive behavior in a stimulating environment like school. Helpful resources are available on Sensory Processing Disorder, ADHD, etc.)

When Kids Lie

Mom is taking a break from her household projects to watch her eleven-year-old daughter, Amanda, play soccer with the neighbor kids in the back yard. She cringes a bit as their game edges closer to her garden, which the kids have been told to stay away from. Just as she starts to open the window to remind them, Amanda launches the ball into the garden, flattening some front row annuals. Fear covers Amanda's face. "Oh No!" she exclaims as she runs into the garden to get the ball, trampling more plants on the way. Mom is immediately angered and races down the stairs to the back yard. The neighbor kids scatter, knowing this might get them in trouble.

When Mom reaches the back yard, Amanda is walking toward the house holding the ball. "I told the kids not to play near the garden!" Though mom's anger shows, she is under control. "I didn't do it!" Amanda quickly responds.

Mom's anger flares. She saw Amanda do it, and now she's lying about it.

Think through the principles:

Foundation (What's going on inside me?)
- What might the mom be believing (about the behavior, about her daughter, about her own value or competence)?
- What objective perspectives or truths might Mom recognize if she were to become peaceful?
- What is needed for the mom to become peaceful even though her flowers are flattened and her daughter is lying?

Connection (How can I connect with my child no matter what?)
How might Mom connect through:

- Words?
- Touch?
- Empathy? (Does Mom know what it's like to get carried away with a fun activity? Does she know what it's like to want to cover up her mistakes?)

Proaction (How can I mentor success and teach/train character?)
- Which of Amanda's gifts or traits can be affirmed – even in the misbehavior?
- How could the gifts or traits that contributed to the misbehavior be redirected toward proper behavior?
- How might the proper behavior be reinforced or taught proactively in other settings?
- How could Amanda be taught God's perspective on telling the truth?

Correction (How can I calmly use logical, reasonable boundaries/consequences?)
- What natural consequences of Amanda's behavior could Mom discuss with her?
- What are some possible logical consequences (related, reasonable, and respectful) the mom could communicate and enforce?

Author's perspective

Who among us has not lied? Imagine if every time we did, even in our subtle, sophisticated, adult way, we were rebuked or punished. Perhaps that would be all it would take to keep us from lying again. More likely, it would cause us to avoid those to whom we've lied, or learn to be more careful about when and where we lie. But our hearts would not change. I can say that as one who grew up lying frequently. The thing that has most compelled me to truth telling is not fear and rebuke, it has been the positive example and gentle, loving confrontation of those who love me.

A leading expert on children's lying behavior[2] verified that children learn to lie primarily from their parents' example. "We don't explicitly tell them to lie, but they see us do it... they see us boast and lie to smooth social relationships." In addition, teaching children the value of honesty (**Proaction**) is far more effective than punishing them for lying. "...kids who live in threat of consistent punishment don't lie less. Instead, they become better liars, at an earlier age—learning to get caught less often."[3]

We've not yet met a child who hasn't lied. Persistent lying, however, can be an indication of difficulties with attachment or bonding. It may be helpful to make a strong effort to connect more deeply with a child who frequently struggles to tell the truth. A child who learns to strongly value honesty has almost certainly been handled gently and gracefully, with a strong **Connection** to honest role models.

A Day in the Life of Lynne

The following is an example of how consistent thought and prayer about the principles of **Foundation, Connection, Proaction,** and **Correction** over time can naturally lead to action consistent with these principles, even during stressful times (remember, people's most deeply held frameworks emerge in times of stress).

One Saturday night after a long hard day, Lynne and I settled down for a chat after the kids were in bed. She felt encouraged, despite the difficult day she'd had with the children, "I'm really glad for the parenting stuff we teach. As I look back on today I realize that I used those principles many times, most of the time without thinking directly about them. It didn't make everything smooth and easy, but I felt peaceful and some really good things happened in the process." Though we'd worked at living the framework's principles of **Foundation, Connection, Proaction,** and **Correction** for several years, it was fairly early in our journey to teach and write about them. When she told me about it, I asked her to capture it in writing, believing it might one day help others grasp the power of these ideas.

Scene one - Cartoons

Jim was gone for the day, which started like an all-American Saturday – kids watching cartoons. The problem was they hadn't asked for permission to break a rule we had established of "No TV/computer before chores are done." Daniel, eleven at the time, was quite intense in his belief that watching Saturday morning cartoons was an inborn right, and not a privilege to be requested.

Foundation – I knew it could be a long day if I got off to a bad start, so I stopped to consider, "How can I be merciful, and avoid a power struggle here?"

Correction – I restated the rule, and then added my reason for upholding it: "I know it's Saturday morning, but it seems when we bend the rules we end up with more arguments because it gets confusing."

Connection – "I don't like arguing with you, I like having fun with you and feeling close to you," I stated. This communicated that we were on the same side – wanting to avoid fights (from confusion about rules) and have fun together instead.

Correction – I told him his infraction was not OK. The consequence would be turning the TV off immediately, and leaving it off for an additional hour after chores were done. I asked if he wanted to negotiate. (**Proaction** – In some situations, giving opportunity to negotiate is helpful training and can be more important than getting children to do exactly what you want.) He proposed finishing the show and then turning it off for the day. This got him less cartoon time than he wanted, but more than if he had immediately lost his privilege for disobeying the rule. It also allowed him to practice the desired behavior of making a respectful request for privileges. I accepted his proposal.

Connection – After the TV was off, we started on the tedious job of sorting Daniel's outgrown and out-of-season clothes and replacing them with "new" garage sale clothes I had accumulated. He strongly disliked this process, and I knew it would be a disaster unless I made it fun. He lay on the bed while I pretended to be his slave. When I held up a particularly disgusting item he would say, "Away with it." or worse yet – "Put it in the blender." My line was, "Yes, Sir!" (in military fashion). The humor relaxed tensions as we enjoyed each other during an otherwise unpleasant task.

Scene two – The Bird

All day long (and it was a *long* day) Daniel seemed restless and irritable. He challenged my authority and was harsh with his siblings. That afternoon, when Noah was a little rough with our parakeet, Snuggles, he rushed to institute justice by hitting Noah.

Proaction – I affirmed his "God-given-gift-gone-awry" by stating, "I appreciate your concern for Snuggles, who certainly can't protect himself. You have a compassion for the underdog, don't you?"

Correction – I reminded him that his response of hitting Noah was not an OK way to solve the problem, however. I wanted him to learn from the situation so his consequence was to type a paragraph on the computer about the results of hitting, both for the person who hits and for the person being hit.

Foundation – By this time I needed refreshment, so I worshipped to praise music while I did laundry. When Jim came home in the late afternoon, I hauled him into a quiet room, closed the door, and poured out the frustration of the day. He was supportive and encouraging and took over with the kids while I regrouped and prayed.

Scene three – The Recliner

Foundation – During my time of refreshment, I had an insight into what might have been going on with Daniel, who had definitely been "off his game" that day. I remembered him talking about a nasty rejection he had received earlier that week from an unkind classmate at the middle school.

Connection – I pulled Daniel next to me on the recliner and talked to him about the day we'd had together. "You had kind of a hard day today. You're acting a little bit like I do when I feel discouraged." (Empathy is a powerful form of connection.) I then mentioned a recent struggle I had with feeling rejected. I asked if his behavior that day might have anything to do with some discouragement at school. He seemed relieved to identify his leftover feelings from the week. We then discussed a more helpful perspective on his peer's actions (Proaction).

Scene four – The Haircut (and an outcome)

Later that night, Daniel asked me to give him a haircut. In my exhaustion from the day, I forgot to put the spacer onto the clippers before I started. I was horrified to watch a large, *long* chunk of hair fall to the floor, leaving behind a lovely bald spot in the back of his head. I anticipated some serious rage from a boy already a little sensitive about fitting into the cutthroat culture of middle school. I was surprised and relieved by his gracious response to my profuse apologies – "That's OK. Can you fix it somehow?"

Connection/Proaction – After the repair was done, we reconnected in the recliner briefly. I asked why he gave me such mercy when I shaved his head. He responded, "Because you cared about my frustrations at school." It was not an easy day, but in blessing him with persistent mercy he was convinced of my love and returned the blessing. Imagine what it might have looked like if I wasn't learning to persistently apply the principles we teach.

After the day was over I slumped into the recliner, reflected back on my day, and realized I had unconsciously utilized every layer of the framework numerous times in dealing with my children. It had been exhausting, but there were no blow-ups, no words to retract or wounds to heal. More importantly, my struggling son witnessed and learned some important lessons and at the same time felt loved unconditionally.

Additionally, Daniel's "military cut" was for a few weeks a visible reminder of God's gracious work in our relationship.

This story didn't simply work out this way because Lynne had learned some slick principles in a class the previous week. This outcome is the fruit of years of thinking about and acting on the ideas about which we've become so passionate. This kind of fruit is why we seek so fervently to give the principles away.

We could offer dozens more possible scenarios. We hope by now it is evident that the principles of **Foundation, Connection, Proaction,** and **Correction** can be effectively implemented in almost every challenging situation.

MY RESPONSE...

What behavior challenge in my family is not covered in this chapter? What are some possible actions according to the framework? (It will help to pray through and discuss these questions with your spouse or a trusted friend.)

Foundation (What's going on inside me?)
- What am I believing (about the behavior, about my child, about my own value or competence)?
- What is an objective perspective or truth I might recognize if I were to become peaceful?
- What is needed for me to become peaceful, despite this problem?

Connection (How can I connect with my child no matter what?)
How might I connect through:

- Words?
- Touch?
- Empathy? (When have I had a challenge or emotion similar to what my child is experiencing?)

Proaction (How can I mentor success and teach/train character?)
- Which of my child's gifts or traits can be affirmed – even in the misbehavior?
- How could the gifts or traits that contributed to the misbehavior be redirected in a positive way?
- What appropriate behavior could substitute for the misbehavior?
- How might this appropriate behavior be reinforced or taught proactively in other settings?

Correction (How can I calmly use logical, reasonable boundaries/consequences?)
- What natural consequences (the consequences or results that happen regardless of parent intervention) of the misbehavior could I discuss with my child?
- What are some possible logical consequences (related, reasonable, and respectful) I could communicate and enforce?

Final Thoughts

Writing this text has been perhaps the greatest academic and practical challenge of our lives. Capturing our passion for parenting on pages in writing was no easy feat. Since the passion changes and grows each day, reducing it to a finished product has proven quite elusive. Today, perhaps eight years after we first started filling in the outline of our parenting classes with written content, it is finished. Along the way, we adapted a little song, sung to the tune of "This is the Song That Never Ends." It goes like this:

This is the book that never ends
Yes, it goes on and on, my friends.
Some people started writing it not knowing what it was
And they continued writing it forever just because...
This is the book that never ends...

Though the content is now printed in this book, we are still learning the concepts in its pages. So it really never ends. We are humbled by how God uses these ideas to help us grow and to increase other parents' passion for parenting. Further, we have been privileged to see parents not only learn to think more deeply about their parenting but grow more aware of God's presence and love for them, even in the midst of the tumultuous family journey.

May what you've learned increase your ability to know and love God and others, and raise children to do the same, *so that* faith in Christ may be effectively passed along and shared from generation to generation.

Blessed to Bless,
Jim and Lynne Jackson

Endnotes

Chapter 1 – A Life-Changing Perspective

1. Matthew 7:24 - Jesus' concluding statement following the Sermon on the Mount. From The Message
2. Eugene Peterson, *The Message* (Colorado Springs: NavPress, 1993), 23.

Chapter 2 – Filled to Overflowing

1. Henri Nowen, *The Inner Voice of Love* (New York: Doubleday, 1996), 65.
2. Thrall, Bill, et all. *TrueFaced, trust God and others with who you really are.* (Colorado Springs: NavPress, 2004,) 84.
3. I Timothy 1:14-16; Ephesians 2:1-5; Psalm 51:1,7, 8
4. Psalm 139:1-18, Exodus 33:12, 17
5. Matthew 3:17, 17:5, Exodus 33:12, 17
6. Sandra Krebs Hirsch and Jane A.G. Kise, *Soul Types: Finding the Spiritual Path That is Right for You,* (New York: Hyperion, 1998), 1.
7. Ibid., Any of 16 different personalities/psychological categories of people, based of the work of Carl Jung.
8. Richard Swenson, *Margin – Restoring Emotional, Physical, Financial, and Time Reserves to Overloaded Lives* (Colorado Springs: NavPress, 1992): 79-80.
9. B. Kantrowitz and P. Wingert, "The Parent Trap," *Newsweek* 29 (January 2001): 49-53.
10. http://timeday.org, accessed 5/20/08.

11. (with children ages 8 – 17)

12. Robert Putnam, *Bowling Alone* (New York: Simon and Schuster, 2000), Text, 101.

13. Robert Putnam, *Bowling Alone* (New York: Simon and Schuster, 2000), Graph, 101.

14. Brennan Manning, *Abba's Child* (Colorado Springs: NavPress, 1994), 64-65.

Chapter 3 – Purposeful Parenting

1. We highly recommend Jane A.G. Kise, et al. *LifeKeys* (Minneapolis: Bethany House Publishers), 1996.

2. "Psychologists suggest that for women, even the threat of a disrupted connection can be perceived not as a loss of a particular relationship but as the loss of a sense of self. Women, prone as they are to depression, feel desperate to keep their children loving them." Mary Ellen Ashcroft, *Balancing Act* (Downers Grove, IL: InterVarsity Press, 1996), 132. Reference used by Ashcroft: Marilyn Mason, *Making Our Lives Our Own* (San Francisco: Harper, 1991), 105.

3. Mary Ellen Ashcroft, *Balancing Act* (Downers Grove, IL: InterVarsity Press, 1996), 129.

4. Luke 2:48-49; Luke 8:19-21; Luke 11:27. This concept is insightfully discussed in Chapters 6 and 11 of *Balancing Act*. Mary Ellen Ashcrost, *Balancing Act* (Downers Grove, IL: InterVarsity Press, 1996).

5. Quoted in Robert Bence, *Ordinary Saints: An Introduction to the Christian Life* (Philadelphia: Fortress Press, 1988), 106.

Chapter 4 – It Takes a Team

1. She took great comfort from the beautiful passage in Isaiah 54:4-8.

2. John 13:34

3. Hebrews 3:13

4. Galatians 6:2

5. http://www.30goodminutes.org/csec/sermon/gallup_3915.htm Transcript from "30 Good Minutes Radio," January 14,1996.

6. Robert Putnam, *Bowling Alone* (New York: Simon and Schuster, 2000), 438.

7. Randy Frazee, *The Connecting Church* (Grand Rapids: Zondervan, 2001), 13.

8. Deuteronomy 6:7

9. Galatians 6:2

Chapter 5 – Why Do I Stay Stuck?

1. John Gottman, *Raising an Emotionally Intelligent Child* (New York: Simon and Schuster, 1997), 42.
2. To cite a few examples: Jesus was furious and aggressive with the temple money changers (John 2:15), and called the Pharisees snakes and vipers condemned to hell (Matthew 23:33). He wept over the death of Lazarus (John 11:33 – 35), and was anguished to the point of sweating blood prior to his crucifixion (Luke 22:44).
3. Phillip Yancey, *Soul Survivor* (New York: Doubleday, 2001), 72.

Chapter 6 – Transformed Parenting

1. See Hebrew 13:5
2. Philippians 4:11.

Chapter 7 – Love No Matter What

1. Josh McDowell, *Disconnected Generation* (Nashville: Word Publishing, 2000), 8.
2. From Quintilian's Maxim – Public Domain.
3. Positive Discipline Newsletter, January 13, 2008.
4. Lee Berk, *Loma Linda University School of Medicine News*: March 11, 1999.
5. Some resources to consider: Parent Magazine, Focus on the Family web resources, etc.
6. John Gottman, *Seven Principles for Making Marriage Work* (New York: Crown Publishers, 1999), 8. *We obtained the approval of John Gottman, (via his executive assistant at the Relationship Research Center, Becky Thatcher) to substitute the word "families" for "marriages" in this quote. Dr. Gottman believes the principles apply to either marriages or families with children.
7. John Gottman, *Seven Principles for Making Marriage Work* (New York: Crown Publishers, 1999), 19- 20.
8. Eugene Peterson, *The Message* (Colorado Springs: Navpress, 1993), Mark 9:37.
9. *The New International Version* (Grand Rapids: Zondervan, 1983).
10. *The New American Standard Bible* (Chicago: Moody Press, 1963).

Chapter 8 – Eye to Eye, Heart to Heart

1. *Webster's New World College Dictionary* (New York: Simon and Schuster, 1996).

2. Ross Campbell, *How to Really Love Your Child* (Wheaton, IL: Victory Books, 1992), 57-67.

3. Note: There are times when I may have responded differently to this kind of situation. It is very appropriate to work with children to bring them along into your agenda. But because my original goal in this situation was to give undivided attention and engagement, I adjusted accordingly rather than helping Daniel understand the importance of my agenda.

4. Sandra Hofferth, "How American Children Spend their Time," *Journal of Marriage and Family* 63: 295-308. (Quote is from description of this research by William Doherty, Family Social Science Department, University of Minnesota in "Overscheduled Kids, Underconnected Families: The Research Evidence.")

5. This quote from a popular email that made the rounds. Found at Publish America's Author Message Board, http://www.publishamerica.com/cgi-bin/pamessageboard/data/main/4156.htm 9/30/02

6. Ross Campbell, *How to Really Love your Child* (Wheaton, IL: Victory Books, 1992), 40.

Chapter 9 – Read My Lips – "I love you!"

1. Gary Smalley and John Trent, *The Blessing* (Nashville: Thomas Nelson, 1986), 54, 55.

2. Luke 3:22

3. Luke 2:52

4. Howard Glasser and Jennifer Easley, *Transforming the Difficult Child* (Nashville: Vaughan Printing, 1998), 46 – 52.

5. Gary Smalley and John Trent, *The Blessing* (Nashville: Thomas Nelson, 1986), 58.

Chapter 10 – The "Magic Touch"

1. For a thorough description of the role of touch in the Bible, see Chapter 3 of Gary Smalley and John Trent *The Blessing* (Nashville: Thomas Nelson, 1986).

2. Luke 5:12-14

3. November 3 1997. Tiffany Field, PhD, is director of the Touch Research Institute at the University of Miami School of Medicine (UMSM) and Nova Southeastern University, and professor in the department of pediatrics, psychology and psychiatry at UMSM. This quote is from an online review of her plenary session of the American Academy of Pediatrics (AAP) annual meeting. http://www.pslgroup.com/dg/42772.htm

4. T. Field, et al. *Infant Behavior and Development* 19 (1996): 109-114.

5. Preschoolers who received a 15-minute massage showed better performance on visual perceptual testing. S. Hart, T. Field, M. Hernandez-Reif, & B. Lundy, *Early Child Development & Care* 143 (1998): 59-64.

6. Following five 30-minute massages children/ adolescents had better sleep patterns, lower depression and anxiety and lower stress hormone levels. T. Field, C. Morrow, C. Valdeon, S. Larson, C. Kuhn, & S. Schanberg, *Journal of the American Academy of Child and Adolescent Psychiatry* 31 (1992): 125-130.

7. J. Devito, M. Hecht, *The Nonverbal Communications Reader* (Illinois: Waveland Press, 1990).

8. C. Cullen, T. Field, A. Escalona, & K. Hartshorn, *Early Child Development and Care* 164 (2000): 41-47.

9. R. Baron, D. Byrne *Social Psychology: Understanding Human Interaction.* Quoted in *A Study on the Effects of Touch and Impression Formation,* by Terri D. Barnhouse, Dept. of Psychology, Missouri Western University, 1987.

10. If a child actually has tactile defensiveness, he or she will probably be sensitive to other sensory input as well, such as sound, light, or head movement. More information is available on the Internet under "tactile defensiveness," "sensory integration dysfunction," or "sensory processing disorder." An excellent website is http://www.sensory-processing-disorder.com. There are now many excellent books on the topic as well, including, *The Out-of-Sync Child,* by Carol Stock Kranowitz. Even children with tactile defensiveness will usually enjoy a backrub at a time when they are calm, if the parent asks permission. It may be helpful to get pointers from a massage therapist or in a community education class to make sure the touch is pleasant and not aversive. If that does not alleviate the issue, a doctor can recommend a pediatric occupational therapist trained in tactile defensiveness.

Chapter 11 – When Connection is Difficult

1. stated in Chapter 2

2. A national expert in ADHD states that the stress of having a child with ADHD "is as great or greater than that experienced by parents who have children with autism, a far more serious developmental disorder." Russell Barkley, *Taking Charge of ADHD* (New York: The Guilford Press, 1995), 99. It has been Lynne's experience that parents of children with a clear-cut, well-known diagnosis get sympathy and support, while parents of children with "challenging wiring" get blamed for their children's problems.

Chapter 12 – Training for Life

1. The Hebrew language here suggests a cause/effect relationship. In other words, the blessing of God is designed to not only go to people, but through them to others.
2. George Barna, *Revolutionary Parenting* (Tyndale House, 2007), 38, 39.
3. Josh McDowell, *The Disconnected Generation* (Word Publishing, 2000), 74.
4. Proverbs 23:24
5. It is normal for teenagers to rebel to some degree as they "individuate," or do the work of establishing their own, independent identity. While it may feel like a crisis, it is quite healthy. But when that individuation is driven by years of forced compliance, the crisis is quite likely to be more complex, high-risk, volatile, and long lasting.

Chapter 13 – How to T.E.A.C.H. My Child

1. America Reads, 1995 "verbal interactions with adults are major predictors of how prepared children will be to succeed in school."
2. Strommen and Hardel, *Passing on the Faith,* 98-99 – fifty-three percent of kids whose church-going parents discuss faith regularly embrace faith for themselves. Twenty-two percent of kids whose church-going parents do NOT discuss their faith openly, embrace faith themselves.
3. National Youth Survey - Research shows that kids who learn about the risks of drug abuse from their parents or caregivers are about thirty-six percent less likely to smoke marijuana, fifty percent less likely to use inhalants, fifty-six percent less likely to use cocaine, and sixty-five percent less likely to use LSD than kids who don't. And two-thirds of youth ages 13-17 say upsetting their parents or losing the respect of family and friends is one of the main reasons they don't smoke marijuana or use other drugs.
4. Michael Resnick, *"Building Resiliency, from Concept to National Agenda,"* from a speech given at the Pacific Rim Conference of the International Association for Mental Health (June 25-28, 2000).

Chapter 14 – Nurturing Authentic, Resilient Faith

1. Merton Strommen and Richard Hardel, *Passing on the Faith* (Winona, Minnesota: St. Mary's Press, 2000), 124.
2. Ibid. p. 59.
3. Merton Strommen and Richard Hardel, *Passing on the Faith* (Winona, Minnesota: St. Mary's Press, 2000), 59.

4. George Barna, *Transforming Children Into Spiritual Champions* (Ventura, California: Regal Books, 2003), 109

5. Merton Strommen and Richard Hardel, *Passing on the Faith* (Winona, Minnesota: St. Mary's Press, 2000), 99.

6. Trent, Osborne & Bruhner, *Spiritual Growth of Children.*

7. Joani Schultz, Group Publishing, ISBN: 0764420127.

8. John Wimber http://www.mtit.com/mbvine/articles/deeperlife.htm

9. Merton Strommen and Richard Hardel, *Passing on the Faith* (Winona, Minnesota: St. Mary's Press, 2000), 95. "In a survey in the *Effective Christian Education* study, adults were asked to recall their experiences in church as children and youth. Those who remembered being involved in service projects as children or teenagers showed higher faith scores. Involvement in service proved to be a better predictor of faith maturity than participation in Sunday school, Bible study, or worship services."

10. In the parable of the Good Samaritan, Jesus seemed to intentionally contrast the religious people who ignored the man in need with a non-Jewish person who clearly displayed the character of God.

11. In my experience with "de-churched" at-risk teens, almost unanimously the reason they have quit attending church and question the existence of God is that life has gone badly for them. In their minds, prayer is like a wish for life to go better that hardly ever comes true. They often talk matter-of-factly about how their prayers never came true. So they just quit praying, or quit believing altogether.

12. McCluskey, Christopher. *Professional Christian Coaching: How Professional? How Christian?* Journal of Christian Coaching, Summer 2008, Volume 1, Number 2.

13. Adapted from a Kirk Weaver www.famtime.com activity.

Chapter 15 – Siblings: From Cell Mates to Soul Mates

1. Wendy Cole. *The New Science of Siblings.* Time Magazine, July 02, 2006. http://www.time.com/time/magazine/article/0,9171,1209949,00.html

Chapter 16 – Pals, Peers, Adults and Relatives

1. Robert Putnam, *Bowling Alone* (New York: Simon and Schuster, 2002), 204.

2. www.grandconnect.com A journaling/letter kit created specifically for out-of-town grandparents to have a deeper relationship with their grandchildren through the mail.

    http://www.grandparenting.org/ **Dedicated to raising grandparent consciousness to better the lives of grandchildren, parents, and grandparents.**

http://www.gu.org/ Generations United (GU) is a national organization that focuses solely on promoting intergenerational strategies, programs, and policies.

http://www.grandkidsandme.com Their mission is to build and support meaningful supportive relationships for grandparents and their grandchildren through media resources, camps, and special events.

3. Peter Scales, *Other People's Kids* (New York: Klewer Academic/Plenum Publishers, 2003), 1.

4. From YMCA/Search Institute Study: *Building Strong Families*, November 2002.

5. http://www.search-institute.org/norms/FinalGG02LongReport.pdf From YMCA Search Institute Study: *Grading Grown-ups*, 2000.

Chapter 17 – Raising World Changers

1. Gary Smalley Gary and John Trent, *The Blessing* (New York: Simon and Schuster, 1979), 88f.

2. An excellent resource is: Florence Littauer, *Personality Plus for Parents: Understanding What Makes Your Child Tick.* (Grand Rapids, MI: Revell Publishing, 2000).

3. Websites to look for equipment: flaghouse.com; abilitations.com; southpawenterprises. com

4. B.Kantrowitz and P.Wingert, "The Parent Trap," Newsweek 29 (January 2001): 50.

5. Carol S. Dweck, *American Educator*, "Caution – Praise Can Be Dangerous" (Spring, 1999).

6. Henry Cloud and John Townsend, *Raising Great Kids* (Grand Rapids: Zondervan Publishing, 1999), .86.

7. Ibid. 95,96.

Chapter 18 – Swimming Against the Current

1. Daniel Goleman. *Emotional Intelligence.* New York: Random House, p. 81,82

2. Sandra Whitehead, How to Teach Kids Self-Discipline http://www.parenthood.com/articles. html?article_id=9736

3. http://www.publicagenda.org/specials/parents/parents.htm Accessed 01/22/08.

4. http://health.usnews.com/articles/health/2007/09/09/its-tough-but-you-can-do-it.html

5. http://www.publicagenda.org/specials/parents/parents.htm Accessed 01/22/08.

6. Sherry Benton, et al., "Changes in Counseling Center Client Problems Across 13 Years." *Professional Psychology: Research and Practice* 34, no.1 (2003): 69.

7. http://www.aacap.org/publications/factsfam/79.htm

8. http://www.surgeongeneral.gov/topics/obesity/calltoaction/fact_adolescents.htm

9. *Star Tribune* newspaper, (February 10, 2004): A9 "Teens like that fizzy feeling."

10. http://www.surgeongeneral.gov/topics/obesity/calltoaction/fact_adolescents.htm

11. Richard. Swenson, *Margin* (Colorado Springs: NavPress, 1992), 165.

12. http://creditcounselingbiz.com/credit_counseling_statistics.htm

13. George Barna, *What Americans Believe* (Ventura, CA: Regal books, 1991), 157

14. "National College Health Risk Behavior," *National survey* (1995).

15. "National College Health Risk Behavior," *National survey* (1995).

16. Claire M. Kamp Dush, et al, *Journal of Marriage and Family* 65 (August 2003): 539-549.

17. Sharon Jayson, *USA TODAY*, (July 18, 2005).

18. Bill Hybels, *Tender Love* (Chicago: Moody Press, 1993), 17-18.

19. Kaiser Family Foundation (2005, March). Generation M: Media in the lives of eight to eighteen year olds. Available online at: www.kff.org/entmedia/entmedia030905pkg.cfm

20. http://www.publicagenda.org/specials/parents/parents.htm Accessed 01/22/08.

21. Strasburger, Victor C. (2001, June). Children and TV advertising: Nowhere to run, nowhere to hide. *Journal of Developmental & Behavioral Pediatrics*, 22, 185.

22. David Walsh, Keynote address for 12-1-2006 Minnesota Council on Family Relations.

23. *Star Tribune* newspaper, (February 10, 2004): A9. "Doctors get 'call to action' on obesity."

24. Richard Swenson, *Margin*, Quoting Dolores Curran, "Stress and the Healthy Family" (San Francisco: Harper and Row, 1985), 62.

25. Jay Teachman, *Journal of Marriage and Family* 65 (May 2003): 444-455.

26. PEDIATRICS Vol. 113 No. 4 April 2004, pp. 708-713

27. "We found that both content exposure and screen time had independent detrimental associations with **school performance.**" PEDIATRICS Vol. 118 No. 4 October 2006, pp. e1061-e1070

28. Tiggemann, M., and Pickering, A. S. (1996). Role of television in adolescent women's body dissatisfaction and drive for thinness. *International Journal of Eating Disorders*, 20, 199-203.

29. Tremblay, M.S., Willms, J.D. (2003). Is the Canadian child obesity epidemic related to physical inactivity? International Journal of Obesity, 27, 1100-1105.

30. Anderson, C. A., Gentile, D. A., & Buckley, K. (2007). Violent video game effects on children and adolescents: Theory, research, and public policy. New York: Oxford University Press.

31. Josh McDowell, *Right from Wrong* (Dallas: Word Publishing, 1994).

Chapter 19 – Media, Materialism, Meals (picky eaters)

1. http://www.uncp.edu/news/2002/henry_winkler_2.htm, accessed 02/07/08.
2. Calvert, S. (1999). Children's journeys through the information age. New York: McGraw-Hill.
3. Dorr, A., & Rabin, B. E. (1995). Parents, children, and television. In: M. Bornstein (Ed.), Handbook of parenting, (vol. 4, pp. 323–351). Mahwah, NJ: Erlbaum.
4. Anderson, C. A., Gentile, D. A., & Buckley, K. (2007). Violent video game effects on children and adolescents: Theory, research, and public policy. New York: Oxford University Press.
5. Tiggemann, M., and Pickering, A. S. (1996). Role of television in adolescent women's body dissatisfaction and drive for thinness. *International Journal of Eating Disorders*, 20, 199-203.
6. Hargreaves, D. (2002). Idealized Women in TV Ads Make Girls Feel Bad. *Journal of Social and Clinical Psychology*, 21, 287-308.
7. Iman Sharif and James D. Sargent. Association Between Television, Movie, and Video Game Exposure and School Performance. PEDIATRICS Vol. 118 No. 4 October 2006, pp. e1061-e1070.
8. McDowell, Josh. *The Disconnected Generation.* Word Publishing, Nashville: 2000. p. 28, 29.
9. *Hardwired to Connect, The New Scientific Case for Authoritative Communities.* The Institute for American Values, New York: 2003. p. 31, 38, 39.
10. D. Kunkel, "Children and Television Advertising," in *Handbook of Children and the Media*, edited by D. Singer and J. Singer (Thousand Oaks, Calif.: Sage, 2001).
11. Sandra L. Calvert. *Children as Consumers: Advertising and Marketing,* The Future of Children, Children and Electronic Media. Volume 18 Number 1 Spring 2008, p. 207.
12. Lan Nguyen Chaplin and Deborah Roedder John, *Growing up in a Material World: Age Differences in Materialism in Children and Adolescents.* Journal of Consumer Research: December 2007.
13. Coleman, Paul. *How to Say it to Your Kids.* Penguin Putnam, Inc. New York, 2000.
14. Sandra L. Calvert. *Children as Consumers: Advertising and Marketing.* The Future of Children, Children and Electronic Media. Volume 18 Number 1 Spring 2008; p. 218.
15. www.diabetes.org

16. Ellyn Satter, *How to Get Your Kid to Eat, But Not Too Much* (Boulder, Colorado: Bell Publishing Company, 1987), 45. Quoting P.R. Costanzo and E.Z. Woody, Domain-specific parenting styles and their impact on the child's development of particular deviance: "The example of obesity proneness," *Journal of Social and Clinical Psychology* 3 (1985): 425-445.

17. Ibid., 45. Quoting M. Kinter, P.G. Boss and N. Johnson, "The relationship between dysfunctional family environments and family member food intake," *Journal of Marriage and the Family* 43 (3) (1981): 633-641.

18. Ibid., 44. Quoting L.L Birch, D.W. Marlin, and J. Rotter, "Eating as the 'means' activity in a contingency: Effects on young children's food preference," *Child Development* 55 (2) (1984): 431-439.

19. Ibid., 14

20. Kay Toomey, *When Children Won't Eat: The SOS Approach to Feeding* (Denver: Self Published, 2002), 1

21. The study was done on children ages 9 – 14. Quote from William Doherty, "Overscheduled, Underconnected Families," the Research Evidence. "Changes in Children's and Families," *Time* www.timeinforfamily.org Researchers: M.W. Gillman, et al., "Family dinners and diet quality among older children and adolescents," *Archives of Family Medicine* 9 (2000): 235-240.

22. Note: Approximately five percent of children are defined as "problem eaters" who will repeatedly choose not to eat other food if their preferred foods are unavailable. This minority of children needs professional help.

Chapter 20 – Talking about S-E-X with K-I-D-S

1. Bill Hybels, *Tender Love* (Chicago: Moody Press, 1993), 17.

Chapter 21 – Grace-filled, Biblical Correction

1. John Gottman, *Raising an Emotionally Intelligent Child* (New York: Simon and Schuster, 1997), 32.

2. Merton P. Strommen and Richard A. Hardel, *Passing On the Faith* (Winona, MN: Christian Brothers Publications, 2000), 58-59.

3. Ibid., 59, quoting Strahan, *Parents, Adolescents and Religion,* 25.

4. Ibid., 59.

Chapter 22 – Stop before Starting

1. Murray Straus and Carolyn Field, "Psychological Aggression by American Parents: National Data on Prevalence, Chronicity and Severity," *Journal of Marriage and Family* 65 (November 2003): 795 – 808.

2. Howard Glasser and Jennifer Easley, *Transforming the Difficult Child* (Nashville, TN: Vaughan Printing, 1998), 9-10.

3. Howard Glasser and Jennifer Easley, *Transforming the Difficult Child* (Nashville, TN: Vaughan Printing, 1998), 14.

4. John Gottman, *The Seven Principles for Making Marriage Work* (New York: Random House, 1999).

5. John Gottman, *The Seven Principles for Making Marriage Work* (New York: Random House, 1999), 27. "Ninety-six percent of the time you can predict the outcome of a conversation based on the first three minutes of a fifteen-minute interaction."

Chapter 23 – Don't Waste a Good Crisis

1. John Gottman, *Raising an Emotionally Intelligent Child* (New York: Simon and Schuster, 1997), 93.

2. Kay Toomey, *When Children Won't Eat: The SOS Approach to Feeding* (Denver: Self Published, 2002), 1.

3. Adapted from Hebrews 12:10

4. Jane Nelsen, *Positive Discipline,* (New York: Ballantine Books, 1987), 73.

5. Grace Chou, "Should I Spank My Child?" *Christian Parenting Today* (Summer 2003): 50-53.

Chapter 24 – So What Do I Do When...!?

1. Jane Nelsen, *Positive Discipline* (New York: Ballentine Books, 1987), xvii .

2. Dr. Victoria Talwar, Asst. Professor, McGill University. Quoted in Po Bronson's article, Learning to Lie, New York Magazine, February 18, 2008. http://nymag.com/news/features/43893/index4.html

3. Ibid.

To order additional copies of this book, please visit www.redemption-press.com
www.connectedfamilies.org

CPSIA information can be obtained
at www.ICGtesting.com
Printed in the USA
FFOW05n0018270916

9 781632 320124